MW01234967

"'Cannabis vs Marijuana' is a trailblazing work at a crucial juncture in the cannabis industry. As cannabis shifts from Prohibition to acceptance, the words we use to describe it carry immense weight. This book sparks the essential dialogue needed to reshape our language, challenge stereotypes, and build a more inclusive and informed future for cannabis. It's a must-read for anyone committed to this industry's growth and responsible communication."
— Dale Sky Jones, Executive Chancellor, Oaksterdam University

"Years of misinformation about cannabis is reflected in the colorful but misleading "dope" vocabulary. Shedding the War on Drugs requires new and positive terminology. Paleschuck's work demonstrates how you can make the transition with ease."
— Jorge Cervantes, Author, The Cannabis Encyclopedia

"In the cannabis industry, words are our bridge to the world beyond. To normalize cannabis and gain acceptance, we must speak a language that politicians, scientists, and society recognize and understand. Our words can bridge gaps, dismantle the stereotypes, and shape a responsible, informed industry. In his book 'Cannabis vs. Marijuana,' David Paleschuck starts the conversation and points us in the right direction. I highly recommend it."
— Steven Phan, Co-Founder, Come Back Daily

"At last, 'Cannabis vs. Marijuana' tackles the linguistic divide that has long hindered the cannabis industry. This book is essential reading for everyone in the field as it lights the path to a more informed, inclusive, and scientifically grounded discourse. To normalize this remarkable plant, we must speak a language understood by industry insiders, consumers, researchers, scientists, and politicians."
— Christian Gray, Partner, Atlas Consulting Inc.

"In the world of cannabis semantics, the battle rages on, a clash of connotations that mirrors the complexity of the plant itself. As we weigh these words, let's remember that language not only labels but also shapes attitudes. It's vital to have books like 'Cannabis vs Marijuana' and authors like David Paleschuck to help untangle these thorny issues and illuminate the path toward a more nuanced conversation."
— Jordan Isenstadt, SVP, Marino PR

CANNABIS vs. MARIJUANA

Language, Landscape And Context

By
DAVID A. PALESCHUCK

Little Giant Press
Seattle, WA

Little Giant Press
Seattle, WA, USA

While the author has made every effort to provide accurate information and internet addresses at the time of publication, neither the publisher nor the author assumes any responsibility for errors or changes after publication. Further, the publisher and author do not have any control over nor assume any responsibility for third-party websites or their content.

Cover Design: Stuart Narduzzo
Interior Design: Dawn Black
Editor: Ruth Shamai

Little Giant Press
Seattle, WA 98105
info@littlegiantpress.com
www.littlegiantpress.com

Ordering information:
Special discounts are available on quantity purchases by corporations, institutions, associations, and others. Contact info@littlegiantpress.com for details.

Cannabis vs. Marijuana: Language, Landscape And Context

David Paleschuck — 1st edition / April 2024

Library of Congress Control Number: 2024904287
ISBN: 979-8-9900420-0-1 (Paperback edition)
ISBN: 979-8-9900420-1-8 (eBook edition)

1. Social Sciences 2. Language Arts 3. Green Business

Printed in the United States of America on acid-free paper

DEDICATED

To all those who have suffered, been prosecuted, and incarcerated due to unjust cannabis laws, this book is dedicated to you. Your stories are not forgotten, and your pain and trauma have not gone unnoticed. Your sacrifices and struggles have been the catalyst for change, and your resilience and determination have paved the way for a more just and equitable society.

This book is a tribute to your strength and courage and will serve as a reminder of the injustices that have occurred and as a call to action to a new generation, ensuring they never happen again.

With respect and gratitude.

TABLE OF CONTENTS

FOREWORD

By Dale Sky Jones
Executive Chancellor, Oaksterdam University
Cannabis Activist

No humans were physically harmed during the birthing of this book, mainly because the discussions were born while talking from relative safety through electronic devices during the depths of digital communication during the pandemic. Cannabis suddenly went from being considered criminal at worst (and a nuisance at best) to being declared an *essential service* by several states. No one knew the future, and we were yearning for connection. These are the days I truly got to know David and his verbal sparring skills, quick wit, and sharp observations. He's my kind of intellectual wonk — fun to talk with and unafraid to engage with people who disagree and bring the heat. But I'm getting ahead of myself!

As a legal and commercial cannabis industry emerges in the United States and worldwide, standards around terminology and jargon — the language we use to describe the plant and its derivatives and properties scientifically — become more important than ever. We legalization pioneers formed the Medical Cannabis Safety Council in 2008 to tackle organoleptic methods, lab testing, and nomenclature concerns. Medicinal cannabis varietals with names like "Cat Piss," "Alaskan Thunderf*ck," and "Green Crack" were unhelpful and often offensive to "Aunt Betty," who ostensibly wanted to treat her medicine with more respect and was already put off by the security man-cage she had to walk through at her dispensary.

Oaksterdam University coined the "cannabis industry" in our mission statement to provide quality training for a group who still considered ourselves a movement. We needed regulators to take our actions more seriously (take off the tie-dye and put on a tie), and we used the scientific name "cannabis" when we put legalization before the voters in 2010, a big gamble. Politically charged language loaded with prejudice and bias was one of the first weapons of Prohibition used to demonize the plant and the people around it. Slang and humor were how decades of consumers hid their activities with cultural references and gently tested strangers to see if they were "cool." We are just beginning to unravel this legacy and establish new, more scientific, peer-reviewed standards. I was thrilled when Oaksterdam University alumni David Paleschuck told me he was writing this book.

David and I have shared countless conversations about terminology and the study of how it affects human nature, from promoting positive political action to implementing scare tactics, and we are on the same page — words have power. David's journey through the corporate world, his expertise in giving voice to top cannabis brands since leaving his "real job," and his experience as a writer position him to make an impact in shaping communication in a fully legal future. Reading this book will highlight the unseen influence of your chosen words, especially on this sensitive subject.

David once mentioned that when he first started at Parsons School of Design in his hometown of New York City, a gallery owner told him, "Just remember, it's not really what you're going to learn there. It's who you'll meet because all those people will be people in the industry you'll know, and as you grow and blossom, so will they."

David told me he took that advice to heart as he ran his gallery in Manhattan for a decade, then worked in branding and marketing serving companies like American Express, Mastercard, Pepsi, and Microsoft. Twelve years ago, when he transitioned into the cannabis industry, the message stuck with him. That's why he sought out Oaksterdam University — to network with like-minded people.

Coincidentally, David moved from New York to Seattle in 2006, the year after I moved to Seattle. Shortly after, I left my corporate career and moved to Orange County, California, in 2007 to work with doctors recommending cannabis to medical-necessity patients. I knew I needed education and discovered Oaksterdam's founders, Jeff Jones and Richard Lee while looking for professional development before the school opened. Six years later, when voters approved I-502, making Washington the first state to legalize cannabis for adult use (along with Colorado), David saw many of his corporate colleagues defect to the promising cannabis industry. Always a fan of the plant, David decided to "come out of the cannabis closet." Believing that knowledge is power, the first thing David did to launch his new career path was seek out cannabis education. By 2012, Oaksterdam University was (in)famous.

Cannabis legalization has deep roots in Oakland, California, where Richard, a cannabis activist, and my husband Jeff, a cannabis horticulture expert, started teaching people how to grow, obtain, transport, and consume cannabis safely, and where I joined them as a teacher and advocate soon after. Oaksterdam University first formalized classes on November 10th, 2007, after Richard took out an ad in the East Bay Express. The phone rang off the hook. People longed to emerge from the veil of Prohibition and celebrate their love of cannabis, their belief in its healing power, and their conviction that no one should be incarcerated over this plant. I started volunteering for the first classes held in our Los Angeles satellite campus on February 2nd, 2008. I fell in love with the school's mission, and my husband — Oaksterdam University, is responsible for connecting many partnerships!

In 2010, we ran the first voter initiative in 35 years to legalize cannabis for adult use in California, the fifth-largest economy on the planet. The election heard worldwide (and Oaksterdam leadership moving the political needle) likely triggered the federal crackdown, initiated before dawn on a clear, crisp April morning. The Obama administration raided OU, and in a long, traumatizing day, four federal agencies seized everything of value — our bank account, plants, computers, and sense of safety. School founder Richard Lee's multiple businesses were forfeited — he was forced to retire under threat of "continuing criminal enterprise" charges carrying a sentence of a lifetime in prison in his wheelchair — or even the death penalty.

I could not fathom quitting the mission amid this crippling federal raid. I soldiered with Richard's blessing and regrouped with a fierce group of dedicated volunteers. Oaksterdam University continued holding public classes two days after the raid. We remained the only campus in the world working with live plants for years — the students grew medical cannabis for a local multiple sclerosis patient. We refused to allow the federal raid to stop our mission to educate and change cannabis law and policy worldwide.

The school expanded to Michigan, Los Angeles, NorCal, and East to New Jersey, D.C., and more. The demand for information and camaraderie around the plant was so strong that we drew people from across the country and around the globe who couldn't believe there was a place that was teaching people how to (illegally) grow and consume safely, as well as protect from illegal search and seizure and advocate to change the law and end the War on Drugs. OU has now educated over 80,000 people from 110+ countries. Among our many alums is David Paleschuck, and I couldn't be prouder of him — and his impact.

David found us and, like so many others from around the world, came to Oakland, California, because he wanted to be part of something bigger than himself. He wanted to be part of the movement. David is a piece of the secret to our success and is helping to change the world.

We met David when he first came to Oaksterdam for a four-day seminar at our Oakland campus. He studied history and policy, extractions, and cooking with cannabis. He learned about terpenes, THC, and CBD and how they affect the endocannabinoid system. He even took a horticulture class with cultivation pioneer Ed Rosenthal, author of *The Cannabis Grower's Handbook*.

David says his connections were equally valuable to the knowledge he gained from classes. Entering the cannabis space back then was still a dangerous proposition. You risked being imprisoned as so many still are — disproportionately people of color. Even as medicinal and adult use legalization makes inroads, you can still be arrested, lose your kids, and become stigmatized in your profession over cannabis. And there was David, contemplating leaving his comfortable corporate job for a career in cannabis. "It was a lonely road," he said.

Oaksterdam University helped make David feel less isolated. As that gallery owner promised, David has grown and blossomed in the industry, as have so many people he met at OU. Cannabis is now a multi-billion-dollar global industry, and as the rest of the world catches up with us rebels out here on the leading edge, I would love to see OU alums grow to do amazing things in the world. David is a great example.

He absorbed the knowledge from Oaksterdam University and melded it with his corporate experience to become a force to be reckoned with. He started as vice president of licensing and brand partnerships for DOPE Magazine. Then, he served as Chief Marketing Officer for Evergreen Herbal, creating some of Washington state's leading cannabis-infused edibles, tinctures, and beverages.

In 2021, he launched his company, Branding Bud Consulting Group, to help clients build their brands and grow across state lines and international borders. That same year, David wrote the book *Branding Bud: The Commercialization of Cannabis* to explore what companies are doing to introduce their products to the hearts and minds of consumers. The book became a bestseller on Amazon in two categories ("Logo & Brand Design" and "Green Business") for nine months. He has gone from a student at Oaksterdam University to an esteemed faculty member, teaching branding and marketing in our business department.

David has also spoken at many industry events and trade shows. Mr. Jones and I bumped into him again at one of the largest, MJBizCon, in Las Vegas after several Clubhouse conversations on his show "Branding Bud Live." David's show attracts an array of people looking to break into the industry, as well as those who've already established themselves and want a safe place to network, ask questions, and learn how to grow their companies.

Someone asked David if he "uses recreational marijuana." It triggered such a passionate reaction in him I was taken aback. It wasn't the question itself but the way it was asked. David stopped everything. "Absolutely not," he replied. "I don't 'use marijuana,' I 'consume cannabis.'"

I was right there with him. Hearing the term "recreational" made me want to wash that man's mouth with soap. It makes cannabis sound fun for kids and scares soccer moms in Kansas — it's irresponsible of a responsible industry to use that term. Hearing "professionals" use the wrong terminology regarding cannabis was just as painful to David! It had become a personal pet peeve for him and a glaring red flag that the person was either uneducated, unprofessional, or both. How can you be taken seriously in this industry if you don't know and use the proper vocabulary? Moreover, how can this fledgling industry, still so precarious, be taken seriously by lawmakers and regulators, never mind neighbors and voters?

The modern use of the term "marijuana" originated in Mexico and was popularized in American culture through racist propaganda. In the days of xenophobic yellow journalism, William Randolph Hearst used the slang word to fearmonger and identify marijuana with the "others," insinuating we were to be frightened of foreigners. It is a controversial term today because of its use to create a negative association with hemp and cannabis, leading to Prohibition. Although written into many federal and state laws, it is not scientifically accurate. This negative association was believed to obscure that "marijuana" is cannabis and hemp and garnered support for the Prohibition of a "scary new drug" coming from the Mexican border.

We share a passion for this topic, and that's why OU publishes the *Oaksterdam Cannabis Terminology Style Guide* to organize and formalize our industry's nomenclature. With more media reporting on cannabis than ever, we saw the need to reference common-use definitions of the words and concepts core to writing about its complexities.

Cannabis isn't a simple subject. More than 80 years of Prohibition has muddled knowledge of the plant's taxonomy, culture, therapeutic use, cultivation, history, law, and scientific study. Our first terminology guide was published in 2021. The Associated Press Style Guide for journalists and public relations professionals and The Chicago Manual of Style for educators offer minimal guidance on the topic, so experts at Oaksterdam University composed and edited a style guide designed for use by academics and writers of all kinds.

I was ready to chime in on the Clubhouse audio app with David and other thought leaders based on our expert-generated curricula and my personal campaign trail experiences. Our spirited discussion in the room those many days — which bordered on verbal sparring — inspired an entire *Branding Bud Live* episode called "Cannabis vs. Marijuana," where David addressed words people use and how important it is for us in the cannabis industry to be united as we forge a standardized way of talking about our industry. That very conversation planted the seed that was the inception of this book.

Cannabis vs. Marijuana contains a wealth of information on appropriate, enlightened vocabulary. Chapters cover specific terms like Legalize vs. Decriminalize; Reschedule vs. Decontrol; Medical, Medicinal, or Therapeutic; Adult Use vs. Recreational; Entourage vs. Ensemble Effect; Strain vs. Cultivar, among others.

The book goes beyond word usage and takes a deep dive into the history and culture surrounding the plant, how stereotypes were created, the future of the language of cannabis, and how to choose words carefully to get your message across.

With his corporate background, David sees the industry's potential and knows that anyone who wants to be a part of it better know their stuff. Reports have shown double-digit job growth year over year. Once states legalize, there is instant demand for cultivators, lab testers, extractors, product manufacturers, and retail workers to grow hemp and cannabis and bring it to market.

There also are countless ancillary positions related to the field — the real estate agents finding commercial spaces for cannabis businesses, the contractors building them out, the accountants preparing their taxes (another subject entirely), and the publicists hired to help spread the word. Chances are you're coming into contact with cannabis clients at work and consumers in your circle of friends and family. Knowing how to speak about the industry and the plant is crucial as you enter job interviews, boardrooms, and conversations with your relatives considering topicals for joint pain (please, talk to your grandma!). David's book is for all these people and anyone else who needs to speak or write intelligently about the plant and its burgeoning industry. This book will not and should not be the end (because David will write more awesome books).

Language is constantly evolving and changing and is an amalgamation of the fabric of human experience with all its diversity, creativity, and messiness. In the *Oaksterdam Terminology Style Guide*, we invite feedback, input, questions, and requests for clarification, and we update the style guide each year because language is not stagnant. Involving many diverse stakeholders in developing standards is crucial. Ultimately, the jury is out even regarding the words' cannabis' versus 'marijuana.' In convicted discussions, Mexican students have expressed they are not at all offended by the word "marijuana," but only the way it was co-opted during Prohibition and imbued with racist connotations. Today, they want to take the word back from their heritage and not be made to feel "evil" by American "latte liberals" deciding that the word is evil and that no one should ever use it. To demonize the term now, especially for a Mexican-American, is reverse-engineering a second assault by making it "bad."

Verbiage is nuanced and changes meaning over time. This book starts a crucial conversation in chatrooms, classrooms, and boardrooms as we forge this brave new industry together. Words matter in framing our advocacy and communicating clearly to discover what we can agree on regarding cannabis freedom, even if our "whys" are different. I hope you enjoy David's book as much as I do and that you use the information inside to become a more educated and ethical consumer of information (and cannabis) and join us in changing the world.

***

INTRODUCTION

THE IMPACT OF LANGUAGE ON ATTITUDES AND PERCEPTIONS

The study of global cannabis terminology is a study of the world's cultural, historical, and political intricacies as they intersect with this ancient and complex plant. Understanding this intersection is essential for anyone involved in the global cannabis conversation, from policymakers and diplomats to educators and advocates. It's a reminder that words are not just communication tools but windows into the diverse and nuanced worldviews that shape our understanding of cannabis.

In the vast tapestry of human existence, one thread has consistently woven itself through the fabric of our history, culture, and society: language. Language, often taken for granted daily, is the cornerstone of human communication and interaction. It's a tool that enables us to bridge the chasms that separate us and to share our experiences, thoughts, and emotions. Yet, language is far more than a mere tool; it's an intricate web of symbols, sounds, and meanings encapsulating the essence of who we are as individuals, communities, and collective species. Throughout the book, I delve into the profound impact of words and language on our lives, examining how they serve as conduits for conveying information, reflections of our values and beliefs, and mirrors of the ever-evolving cultural landscapes in which they thrive.

Language is humanity's communication bridge, stretching across the vast and turbulent river of misunderstanding. It's our tool for sharing knowledge, telling stories, and expressing the intricacies of our inner worlds. In the early stages of our evolution, humans grasped the power of words to convey simple ideas and needs. Across countless ages, this basic system of communication has blossomed into the diverse array of languages that weave the vibrant linguistic fabric of our world today. Language encapsulates the unique experiences and worldviews of its speakers.

Words not only convey meaning but also shape our identities. They are the essence of our self-expression, reflecting our beliefs, values, and emotions. Every linguistic community, from the vast tribes of the Amazon to the bustling streets of New York City, carries a unique linguistic fingerprint within it. Through language, we transmit our cultural heritage, defining who we are and where we come from. The cadence of our speech, the idioms we employ, and the vocabulary we cherish all contribute to the mosaic of our linguistic identity.

Language holds the power to both divide and unite. Throughout history, the choice of words has ignited revolutions, resolved conflicts, and kindled the fires of social change. The American Civil Rights Movement, fueled by the eloquence of Dr. Martin Luther King Jr., stands as a testament to the transformative power of language. Conversely, words have been wielded as weapons, inciting hatred, discrimination, and violence. By understanding this duality, we can harness language to heal rather than harm, to build bridges rather than barriers.

Language is not static; it is a living entity that evolves with society. New words emerge to describe technological advancements, cultural phenomena, and shifting paradigms. In the digital age, terms like "tweet," "selfie," and "emoji" have become commonplace, shaping how we interact and communicate. Adapting language to our ever-changing world reflects our innate creativity and adaptability as a species.

One of the most intriguing facets of language lies in its nuanced expressions and the challenge of translation. Each language holds a treasure trove of words and phrases that are difficult to convey accurately in another tongue. From the untranslatable Portuguese *"Saudade,"* a term that doesn't have a direct English translation but described as a complex and deep emotional state of intense longing, nostalgia, and melancholy, to the Japanese phrase *"mono no aware"* - roughly translated to "the beauty of impermanence" or "the pathos of things." These terms encapsulate profound emotions and experiences that transcend the boundaries of simple definition. Exploring these linguistic treasures enriches our understanding of language and offers a glimpse into the kaleidoscope of human emotions.

As we navigate the complexities of the 21st century, language remains at the forefront of societal change. The digital age has birthed a new lexicon that traverses borders and cultures at the speed of light. The implications of this linguistic globalization are profound, affecting everything from international diplomacy to everyday conversations.

Beyond their capacity for conveying information, words serve as mirrors reflecting our individual and collective identities, bridges connecting disparate worlds, and living entities evolving alongside society. The power of words is as boundless as the human spirit itself. How we wield this power is our choice: whether to divide or unite, harm or heal, communicate or miscommunicate.

The importance of words in bridging gaps and correcting misunderstandings must be considered. Language's ability to convey thoughts, emotions, and intentions is the linchpin of effective communication. It's a tool that facilitates understanding, fosters empathy, and allows for the exchange of perspectives.

One of the most profound functions of language is its capacity to invoke empathy. Through words, we can step into another's shoes, gaining insights into their experiences, fears, hopes, and dreams. When words are used with empathy, they become instruments of connection, dissolving the barriers that often divide us.

THE POWER OF CONTEXT

The context within which we choose our words is paramount. Language is humanity's bridge across the vast river of misunderstanding, allowing us to share knowledge, stories, and the intricacies of our inner worlds. Over epochs, our primitive communication evolved into the diverse tapestry of languages we know today, encapsulating speakers' unique experiences and perspectives.

Context provides the necessary framework for understanding the meaning, intention, and nuances behind words. Words on their own can have multiple interpretations or meanings. Context helps us navigate these interpretations by providing information about the situation, setting, tone, and the people involved in a conversation or written piece.

Context shapes the evolution of language. Navigating the complexities of the 21st century, language remains at the forefront of societal change, especially in the digital age, where linguistic globalization affects diplomacy, policy, and everyday conversations.

Words are profoundly important in bridging gaps and correcting misunderstandings. Language's ability to convey thoughts, emotions, and intentions is vital for effective communication. Context informs the selection of words, ensuring they foster understanding, empathy, inclusion, and diverse perspectives.

In an age characterized by an avalanche of information, the role of words in correcting misinformation and disinformation is paramount. With the spread of falsehoods facilitated by the digital realm, the ability to critically assess and respond to information has never been more crucial. In this context, language serves as both a shield and a sword. It empowers individuals to dissect, challenge, and rectify misunderstandings while also being the vehicle for disseminating truths.

Words can be healing elixirs in moments of conflict and misunderstanding. Our vocabulary has the power to apologize, forgive, and extend an olive branch. When chosen carefully and delivered sincerely, words can mend broken bonds and rebuild trust. Conversely, a lack of communication or the careless use of words can deepen rifts and perpetuate fabrications and falsehoods.

As technology continues to reshape the communication landscape, words play a central role in navigating this shifting terrain. The digital age has ushered in new forms of discourse, from the succinct expressions of social media to the nuanced conversations of online forums. With these changes come challenges and opportunities. The brevity of tweets and status updates demands precision in language, while the expansiveness of long-form content allows for deeper exploration of complex topics.

ALIGNING LANDSCAPES AND PERSPECTIVES

The evolution of language is inherently linked to the dynamic nature of culture, society, and human experiences. Words and their definitions change and evolve in response to cultural shifts, technological advancements, and societal transformations. New concepts, inventions, and ideologies continuously emerge, necessitating the creation of new vocabulary or the adaptation of existing words to encompass these novel ideas. Similarly, the changing socio-cultural landscape influences the connotations and associations of specific words, leading to shifts in their semantic meanings and societal interpretations. As societies progress and evolve, language adapts to reflect the evolving values, beliefs, and priorities of the communities it serves, illustrating the interconnected relationship between language and the human experience.

Words stand as both a gift and a responsibility. They are the conduits of our thoughts, the architects of our relationships, and the keys to unlocking understanding and empathy. It's clear that words are not mere tools; they are the heartbeat of human connection, the compass that guides us through the labyrinth of existence. We must wield them with care, for they can illuminate, obscure, unite, divide, and ultimately define us as individuals, communities, and species. The responsibility is ours, and the gift is immeasurable.

The urgency of using the right words in the cannabis industry is underscored by the need to bring together individuals from all walks of life, including scientists, researchers, politicians, and policymakers. To bridge the divide between the industry and those outside it, we must adopt a lexicon that speaks to the core values of precision, accuracy and shared knowledge.

The use of words related to cannabis exemplifies the crucial role of context in shaping the perception and understanding of the plant throughout history. Depending on the cultural, legal, and social contexts in which they are employed, terms like "cannabis" and "marijuana" have carried diverse connotations, evoking varying responses and perceptions among different communities and societies.

In the past, the term "marijuana" was predominantly utilized in a derogatory manner, often associated with negative stereotypes and racial biases, particularly in the context of early 20th-century America. Its derogatory connotations were intertwined with xenophobic and racially discriminatory sentiments, contributing to the stigmatization and criminalization of cannabis use within specific communities. Conversely, the term "cannabis" has been utilized in a more neutral and scientific context, often associated with its botanical properties and medicinal potential, transcending the negative cultural associations attached to "marijuana."

ASKING THE RIGHT QUESTIONS

By considering the role of language, context, culture, and community, we can choose words that foster empathy, understanding, and solidarity among diverse groups, facilitating meaningful connections and mutual appreciation. To better understand the benefits of the plant and to normalize it, as individuals and as an industry, perhaps we should ask ourselves the following questions:

- How does language shape perceptions and attitudes towards cannabis within and across cultures?
- What cultural contexts surround cannabis consumption, and how do these differ within specific communities?
- How can language, cultural context, and intent be harmonized to promote informed, respectful, and normalized discussions about cannabis?
- Perhaps the most crucial question is how adequate communication can bridge gaps between scientists, researchers, policymakers, and the industry itself.

Only through words that resonate with all stakeholders can we hope to build a foundation of trust, dismantle misconceptions, and foster collaboration that will propel the cannabis industry forward. I hope this book serves as a compass, guiding us toward a future where cannabis is comprehended, celebrated, and responsibly integrated into our society. Let us join together to forge a path toward unity and progress.

***

CHAPTER 1

CANNABIS vs. MARIJUANA

THE VEIL OF WORDS

Cannabis and marijuana may be two names for the same plant; the difference is one represents the future, and the other the past.

Using words and language is an essential aspect of human communication and interaction. Words convey information and reflect the values, beliefs, and culture of the society in which they are used. In the context of cannabis, words have played a significant role in shaping attitudes and perceptions towards the plant, and how they are discussed and referred to has evolved.

> *"I have opted to use 'cannabis' over 'marijuana' for a while now. This conscious effort is a step towards the future and away from "marijuana's" historically racist roots. It's more than a name change; it's embracing the plant's formal and legitimate name to leave outdated biases in the past."*
> — Rusty Wilenkin, Co-Founder & CEO, Old Pal

Euphemisms and slang have been a common feature of cannabis culture for many years. These terms have been used to describe the effects of cannabis, as well as to obscure its true meaning. While some euphemisms and slang terms have become mainstream and widely accepted, others have been criticized for reinforcing negative stereotypes and stigmatizing individuals who consume the plant.

Historically, marijuana has been associated with negative connotations, often linked to criminal activity and deviant behavior. As such, the language surrounding the plant is characterized by negative and stigmatizing terms, such as "pot" and "dope." These terms are used to demonize and marginalize individuals who consume the plant, contributing to a broader societal narrative that it is dangerous and should be avoided.

However, as attitudes towards cannabis have evolved, so has the language used to describe it. Terms such as "medical marijuana" and "recreational cannabis" have become more widely accepted, reflecting a growing awareness of the plant's potential benefits for both therapeutic and adult consumption. These terms reflect a more positive and accepting attitude towards cannabis and indicate a broader shift in societal attitudes towards the plant.

LANGUAGE AND PURPOSE

Using euphemisms and slang to describe cannabis is not a new phenomenon. The plant has been subject to many euphemisms and slang terms throughout history, reflecting changing attitudes towards it.

In the early 20th century, cannabis was commonly called "Indian hemp" or "loco weed," reflecting its association with marginalized communities and the perception that deviant or criminal individuals consumed it. However, as the plant became more widely consumed and accepted, so did the language used to describe it. Terms such as "pot" and "weed" emerged in the 1960s and 1970s, reflecting a growing acceptance of cannabis consumption among counterculture communities.

Since then, many euphemisms and slang terms have emerged, reflecting the change in attitudes towards cannabis. Words such as "chronic," "dank," and "loud" are commonly used to describe high-quality cannabis, while terms such as "mids," "regs," and "boof" are used to describe lower-quality cannabis. These terms reflect a broader cultural fascination with cannabis and demonstrate how language has evolved to reflect changing attitudes and perceptions.

Euphemisms, words, and phrases used to avoid terms considered too blunt or offensive have been used to soften the perceived impact of cannabis consumption. For example, terms like "medical marijuana" or "cannabis therapy" are used to describe the consumption of cannabis for medicinal purposes, which have helped to destigmatize its consumption and highlight its potential benefits. Similarly, the term "recreational cannabis" is often used to describe the consumption of cannabis for non-medicinal purposes (i.e., adult use), which can help to shift the focus away from the negative stereotypes associated with recreational drug use.

However, using euphemisms can also be problematic when it comes to cannabis. For example, the term "marijuana" has a long and complicated history, and its use can be seen as reinforcing negative stereotypes and racial biases. The term was popularized in the early 20th century as part of a campaign to demonize cannabis and associate it with Mexican immigrants. Its continued use can be seen as perpetuating these stereotypes. Similarly, terms like "stoner" or "pothead" can reinforce negative stereotypes and stigmatize cannabis consumption, particularly for those who consume it for medicinal purposes.

Terms like "weed," "pot," and "bud" have become ubiquitous in popular culture and are often used to refer to cannabis in a casual or colloquial context. While these terms can help to create a sense of community and shared experience among cannabis consumers, they can also be seen as reinforcing negative stereotypes and limiting the public's understanding of the plant and its potential benefits.[1]

> *"This industry is like no other. I've witnessed how a solitary word wields power and can swiftly alter perceptions and shape advancement. Beyond semantics, distinctions like 'cannabis vs. marijuana' signify purposeful steps in erasing outdated mindsets, all while honoring the struggles of those who paved our path. In the world of cannabis, language should be rolled with care – misused words can be a joint venture into misunderstanding."*
>
> — Carolyn Matthies, CMO, The Arcview Group

In recent years, there has been a growing recognition of the importance of language in the cannabis industry and culture. Many advocates and activists are pushing for more thoughtful and intentional language use, focusing on promoting understanding and dismantling harmful stereotypes. Similarly, many businesses and organizations in the legal cannabis industry are adopting more neutral, professional, or scientific language to destigmatize cannabis consumption and promote its potential benefits.

As society progresses in its understanding and acceptance of cannabis, the language surrounding it evolves. The shift from "marijuana" to "cannabis" in public and legal discourse signifies a deliberate move towards a more neutral, scientific lexicon that reflects the plant's legitimate uses and distances it from historical prejudices and legal stigmatization. "Cannabis" invites a perspective that respects its medicinal and adult use, aligning with a global trend toward legalization and regulation.

Despite this progress, the persistence of slang terms like "ouid" and coded language such as "c4nn4b1s" on social media platforms underscores an ongoing dichotomy. In regions or forums where cannabis discussions are censored or culturally taboo, these linguistic contortions reveal that while the plant gains formal acceptance, there remains an undercurrent of necessity to veil dialogue, indicating that normalization is still a work in progress. This linguistic duality showcases the complex relationship between legal developments, cultural acceptance, and the continuous push for broader societal normalization of cannabis.

As attitudes towards cannabis continue to shift and as legalization efforts gain traction, it is clear that the language we use to talk about the plant will play an essential role in shaping public perceptions and policy. By taking the time to reflect on the language we use to talk about cannabis and the cultural context in which that language exists, we can help to build a more informed and thoughtful cannabis culture and a more equitable, just, and legal cannabis industry.

One of the challenges facing the cannabis industry and culture is the need to balance the desire for openness and transparency with the need for responsible and thoughtful language use. On the one hand, many advocates and activists are pushing for greater transparency and honesty around cannabis consumption, focusing on promoting understanding and reducing stigma. On the other hand, there is a concern that overly casual or flippant language can reinforce negative stereotypes and undermine efforts to promote the responsible and safe consumption of cannabis.

The legalization of cannabis has created a complex regulatory landscape, which can make language use even more important. In most jurisdictions, cannabis is still subject to strict regulations around advertising and marketing, which can limit the language used to describe the plant and its by-products. For example, many legal cannabis businesses must use neutral or clinical language when describing their products to avoid making unsubstantiated health claims or promoting excessive consumption.

> *"Originally introduced to Mexico by Spanish conquistadors as 'cañaba,' the plant gained respect among indigenous people who referred to it as 'marijuana.' However, in the US, Harry Anslinger, the first commissioner of the Federal Bureau of Narcotics and known for his xenophobic views, appropriated the term to promote anti-Mexican sentiment during Prohibition. Today, we revert to the scientific term 'cannabis,' shedding the baggage that has damaged this healing plant's reputation for decades.*
>
> — Gary Stein, Executive Director, Clarity PAC

At the same time, that complex regulatory landscape often requires cannabis businesses to use specific words (i.e., marijuana, marihuana, etc.) in their applications for production and processing licenses, as well as on their products' labels.

A MULTITUDE OF PERSPECTIVES

Another challenge facing the cannabis industry and culture is balancing different communities' diverse perspectives and experiences. Cannabis has a long and complex history, shaped by various cultural, social, and economic factors. As a result, the language used to talk about cannabis can have different meanings and associations depending on the context and the community.

Some advocates and activists are pushing for greater recognition of the historical and cultural significance of cannabis for marginalized communities, particularly BIPOC communities. These advocates argue that terms like "marijuana" can be seen as disrespectful or offensive and that more respectful and culturally appropriate language should be used instead.

Using language to describe cannabis is not simply a matter of individual preference. Various cultural and societal factors shape language use, media representation, legal frameworks, and social norms.

For example, media representation of cannabis has significantly influenced the language used to describe the plant. In the past, media coverage of the plant has been characterized by sensationalism and fear-mongering, with terms such as "gateway drug" and "dangerous narcotic" used to describe cannabis. However, as media coverage has become more balanced and nuanced, so has the language used to describe the plant.

> *"The stigma surrounding cannabis persists in all sectors of society, particularly within the media. While several major outlets, primarily print and online, have begun to report on cannabis in an educational manner, the television industry either avoids discussing it entirely or perpetuates stereotypes rather than presenting the current reality. This remains the next challenge if we aim to achieve widespread acceptance of cannabis."*
> — Stu Zakim, CEO, Bridge Strategic Communications

Legal frameworks also have a significant influence on language use. In jurisdictions where cannabis is illegal, terms such as "weed" and "pot" are commonly used to describe the plant, reflecting the criminalization and stigmatization of their consumption. In contrast, in jurisdictions where the plant is legal, terms such as "cannabis" are more commonly used, reflecting a more positive and accepting attitude towards the plant.

Social norms also play a significant role in shaping language use. In many communities, the use of cannabis is stigmatized, and individuals who consume the plant may be subject to social ostracism and discrimination. As a result, language use can serve as a way of signaling acceptance or rejection of the plant, with individuals who use more positive or neutral terms such as "cannabis" viewed more positively than those who use more negative words such as "weed," "pot," or "marijuana."

CODED NARRATIVES

The language used to describe cannabis significantly impacts attitudes and perceptions toward the plant. Negative and stigmatizing language reinforces negative stereotypes and contributes to a broader societal narrative that the plant is dangerous and should be avoided. In contrast, more positive and accepting language can help to change attitudes and perceptions towards the plant, contributing to a broader acceptance of its consumption.

The term "medical marijuana" has significantly changed attitudes towards cannabis consumption for medicinal purposes. This term has helped to shift the conversation away from the stigmatization of the plant towards a more positive and accepting attitude relative to its medicinal benefits.

Similarly, using more positive and accepting language can help reduce the stigma associated with cannabis consumption, making it easier for individuals who consume the plant to access support and treatment if necessary. By using more positive and accepting language, we can help to create a more supportive and accepting environment for individuals who consume the plant.

In the world of cannabis, a peculiar phenomenon has taken hold—a maze of insider jargon and euphemisms carefully crafted to conceal the true nature of the conversation. This intricate web of language, born out of necessity during times of prohibition and social stigma, has inadvertently given rise to a significant consequence: a lack of shared understanding and frequent disagreements among laypeople and experts alike.

For decades, cannabis has remained shrouded in secrecy. Coded language, such as "grass," "pot," or "weed," was employed to disguise the plant itself. This clandestine lexicon was a means of survival, enabling individuals to discuss cannabis without arousing suspicion or inviting legal repercussions. However, as the legal landscape surrounding cannabis transforms, the need for this secrecy diminishes. It is time to emerge from the shadows and engage in open, informed conversations.

Within the cannabis community, a rich tapestry of terms and expressions has blossomed. Words like "sativa," "indica," "CBD," and "THC" have become synonymous with the plant. However, their proper definitions and effects have become obscured amidst many conflicting opinions. Are these distinctions accurate? Or have we collectively adopted oversimplified narratives that fail to capture the complexity of the plant and its properties? It is imperative to untangle the intricacies and dispel misconceptions to foster a more nuanced understanding.

"Words evoke emotions and feelings. Utilizing the more scientific word, cannabis, allows people to talk about the plant more freely without it carrying the heavy stigma that the slang term, marijuana, brings with it."
— Kim Prince, Founder & CEO, Proven Media

CULTURAL IDENTITY AND CANNABIS

Cannabis, more than just a plant, has evolved into a cultural phenomenon. It has inspired art, music, and a vibrant community. However, as cannabis gains mainstream acceptance, questions arise about cultural appropriation and commodification. Is there a risk of losing the essence of cannabis culture amidst corporate co-optation? It is crucial to explore how we can preserve the integrity and diversity of cannabis culture while embracing its evolution.

The beneficial properties of cannabis have captivated scientists, patients, and consumers alike. However, the absence of standardized research and medical guidelines has led to contentious debates within the medical community. While some advocate for rigorous clinical trials and FDA approval, others emphasize the importance of patient experience and anecdotal evidence. We must bridge the gap between traditional medicine and alternative therapies to find common ground.

CULTIVATING UNITY AMIDST DIVERSITY

Throughout history, marginalized communities have borne the brunt of cannabis criminalization. As legalization spreads across jurisdictions, addressing the inequities perpetuated by the War On Drugs is imperative. How can we rectify past injustices and ensure a fair and inclusive cannabis industry? We can forge a more just and inclusive future by examining social equity initiatives, restorative justice measures, and empowering affected communities.

The time has come for a collective effort to foster understanding, bridge divides, and cultivate unity within the cannabis industry and its communities. In exploring cannabis-related issues, we see the layers of secrecy, differences in language, and the challenges arising from conflicting viewpoints.

To achieve this, unity, education, and open dialogue must prevail. We must prioritize disseminating accurate information grounded in scientific research and shared experiences. By debunking myths, challenging misconceptions, and promoting evidence-based discussions, we can establish a foundation of knowledge that enables us to move forward collectively.

> *"If cannabis were a new discovery rather than a well-known substance carrying cultural and political baggage, it would be hailed as a wonder drug."*
> — Dr. Lester Grinspoon, MD, Harvard Medical School

Summary

Cannabis is more than a plant; it is a culture, a medicine, an industry, and a social movement. As it becomes increasingly integrated into mainstream society, preserving its cultural identity while embracing its evolution is a delicate balance. We must honor its rich history and the diverse communities that have championed it while navigating the changing landscape of legalization and commercialization.

Yet, perhaps the most critical aspect of our journey is the recognition of the inequities and injustices perpetuated by the War On Drugs. To move forward, we must rectify past wrongs through social equity initiatives, restorative justice, and inclusive practices. We must create an industry that is not only economically viable but also fair and inclusive, offering opportunities to those who have borne the brunt of prohibition.

We can select words that nurture empathy, comprehension, and unity among varied groups, enabling significant bonds and shared respect.

To deepen our comprehension of the plant's advantages and to integrate it more naturally, both individually and within the industry, it might be valuable to reflect on the following questions:

- What specific language is legally recognized or required within the applicable laws and regulations?
- How do the chosen words resonate within the cultural context or informal settings and facilitate open dialogue?
- What language choices might best address societal perceptions and sensitivities surrounding cannabis?
- What terms align with personal comfort levels or preferences, considering potential impacts on communication effectiveness?

The path forward is clear: unity, education, and open dialogue. By fostering a collective commitment to transparency, understanding, and responsible action, we can navigate the complexities of the cannabis industry with clarity and purpose. It is a call to action, a collective endeavor to create a more equitable, just, and informed future where cannabis can thrive in all its forms.

CHAPTER 2

CANNABIS, CULTURE & CONTEXT

WHAT IS CULTURE?

Culture refers to the shared beliefs, values, customs, behaviors, and artifacts that characterize a group or society. It encompasses many elements, such as language, art, music, cuisine, religion, social norms, and traditions.[1]

> *"Cannabis is a unifying force, fostering connections and building vibrant communities across diverse backgrounds. Whether it's the shared exploration of unique cultivars or the coming together of like-minded individuals, cannabis enriches our experiences and pays homage to its culturally diverse roots."*
> — Amy Deneson, Co-Founder, Cannabis Media Council

It is often learned through socialization and transmitted from generation to generation. It can vary widely between different societies and can also change over time. Culture is critical in shaping individuals' perceptions, attitudes, and behaviors. It is integral to a society's identity and sense of belonging and can be classified into two main categories: material and non-material. Material culture includes physical objects such as clothing, tools, buildings, and artwork, while non-material culture refers to the intangible aspects of culture, such as beliefs, values, and norms.

Cultural diversity refers to the variety of different cultures that exist in the world. Each culture has its unique characteristics and perspectives, which can enrich our understanding of the world and our interactions with others. Cultural diversity is essential because it allows us to learn from and appreciate different perspectives and traditions, and it helps to promote tolerance and acceptance of differences.

Cultural beliefs and values can also significantly shape social, political, and economic systems. For example, they can influence the development of laws and policies and how people interact in the workplace and social settings.

It is important to note that culture is not static and can change over time as societies evolve and interact. The study of culture is a complex and dynamic field, and researchers in anthropology, sociology, and other social sciences continue to explore the many facets of this vital topic.

One important concept related to culture is cultural relativism. It is the idea that we should approach other cultures without judging them based on our cultural norms and values. Instead, we should strive to understand and appreciate different cultures on their terms, recognizing that what may seem strange or even wrong to us may be perfectly acceptable and even essential in another culture.

However, cultural relativism can sometimes conflict with universal human rights, which suggests that certain fundamental rights and freedoms should apply to all people regardless of their cultural background. Finding a balance between cultural relativism and universal human rights can be challenging and lead to complex ethical questions.

In today's globalized world, cultures are increasingly interacting and blending, which can create new and exciting opportunities for cross-cultural exchange and learning. Still, it can also lead to challenges and conflicts as different cultures and values clash. Understanding and appreciating cultural diversity can help us to navigate these challenges and promote a more harmonious and peaceful world.

In addition to cultural relativism, ethnocentrism is another crucial concept in the study of culture. It is the tendency to judge other cultures based on the standards and values of our own culture, often leading to a belief that our culture is superior to others. Ethnocentrism can lead to misunderstandings, prejudice, and discrimination and hinder cross-cultural understanding and cooperation.

Engaging in intercultural communication is essential to understand and appreciate other cultures. It involves developing the skills to communicate effectively with people from different cultural backgrounds, including awareness of cultural differences in nonverbal communication, values, beliefs, and norms. It also involves having an open mind and a willingness to learn from and appreciate different cultural perspectives.

It is noteworthy that culture is not limited to national or ethnic groups. Subcultures, or smaller groups within a larger culture that share specific beliefs, values, and behaviors, also exist. Examples of subcultures include religious groups, social classes, and professional groups. The study of subcultures can provide further insight into culture's complex and diverse nature.

Another important aspect of culture is the role it plays in shaping identity. Culture gives individuals a sense of belonging and can help define who they are. For example, language is a critical component of culture and is often closely tied to an individual's sense of identity.

Culture can also influence how individuals perceive themselves and others, as well as their attitudes and behaviors. For example, cultural norms and values can shape an individual's attitudes toward gender roles, sexuality, and race. Understanding the cultural context in which attitudes and behaviors are formed is essential in promoting understanding and acceptance of diversity.

In today's interconnected world, cultural exchange is increasingly common. Travel, international trade, and the internet have all contributed to the mixing of cultures, leading to a phenomenon known as "globalization." It has both positive and negative impacts on cultures, as it can lead to new opportunities for communication and exchange but can also lead to cultural homogenization and loss of traditional cultures.

> *"Cannabis has always played a pivotal role in culture, serving as a unifying force that transcends boundaries and brings communities together. Its remarkable ability to foster transformative dialogues and bridge diverse groups is a testament to its profound impact."*
> — Kristina Adduci, Founder, House of Puff

Finally, it is worth noting that culture is not static but constantly evolving and changing. It means that cultures can adapt and respond to new challenges and circumstances. Therefore, the study of culture is an essential field of inquiry, helping us better understand and appreciate the complexity and diversity of human societies.

WHAT IS CANNABIS CULTURE?

Cannabis has been consumed for various purposes for thousands of years, and its consumption has been intertwined with culture and context throughout history. Today, the cultural and social context of cannabis consumption is still an important consideration, as attitudes and perceptions towards the plant vary depending on various factors, including geography, age, race, and socio-economic status.[2]

A critical aspect of the cultural and social context of cannabis consumption is its historical and cultural significance. Cannabis has been consumed for medicinal, spiritual, and recreational purposes in many different cultures and societies throughout history. For example, in ancient China, cannabis was consumed for medicinal purposes and was considered one of the "five grains" alongside rice, wheat, barley, and soybeans. Similarly, in India, cannabis has a long history of consumption in Ayurvedic medicine and spiritual practices and is considered a sacred plant in some religious traditions.

> *"Cannabis has woven itself into the fabric of American culture, serving not just as a plant, but as a symbol of progressive thought, political discourse, and a challenge to the status quo. Against all odds and under the pressures of social ousting and aggressive political efforts, cannabis has persevered. Its journey from taboo to acceptance mirrors our society's evolving perspectives on health, wellness, and social justice."*
> — Juliana Whitney, Founder & CEO, Cann Strategy

Despite this long history of use, cannabis has also been stigmatized and criminalized in many cultures and societies. It has often been due to political, economic, and social factors rather than any inherent danger or harm associated with the plant. For example, in the United States, cannabis was criminalized in the early 20th century, partly due to racist and xenophobic attitudes towards Mexican immigrants who were thought to consume it. Similarly, the criminalization of cannabis in the 20th century has been linked to broader social and political movements, including the "War On Drugs" and the influence of pharmaceutical companies.

Attitudes towards cannabis use may vary depending on a person's geographic location, with some areas having more permissive attitudes towards the plant than others. Similarly, younger generations may have more positive attitudes towards cannabis consumption than older generations due to changing social and cultural norms.

Research has shown that BIPOC individuals are more likely to be arrested and incarcerated for cannabis-related offenses despite similar consumption rates among other groups. It has been linked to systemic racism and discriminatory law enforcement practices that target marginalized communities.

The cultural and social context of cannabis consumption is essential when discussing the plant and its use. The historical and cultural significance of cannabis and its criminalization and stigmatization have all played a role in shaping attitudes and perceptions. Understanding the cultural and social context of cannabis consumption is an essential step toward promoting more inclusive and accepting attitudes toward the plant and the individuals who consume it.

In recent years, as attitudes toward cannabis consumption have shifted and legalization efforts have gained momentum in some countries, the cultural and social context of cannabis consumption continues to evolve. With the emergence of legal cannabis markets and increased access to information about the plant, there has been a growing interest in cannabis culture and its associated traditions and practices.

One aspect of cannabis culture that has received increasing attention is using slang and euphemisms to describe the plant and its effects. These terms can vary depending on the cultural and social context in which they are used and can be influenced by various factors.

For example, some standard slang terms for cannabis include "weed," "pot," "marijuana," and "grass," among others. These terms have been used for decades and have become deeply ingrained in popular culture, often associated with images of counterculture and rebellion. Similarly, words like "high," "stoned," and "baked" are often used to describe the effects of cannabis and can vary in their connotations depending on the context and the individual consuming them.

> "The plant has the potential to both ravage and reshape society as the industry matures. We must evolve from the extractive, hyper-consumption, egocentric culture model to a revolutionary, eco-focused healing practice, creating paths for conscious life integration, manufacturing, regenerative farming, and sustainability rooted in repairing communities and the planet. Releasing the shackles of antiquated processes allows for a full spectrum of connection, creativity, innovation, and inspiration. Much of our liberation is connected to the plant's."
> — Solonje Burnett, Chief Culture & Community Officer, Erven

In addition to slang and euphemisms, there are also a variety of cultural practices associated with cannabis consumption that have emerged over time. For example, "420" has become a widely recognized symbol of cannabis culture, with April 20th (4/20) being celebrated by many as a day to consume cannabis. Similarly, the "joint" has become a ubiquitous symbol of cannabis consumption and has been incorporated into popular culture through music, movies, and other forms of media.

However, it is essential to note that not all aspects of cannabis culture are universally accepted or celebrated. For example, some individuals and communities may view certain aspects of cannabis culture as perpetuating harmful stereotypes or contributing to the stigmatization of cannabis consumers. Similarly, cultural practices that involve sharing cannabis products, such as passing a joint or pipe, may have become less common or acceptable in the wake of the COVID-19 pandemic.

The cultural and social context of cannabis consumption is a complex and dynamic phenomenon shaped by various historical, cultural, and social factors. As attitudes towards cannabis continue to evolve, so will the cultural practices and traditions associated with its use. By understanding and respecting the cultural and social context of cannabis consumption, we can work towards creating a more inclusive and accepting society for all individuals, regardless of their relationship with the plant.

> *"Cannabis deeply influences American culture, impacting social attitudes, politics, the economy, and media. A vital aspect is its profound connection to music, spanning genres like reggae, hip-hop, rock, and more. Artists from diverse backgrounds have integrated its healing and spiritual essence into their work, significantly shaping our culture and enriching the American experience."*
>
> — Jocelyn Sheltraw, Co-Founder, Budist

As the legalization and normalization of cannabis consumption continue, it is essential to consider the impact of language and cultural practices on how individuals and communities perceive and interact with the plant. Using slang and euphemisms to describe cannabis can be a double-edged sword, providing some individuals a sense of community and belonging while perpetuating negative stereotypes and stigmatizing those who consume the plant.

One example of this can be seen in using terms like "dank" or "loud" to describe high-quality cannabis products. While some individuals may use these terms to express enthusiasm or appreciation for the plant, they can also perpetuate the idea that cannabis consumption is solely for recreational purposes – and that those who consume it are "stoners" or "druggies." It can be particularly damaging for individuals who consume cannabis for medicinal purposes or responsibly and conscientiously.

Similarly, the use of cultural practices like passing a joint or pipe can be seen as promoting social connection and community among cannabis consumers. However, in a global pandemic, these practices may also be seen as irresponsible and potentially dangerous.

As the cultural and social context of cannabis consumption continues to evolve, it is also essential to consider the impact of language and cultural practices on equity and justice. Historically, the criminalization of cannabis has been used as a tool for racial and social control, with

BIPOC communities and low-income individuals disproportionately targeted for arrest and incarceration. While the legalization of cannabis has the potential to reduce these disparities, it is vital to ensure that language and cultural practices do not perpetuate these inequalities.

It can be seen in the case of the term "marijuana," which has its roots in racist and xenophobic attitudes towards Mexican immigrants in the early 20th century. While the term is still commonly used today, many advocates and activists have pushed for the use of more neutral or positive language, such as "cannabis," "hemp," or "plant medicine." By reframing the language used to describe cannabis, shifting the cultural and social context in a more positive and equitable direction is possible.

Words' importance, meaning, and intent in the context of cannabis culture and language cannot be overstated. As legalization and normalization of cannabis consumption continue, it is crucial to consider the impact of language and cultural practices on individuals and communities. Promoting inclusive and equitable language and cultural traditions can help create a more accepting and respectful society for all individuals, regardless of their relationship with the plant.

> *"Cannabis symbolizes restorative justice, having once marginalized and criminalized communities. In recent decades, it has gained mainstream acceptance and stands as an industry where ordinary people can build generational wealth. While it caused incarceration, it now offers opportunities for redemption. Despite the arduous path to ending Prohibition, significant progress has been made, promising a more inclusive and equitable cannabis industry in the future."*
> — Anthony Alegrete, Founder & COO, 40 Tons

WHY IS CULTURAL CONTEXT IMPORTANT?

Cultural context is essential for a variety of reasons. It influences how people interpret and respond to different situations, shaping their attitudes and behaviors. Understanding cultural context is necessary for effective communication and interaction between individuals and groups from different cultural backgrounds. Here are some reasons why cultural context is important:

Communication: Cultural context can affect how people communicate with each other. It includes language, nonverbal communication, and cultural norms around communication. Understanding these cultural differences is essential for effective communication and avoiding misunderstandings.

Behavior And Values: Cultural context can influence an individual's attitudes and behaviors, as well as their values and beliefs. For example, different cultures may have different attitudes toward time, personal space, family, and authority. Understanding these differences is vital for building relationships and working effectively with people from different cultural backgrounds.

Conflict Resolution: Understanding cultural context is essential for resolving conflicts between individuals or groups from different cultural backgrounds. Cultural differences can cause misunderstandings and disagreements, and understanding these differences can help to identify solutions that work for everyone.

Business And Trade: Cultural context is essential for business and trade relationships. Understanding cultural differences in business practices, negotiation styles, and communication can help to build strong relationships and achieve successful outcomes.

Diversity And Inclusion: Cultural context is vital for promoting societal diversity and inclusion. Understanding and appreciating different cultures can help to reduce prejudice and discrimination and promote a more tolerant and inclusive society.

Health And Wellness: Cultural context is also crucial for health and wellness. Different cultures may have different attitudes and beliefs around health and wellness and other practices for maintaining health and treating illnesses. Understanding cultural differences in health practices can provide more effective and culturally sensitive healthcare.

Education: Cultural context is essential in education, as it can influence how students learn and what they know. Different cultures may have different educational approaches and expectations for students and teachers. Understanding cultural differences in education can promote more effective and culturally responsive teaching.

Art & Creativity: Cultural context can also influence art and creativity. Different cultures may have other artistic traditions, styles, and creative expression methods. Understanding cultural differences in art can promote cross-cultural appreciation and understanding.

Historical & Social Context: Cultural context can also provide important historical and social context. Understanding cultural traditions and practices can provide insight into the history and social context of a particular group or society. It can promote understanding and appreciation of different cultural experiences.

Summary

The profound significance of culture and context within the realm of cannabis cannot be overstated. This dynamic and evolving cultural landscape, deeply rooted in historical traditions and societal attitudes, demands a thoughtful and deliberate approach. As attitudes towards cannabis continue to shift, it is imperative to acknowledge the power of culture and language to perpetuate harmful stereotypes or promote inclusivity and understanding. By reframing the terminology surrounding cannabis and recognizing the cultural nuances, we can contribute to a more equitable, respectful, and accepting society that bridges the gaps between diverse communities and fosters a culture of appreciation and unity.

Moreover, understanding the broader context of culture, beyond just language, is crucial in our increasingly interconnected world. Cultural context shapes how we communicate, how we behave, and how we view the world. It influences everything from business and healthcare practices to education and art.

Taking into account the impact of culture and community with regard to cannabis, we can foster profound connections and mutual respect.

To enhance our understanding of how we can promote tolerance and reduce prejudice by appreciating and respecting diverse cultural contexts, it could be beneficial to contemplate the following questions:

- How does cultural heritage influence the perceptions and traditions surrounding cannabis use, and how can this understanding guide more respectful and inclusive dialogue?
- What role does reframing the discourse around cannabis terminologies play in bridging gaps between diverse communities and promoting a more equitable and appreciative society?
- Beyond language, how does cultural context impact the broader societal view of cannabis, and what steps can be taken to navigate these nuances to foster unity and appreciation?
- In what ways can an awareness and appreciation of diverse cultural contexts surrounding cannabis contribute to reducing prejudice, promoting tolerance, and cultivating a more harmonious societal landscape?

As we navigate the complex landscape of cannabis culture and its impact on society, let's remember the power of words and the importance of cultural context in shaping our collective future.

CHAPTER 3

A BRIEF U.S. CANNABIS HISTORY

HISTORY AT ODDS

The historical and cultural context surrounding the controversy over the use of the term "marijuana" is rooted in the complex and often troubled history of cannabis prohibition in the United States. Cannabis was initially brought to the United States in the 17th century by European colonizers, who used it for various purposes, including fiber production and medicinal uses.

> *"Make the most you can of the Indian hemp seed and sow it everywhere."*
>
> — George Washington, 1st U.S. President

In the early 20th century, however, attitudes towards cannabis began to shift, partly driven by racial and ethnic stereotypes and fears of drug addiction. In the 1930s, politicians and government officials, including Harry Anslinger, the head of the newly-created Federal Bureau of Narcotics, began a campaign to demonize and criminalize cannabis, which was increasingly associated with Mexican immigrants and African-American jazz musicians.[1]

As part of this campaign, government officials began to use the term "marijuana," which was less well-known than the term "cannabis," to refer to the plant. By associating the plant with Mexican culture and using a less prominent term, officials could paint cannabis use as a foreign and dangerous practice that threatened American values and fueled xenophobic fears.

The history of cannabis in the United States is long and complicated, dating back to the 17th century when the plant was first brought to the colonies for hemp production. Cannabis was widely cultivated and used for industrial purposes throughout the 18th and 19th centuries, with early American farmers even being legally required to grow hemp.

In the following decades, the term "marijuana" became increasingly widespread, and it was eventually codified in federal drug laws, including the Marihuana Tax Act of 1937 and the Controlled Substances Act of 1970, classifying cannabis as a Schedule I drug, meaning it was considered to have no medicinal value and a high potential for abuse. This classification made it illegal under federal law and led to a massive increase in cannabis-related arrests and incarceration rates, particularly for BIPOC communities. The term "marijuana" was cemented in the public consciousness, and it has continued to be the most common term used to describe the plant in the United States, even as attitudes towards cannabis have begun to shift. [2]

Despite the federal crackdown, some states began to push back against the strict regulations and prohibitions on cannabis use. California was the first state to legalize medical cannabis in 1996. Since then, more than 38 states, three territories, and the District of Columbia have allowed the medical use of cannabis products.

The federal government's position on cannabis has shifted recently, with many lawmakers and officials pushing for legalization and reform. In 2018, the Agriculture Improvement Act, commonly known as the Farm Bill, legalized hemp production and sales. In 2021, the House of Representatives passed the Marijuana Opportunity Reinvestment and Expungement Act (also known as the MORE Act), which would remove cannabis from the list of federally controlled substances. This legislation aims to decriminalize cannabis at the federal level, propose the expungement of certain cannabis offenses, and create funding for communities affected by the War on Drugs.[3]

It must be noted that passing the MORE Act in the House does not mean it became law. For a bill to become law, it must pass both the House of Representatives and the Senate and then be signed by the President. While the MORE Act passed the House, it faced uncertain prospects in the Senate, where a 60-vote majority is (typically) required to overcome a filibuster and bring legislation to a vote. Without passage in the Senate and a presidential signature, the bill has yet to become law.

While the federal government's position on cannabis continues to evolve, it is clear that the history of cannabis in the United States is a complex and ongoing story. The plant has played a significant role in American history and culture, from its early use as an industrial crop to its criminalization and subsequent legalization efforts. It will undoubtedly continue to do so in the years to come.

In recent years, there has been a growing recognition of the injustices and adverse effects of the War On Drugs, particularly on BIPOC communities, and a push for reform and equity in the legal cannabis industry. Many states with legalized cannabis have implemented social equity programs to address past harms and ensure that those most affected by the War On Drugs have access to the benefits of the legal cannabis industry.

At the federal level, much work must be done to address the historical and ongoing injustices related to cannabis. While some lawmakers and officials are pushing for reform and legalization, there is still a lack of consensus on the issue, and the future of cannabis policy in the United States remains uncertain.

Despite the challenges and complexities of the legal and social landscape surrounding cannabis, it is clear that the plant and its cultural significance will continue to play a significant role in society. As attitudes towards cannabis continue to shift and as legalization efforts gain traction, it is essential to understand the history and cultural context of the plant.

By taking the time to reflect on the language we use to talk about cannabis and the cultural context in which that language exists, we can help to build a more equitable and just legal cannabis industry and a more informed and thoughtful cannabis culture.

> *"Prohibition goes beyond the bounds of reason in that it attempts to control a man's appetite by legislation and makes a crime out of things that are not crimes."*
> — Abraham Lincoln, 16th U.S. President

THE RISE OF ANTI-CANNABIS SENTIMENT IN THE UNITED STATES

In recent years, there has been a growing movement towards legalizing cannabis in the United States. With more and more states legalizing cannabis for medicinal and adult use, it may seem like the tide has finally turned in favor of this once-stigmatized plant. However, alongside this progress, there has also been a rise in anti-cannabis sentiment in certain parts of the country. From lawmakers who continue to push for Prohibition to parents who worry about the impact of legalization on their children, many are still deeply skeptical of the benefits of the plant.

One of the main drivers of anti-cannabis sentiment in the United States is a long-standing cultural bias against using any mind-altering substances. For many Americans, cannabis is still associated with the counterculture of the 1960s and the so-called "hippie" movement. This perception has been reinforced by decades of propaganda and misinformation, which portrayed cannabis as a dangerous and addictive drug with no medical benefits.

There are concerns about the potential risks of cannabis use, particularly when it comes to adolescent brain development and the risk of addiction. While research on the long-term effects of cannabis use is ongoing, many parents and healthcare professionals worry that legalization will increase access and use among young people.

Another factor contributing to anti-cannabis sentiment is the political divide in the United States. While cannabis legalization has gained support from both Democrats and Republicans in recent years, many conservative lawmakers still oppose it on moral or ideological grounds. It has resulted in a patchwork of laws and regulations across the country, with some states legalizing cannabis while others continue to prohibit it.

Despite these challenges, many continue to advocate for the benefits of cannabis legalization, from medical professionals who have seen its therapeutic effects first-hand to entrepreneurs who see it as a burgeoning new industry with the potential to create jobs and economic growth.

The rise of anti-cannabis sentiment in the United States is a reminder that the legalization movement is far from over. As advocates continue to make their case for the benefits of cannabis, it will be essential to address concerns and misinformation head-on and to work towards a more nuanced and evidence-based understanding of this complex plant.

It is also important to acknowledge the historical and social factors that have contributed to the stigmatization of cannabis. For many years, cannabis was used to target marginalized communities, particularly communities of color. The War On Drugs, initiated in the 1970s, was often used as a pretext to criminalize and incarcerate individuals for nonviolent drug offenses, disproportionately affecting BIPOC communities.

As a result, many advocates for cannabis legalization argue that legalization can help redress some of the harms caused by decades of punitive drug policies and create opportunities for individuals and communities disproportionately impacted by the War On Drugs.

Many states that have legalized cannabis have implemented social equity programs to support individuals and communities negatively impacted by Prohibition. These programs often include measures such as expunging criminal records, providing training and resources for minority-owned businesses, and earmarking tax revenues for community reinvestment.

While the rise of anti-cannabis sentiment in the United States is concerning, it is not an insurmountable obstacle. By addressing concerns and misinformation and by working towards a more nuanced and evidence-based understanding of cannabis, advocates can continue to make progress toward legalization. Moreover, by recognizing the historical and social factors that have contributed to the stigmatization of cannabis and by implementing policies and programs designed to promote social justice and equity, we can ensure that legalization is not just a matter of economics and public health but also a matter of morality and justice.

FEDERAL APPROACHES TO ALCOHOL AND DRUG PROHIBITION

In the United States, the federal government has historically taken several approaches to (alcohol and drug) Prohibition. Here are some of the critical approaches:

Prohibition: From 1920 to 1933, the federal government implemented (alcohol) Prohibition, making it illegal to produce, sell, or transport alcoholic beverages. This approach failed, leading to increased organized crime and black market activity. Prohibition was repealed in 1933.

Criminalization: The federal government has criminalized the production, sale, and possession of certain drugs, including cannabis, cocaine, and heroin. This approach has led to the incarceration of large numbers of individuals, particularly from minority communities, and has been criticized for its ineffectiveness and disproportionate impact on vulnerable populations.

Regulation: In some cases, the federal government has chosen to regulate the production and sale of alcohol and drugs. For example, the government controls the production and sale of alcohol through licensing requirements and taxes. Similarly, some states have implemented regulatory frameworks for the production and sale of cannabis.

Public Health Approach: More recently, there has been a growing movement to treat drug and alcohol use as a public health rather than a criminal justice issue. This approach focuses on prevention, treatment, and harm reduction and addresses the underlying social and economic factors contributing to substance abuse. This approach has been implemented in several states, particularly in response to the opioid epidemic.

International Drug Policy: The federal government has also developed international drug policy through organizations such as the United Nations Office on Drugs and Crime. The U.S. has played a leading role in advocating for drug prohibition and criminalization worldwide, although this approach has been growing criticism in recent years.

Prescription Drug Monitoring: The federal government has implemented prescription drug monitoring programs to help track and prevent prescription drug abuse. These programs help identify individuals engaging in doctor shopping or other illicit behaviors to obtain prescription drugs.

Prevention And Education: The federal government has implemented several prevention and education programs to address alcohol and drug use, particularly among youth. These programs aim to provide information and support to individuals and communities to prevent substance abuse and addiction.

Treatment And Recovery: The federal government has also implemented various treatment and recovery programs for individuals struggling with substance abuse and addiction. These programs may include medication-assisted therapy, counseling, and other support services.

While some approaches, such as criminalization, have been criticized for their ineffectiveness and negative impact on vulnerable populations, others, such as a public health approach, have shown promise in addressing the complex issues surrounding substance abuse. There are still significant challenges to addressing substance abuse and addiction, including stigma and the lack of access to treatment.

"Penalties against drug possession should not be more damaging to an individual than the use of the drug itself, and where they are, they should be changed. Nowhere is this clearer than in the laws against the possession of marijuana in private for personal use."

— Jimmy Carter, 39th U.S. President

THE PROHIBITION ERA (1900s – 1930s)

The Marijuana Tax Act of 1937 was a federal law that effectively prohibited the sale and use of marijuana in the United States. The law imposed a federal tax on the sale of marijuana and required individuals and businesses that sold or possessed marijuana to register with the government and pay the tax. The law did not technically make marijuana illegal, but it made it difficult and expensive to produce, sell, and consume – effectively driving the industry underground.

Many government officials, including Harry Anslinger, the head of the newly formed Federal Bureau of Narcotics, argued that marijuana consumption could lead to insanity, violence, and addiction and threaten American society's moral fabric.

Before the law, cannabis was widely used for therapeutic purposes. Over the years, the law was strengthened through other federal laws, including the Controlled Substances Act of 1970, which classified cannabis as a Schedule I drug, making it illegal to sell, possess, or consume.

THE WAR ON DRUGS (1970s – 1990s)

Despite the federal Prohibition of marijuana, many states have moved to decriminalize or legalize the plant for medicinal or recreational consumption.

The federal government's approach to cannabis has also evolved in recent years. In 2013, the Department of Justice issued a memo stating that it would not prioritize the enforcement of federal marijuana laws in states that had legalized marijuana. In 2018, President Trump signed the Farm Bill, which legalized the production and sale of hemp, a non-psychoactive form of cannabis.

The current status of cannabis in the U.S. remains complex and varies by state. While many states have legalized cannabis to some degree, it is still classified as a Schedule I drug under federal law, and the federal government maintains strict controls over the production, sale, and consumption of cannabis.

LEGALIZATION AND REGULATION (2000s – PRESENT)

There has been growing momentum to reform federal cannabis laws, particularly in light of the increasing number of states legalizing cannabis. As previously mentioned, in 2021, the House of Representatives passed the MORE Act. While it wasn't passed into law, its objective was to remove cannabis from the list of federally controlled substances and expunge certain cannabis-related criminal records.

In addition to federal law, international treaties govern the production, sale, and consumption of cannabis. The United Nations Single Convention on Narcotic Drugs, signed in 1961, prohibits the production and use of cannabis for non-medical purposes. However, some countries, such as Canada and Uruguay, have moved to legalize cannabis for adult use in violation of the treaty.[4]

The complex patchwork of federal and state cannabis laws has created challenges for individuals and businesses in the industry. For example, cannabis businesses may face difficulties accessing banking services or obtaining loans, as many banks are hesitant to work with companies that technically operate violating federal law. In April 2023, the House passed the Secure and Fair Enforcement Banking Act of 2023, also known as the SAFE Banking Act of 2023.

This bill protects federally regulated financial institutions serving state-sanctioned cannabis businesses. Many financial institutions do not provide services to state-sanctioned cannabis businesses due to the federal classification of cannabis as a Schedule I controlled substance.

Under the bill, a federal banking regulator may not penalize a depository institution for providing banking services to a state-sanctioned cannabis business. For example, regulators may not terminate or limit a depository institution's deposit or share insurance solely because the institution provides financial services to a state-sanctioned cannabis business.

The bill also prohibits a federal banking regulator from requesting or ordering a depository institution to terminate a customer account unless (1) the regulator has determined that the depository institution is engaging in an unsafe or unsound practice or is violating a law or regulation and (2) that determination is not based primarily on reputation risk.

Additionally, proceeds from a transaction involving activities of a state-sanctioned cannabis business are no longer considered proceeds from unlawful activity. (Financial institutions that handle proceeds from illegal activity are subject to anti-money laundering laws. Violators of these laws are subject to fines and imprisonment.) Furthermore, a financial institution, insurer, or federal agency may not be held liable or subject to asset forfeiture under federal law for providing a loan, mortgage, or other financial service to a state-sanctioned cannabis business.

Summary

As the legal and regulatory landscape around cannabis continues to evolve, federal and state policymakers will need to work together to develop a coherent and consistent approach to regulating the production, sale, and consumption of cannabis. This will require addressing many issues, including public health, criminal justice, taxation, and international treaties.

One of the main challenges in developing a coherent approach to cannabis regulation is the lack of consistent and reliable data on the effects of cannabis consumption. While there is growing evidence to suggest that cannabis may have medical benefits for certain conditions, such as chronic pain, epilepsy, and multiple sclerosis, there is also evidence to suggest that it can have adverse effects on mental health, particularly in chronic consumers.

Another challenge is ensuring that the regulatory framework around cannabis is equitable and just. Historically, marijuana prohibition has disproportionately affected BIPOC communities, who have been more likely to be arrested and incarcerated for cannabis-related offenses. As such, many advocates of cannabis legalization have emphasized the importance of expunging criminal records for cannabis-related offenses, providing opportunities for individuals and communities most negatively affected by Prohibition, and promoting diversity and inclusion in the emerging cannabis industry.

There are concerns about the potential risks of cannabis consumption, particularly among youth. As such, many states that have legalized cannabis have put strict regulations around the sale, marketing, and consumption of cannabis – including age restrictions and limits on the amount of cannabis that can be purchased at one time.

Considering the following questions may help unravel the historical and cultural intricacies of cannabis in the U.S. and its changing legal context:

- What cultural shifts in attitudes towards cannabis in the early 20th century led to its criminalization?
- What role did racial and ethnic stereotypes play in the demonization of cannabis in the 1930s?
- How did government officials use language and cultural associations to stigmatize cannabis consumption?
- How has the history of cannabis cultivation evolved from its early industrial use to federal crackdowns and the War on Drugs?

The future of cannabis regulation in the U.S. remains uncertain, with various opinions and perspectives on the appropriate approach to regulating the controversial plant. However, it is clear that the current patchwork of federal and state laws around cannabis is creating significant challenges for individuals and businesses operating in the industry, and there is a need for a more coherent and consistent approach to cannabis regulation that takes into account public health, social justice, and economic considerations.

CHAPTER 4

CULTIVATING MYTHS:
THE ROOTS OF STEREOTYPES

THE CREATION OF CANNABIS STEREOTYPES

The creation of cannabis stereotypes can be traced back to the early 20th century when anti-marijuana campaigns were used to associate cannabis with racial and ethnic minorities. These campaigns portrayed marijuana as a dangerous drug that could lead to madness and violence, often associating it with Mexican and African-American cultures. By associating cannabis with these groups, anti-marijuana campaigners were able to use racial prejudices to drum up support for Prohibition.[1]

> *"Cannabis consumers have often been characterized as individuals seeking a high. This naïve perception is transforming as consumers turn to sophisticated cannabis offerings like edibles and premium cannabis-infused beverages. Consequently, this shift is reshaping the perception of cannabis consumers and the wide array of products they embrace."*
> — Warren Bobrow, Co-Founder & CEO, Klaus

These stereotypes were further reinforced in popular culture in the 20th century. In films like "Reefer Madness," marijuana was portrayed as a "gateway drug" that could lead to moral decay, insanity, and criminal behavior. The media also played a role in perpetuating stereotypes, often focusing on sensationalized stories of marijuana-related crime and violence.

As cannabis has become more mainstream, these stereotypes have started to break down. However, some stereotypes persist, particularly around the consumption of cannabis by young people and certain subcultures. For example, some people still associate cannabis use with "stoner culture," a term often used to describe individuals who are lazy, unmotivated, and unproductive individuals.

These stereotypes can be harmful and inaccurate, contributing to negative attitudes and prejudices towards cannabis consumers. They can also lead to unequal treatment of individuals based on their cannabis consumption, particularly in areas like employment and housing. As such, it is essential to break down these stereotypes and promote a more accurate and nuanced understanding of cannabis consumption and its effects. It includes educating people about the medical benefits of cannabis, promoting responsible use, and emphasizing that cannabis consumption is a personal choice that should not be subject to stigma or discrimination.

Breaking down cannabis stereotypes also involves addressing the social and cultural factors that contribute to these stereotypes. Addressing racial disparities in cannabis enforcement and ensuring that BIPOC communities are not unfairly targeted for cannabis-related offenses can help to reduce the association between cannabis and minorities. Similarly, promoting diversity and inclusion in the emerging cannabis industry can help to break down stereotypes around who consumes and benefits from cannabis.

Promoting a more accurate and nuanced understanding of cannabis consumption can also involve challenging the stigmatization of certain subcultures or groups associated with "marijuana use." By challenging negative stereotypes and promoting a more accurate understanding of the benefits and risks of cannabis consumption, we can help create a more equitable and just society that recognizes individual freedom of choice regarding personal cannabis consumption.

In addition to addressing social and cultural factors, it is also essential to educate the public about the scientific research on cannabis and its effects. It can help to dispel myths and misconceptions and promote a more informed and evidence-based approach to cannabis consumption and regulation.

Research has shown that cannabis consumption can have positive and negative effects, depending on the individual and the context of consumption. While some studies have suggested that cannabis can be effective in treating certain medical conditions, such as chronic pain, epilepsy, and multiple sclerosis, other studies have found that heavy cannabis consumption can be associated with adverse effects on mental health, including increased risk of psychosis and cognitive impairment.

By educating the public about the complexities of cannabis consumption and its effects, we can help promote a more informed and responsible approach to cannabis regulation that considers consumers' health and social considerations while also recognizing the broader public health and safety concerns associated with cannabis consumption.

> *"The war on cannabis hasn't revolved around the plant's impact, family protection, crime, or the numerous reasons presented over the last century. These rationales were tools of propaganda for political and corporate motives. Those most affected by these stereotypes are now tasked with halting this machinery and redirecting its course. As the cannabis industry shifts, we must redefine the narrative, unveiling a truer comprehension of cannabis, untangled from historical biases."*
> — Tyme Ferris, Founder, The Pantheon Perspective

CANNABIS IN COUNTERCULTURE AND THE ANTI-ESTABLISHMENT

Cannabis has a long history within counterculture movements and has often been associated with anti-establishment and rebellion against authority. In the 1960s and 1970s, the hippie movement and other counterculture groups embraced cannabis as a symbol of resistance to traditional social norms and political structures. The consumption of cannabis was seen as a way to reject the status quo and challenge the establishment.

At the same time, cannabis was also associated with the anti-war movement, with many young people consuming the plant to protest the Vietnam War and express their opposition to the government. Cannabis was seen as a way to promote peace, love, and unity and was often used to bring people together and foster a sense of community.

The association between cannabis and counterculture has continued to the present day, with many subcultures and movements embracing the plant as a symbol of resistance to authority and social norms. However, while cannabis has often been associated with rebellion and nonconformity, it has become more mainstream in recent years, increasing acceptance and legalization in many parts of the world.[2]

Today, cannabis use is increasingly seen as a legitimate form of self-expression and individual choice rather than a symbol of counterculture or rebellion. However, the history of cannabis within counterculture movements and anti-establishment protests has played an essential role in shaping attitudes towards the plant and promoting greater acceptance and understanding of its potential benefits.

Research has shown that cannabis use can stimulate creative thinking and enhance divergent thinking, which is the ability to generate new and original ideas. Some researchers have suggested that cannabis use may help break down mental barriers and promote greater openness to new experiences and ideas, leading to more creative thinking.

It is important to note that the relationship between cannabis consumption and creativity is complex and varies depending on individual factors such as dosage, consumption frequency, and individual sensitivity. While some individuals may experience enhanced creativity and new insights due to cannabis consumption, others may experience adverse effects such as impaired cognitive function and decreased motivation.

The stigma surrounding cannabis use has also contributed to negative stereotypes and misperceptions about the plant, with many individuals viewing it as a dangerous and harmful substance. These stereotypes have been perpetuated by mainstream media, government campaigns, and other social institutions, leading to a widespread lack of understanding and misinformation about the plant.

In recent years, there has been a growing movement towards the legalization and decriminalization of cannabis in many parts of the world, as well as increased recognition of the plant's potential therapeutic and adult use benefits. This shift in attitudes towards cannabis has been driven by several factors, including changing cultural attitudes, increased scientific research into the plant, and growing public awareness of the potential benefits of cannabis consumption.

The growing legalization and normalization of cannabis has also led to the development of a new industry around the plant, including the production and sale of a range of cannabis-based products such as oils, concentrates, edibles, beverages, and topicals. It has created new opportunities for entrepreneurs and investors and increased access to the plant for individuals who may benefit from its therapeutic properties without smoking.

The development of this new industry has also raised concerns about issues such as product safety, quality control, and marketing to vulnerable populations. As with any new industry, regulatory frameworks and guidelines are needed to ensure that the production and sale of cannabis-based products are safe and ethical.

> *"The relentless creation of cannabis stereotypes has been a disservice, particularly to those who turn to cannabis for its therapeutic and medicinal potential. These misleading narratives have obscured the profound healing properties of the plant, impeding access to its benefits and perpetuating a disheartening cycle of misinformation and stigma."*
> — Adriana Hemans, Marketing Director, Green Meadows

POT IN POPULAR CULTURE

Cannabis has been a significant presence in popular culture for many decades. From music and movies to television and literature, the plant has been referenced and portrayed in various ways across many forms of media.

One of the earliest examples of cannabis in popular culture can be traced back to the early 20th century when jazz musicians in the United States began to incorporate cannabis use into their music and lyrics. Songs such as "Muggles" by Louis Armstrong and "Reefer Man" by Cab Calloway referenced the plant explicitly and subtly. They helped to establish a cultural association between cannabis and jazz music.

In the 1960s and 70s, cannabis became closely associated with the counterculture and anti-establishment movements of the time. It was referenced in various music and movies related to these movements. Songs such as "Legalize It" by Peter Tosh and "Don't Bogart Me" by Fraternity of Man became anthems for the movement. In contrast, movies such as Easy Rider and The Big Lebowski featured characters who were frequent cannabis consumers.

In recent years, cannabis has remained a prominent feature of popular culture, with references to the plant appearing in everything from television shows like Weeds and Broad City to movies such as Pineapple Express and Harold and Kumar Go to White Castle. The rise of social media and influencer culture has also led to a new generation of cannabis influencers and content creators who promote the plant through their online and social media platforms.

Cannabis has significantly shaped popular culture over the past century and has become a cultural touchstone for many people worldwide. As attitudes towards cannabis continue to evolve and shift, it will be interesting to see how the plant is portrayed and represented in popular culture in the years to come.

Its portrayal in music, movies, and television, cannabis has also shaped popular fashion and style trends. In the 1960s and 70s, tie-dye clothing and psychedelic prints became associated with the counterculture and anti-establishment movements, often linked to cannabis consumption. In recent years, cannabis has become a prominent feature of streetwear fashion, with clothing brands incorporating cannabis imagery and references into their designs.[3]

Cannabis has also been the subject of many books and works of literature. From classic novels such as Jack Kerouac's *"On the Road"* and Hunter S. Thompson's *"Fear and Loathing in Las Vegas"* to more recent works like Michael Pollan's *"Botany of Desire"* and Tommy Chong's *"The I Chong,"* the plant has been a common theme and subject for many writers and authors.

Cannabis has also been the focus of many documentaries and films exploring its cultural, social, and historical significance. Films such as *"The Culture High," "Grass is Greener,"* and *"Super High Me"* examine the cultural and political forces that have shaped the legal and social status of cannabis while exploring its potential benefits and risks.

In addition to its portrayal in popular culture, cannabis has also played a role in developing several subcultures and communities. The medical cannabis community, for example, has emerged as a powerful force in recent years, advocating for the legalization and normalization of cannabis use for medical purposes. This community includes patients, caregivers, medical professionals, and researchers and has played a vital role in advancing our understanding of the potential medical benefits of cannabis.

The legalization of cannabis has also significantly impacted the cultural and social norms surrounding the plant. In places where cannabis is legal, it has become more accepted and normalized, changing how people talk about and perceive it. As a result, there has been a shift in how cannabis is portrayed in popular culture, with more positive and nuanced representations of the plant becoming increasingly common.

One example of this shift can be seen in the growing number of cannabis-themed cooking shows, which have become popular in recent years. These shows typically feature chefs who use cannabis-infused ingredients to create various dishes, from appetizers to desserts. By presenting cannabis in a more normalized and mainstream context, these shows help to challenge the negative stereotypes and stigmas surrounding the plant.

Another way that cannabis legalization has impacted popular culture is through the rise of "cannabis tourism." In places where cannabis is legal, such as certain states in the US, Canada, and now Thailand, cannabis tourism has become a popular niche industry. Visitors can tour cannabis production facilities, sample different cultivars, and attend cannabis-themed festivals and events.

"Cannabis stereotypes perpetuate negative biases and stigmas associated with the industry, which can alienate potential consumers and limit the ability of brands to appeal to a broader, mainstream audience. These stereotypes also obstruct growth opportunities, contribute to ongoing regulatory challenges, and undermine efforts to position cannabis as a legitimate industry."
— Patrick Toste, Co-Founder, Highopes

The legalization of cannabis has significantly impacted popular culture, helping to shift attitudes and perceptions surrounding the plant. As more and more countries, states, and regions move towards legalization, it will be interesting to see how these cultural and social changes continue to evolve and shape our understanding of the plant.

With the legalization of cannabis, however, this trend has become more mainstream and less stigmatized. For example, in the US, several states with legal cannabis have seen the emergence of cannabis-themed music festivals, such as the Northern Nights Music Festival in California and the Mile High Music Festival in Colorado.

The relationship between cannabis and popular culture is complex and multifaceted. It will likely continue to evolve and change in the coming years as legalization and normalization spread.

We can't forget about the development of the "cannabis industry," which encompasses a wide range of businesses and organizations involved in producing, selling, and distributing cannabis products. This industry includes everything from growers and dispensaries to accessory and lifestyle brands and has emerged as a powerful economic force in many parts of the world.

WHERE THE RUBBER HITS THE ROAD

The state of cannabis today varies significantly depending on the country, state, and region in question. In some parts of the world, such as Canada, Uruguay, and several US states, cannabis has been fully legalized for medical and adult use. In these places, individuals can purchase and consume cannabis without fear of legal repercussions, and a thriving cannabis industry has emerged to meet the demand.

In other parts of the world, however, cannabis remains illegal or highly restricted. In many countries, possession or use of cannabis can result in steep fines or even imprisonment, and the plant is often stigmatized and associated with criminal activity.

Despite these disparities, there is a growing global trend towards cannabis legalization and normalization. As more and more countries recognize the medical benefits of cannabis and the failure of prohibitionist policies, many are beginning to explore alternative approaches to drug policy.

The state of cannabis today is one of rapid change and ongoing evolution as societies and cultures worldwide grapple with the complex and multifaceted implications of this influential and controversial plant. As we continue to learn more about cannabis and its effects on our bodies and minds, the debate around its legalization and consumption will likely continue to evolve, and new opportunities and challenges will emerge in the years to come.

There are also significant economic implications associated with the growing cannabis industry. As more and more countries legalize cannabis, a thriving industry is emerging to meet the increasing demand for the plant, creating new jobs, business opportunities, and revenue streams for governments and private companies alike.

Another critical area of development in the cannabis industry is the ongoing innovation in producing and distributing cannabis products. As the industry has grown, entrepreneurs and investors have developed new and innovative ways to cultivate, process, and distribute cannabis products, from advanced indoor cultivation facilities to high-tech extraction methods and innovative delivery mechanisms.

This innovation has led to the development of a wide range of cannabis products, from traditional dried flower and cannabis oil to edibles, beverages, tinctures, topicals, sublingual slips, and transdermal patches. The rise of the cannabis edibles market, for example, has been driven by the growing demand for discrete, convenient, and accurate dosing methods and has led to the creation of a wide range of sophisticated cannabis-infused products.

At the same time, there are also concerns about the potential risks associated with the widespread availability of cannabis products, particularly when it comes to issues like accurate labeling, consistent dosing, and the potential for accidental ingestion by children and pets. As a result, many jurisdictions have implemented strict labeling requirements, packaging restrictions, and other quality control measures to ensure that cannabis products are used safely and responsibly.

Cannabis today is evolving and transforming as entrepreneurs, investors, and regulators explore new opportunities and challenges in the emerging cannabis industry. As the industry continues to grow and mature, we will likely see innovations, new challenges, and new opportunities emerge.

By addressing the social, economic, and scientific factors that contribute to cannabis stereotypes, we can help to create a more inclusive, accepting, and evidence-based approach to cannabis consumption.

The growing movement to break down these stereotypes and promote a more positive and informed view of cannabis consumption has involved a variety of approaches, including:

Advocacy: Advocacy groups, such as the Marijuana Policy Project, NORML, and the Last Prisoner Project, among others, have played a key role in promoting legalization and breaking down stereotypes around cannabis use. These groups work to educate the public about the benefits and risks of cannabis consumption while promoting policies.

Education: Education campaigns, such as the *"Marijuana Is Safer Than Alcohol"* campaign, have helped to challenge stereotypes around cannabis consumption. These campaigns dispel myths and misconceptions while promoting responsible use and harm reduction strategies. Mainstream colleges and universities such as Syracuse University, LIM College, and the Pennsylvania Institute of Technology, among others, have created majors specifically focused on the business of cannabis. In contrast, specialty schools such as Oaksterdam University have existed for years.

Media: The media has played an essential role in breaking down stereotypes about cannabis consumption. An increasing number of television shows, movies, and books portray cannabis consumption in a more positive and nuanced light. For example, shows like "Weeds" and "High Maintenance" have helped to challenge stereotypes about cannabis consumers and promote a more diverse and inclusive view of cannabis consumption. Today, the Cannabis Media Council acts similarly to the Ad Council, laying the groundwork for best practices in cannabis media.

Science: Advances in scientific research on cannabis have helped to promote a more informed and evidence-based approach to consumption and regulation. This research has helped dispel myths and misconceptions while highlighting the potential medical benefits of cannabis and the risks associated with chronic consumption.

As the industry continues to grow and evolve, it is essential to ensure that people from all backgrounds and communities have the opportunity to participate and benefit from the industry. It can involve a variety of initiatives, such as:

Social Equity Programs: Many states with legal cannabis markets have implemented social equity programs designed to promote diversity and inclusion within the industry. These programs assist and support individuals from communities disproportionately impacted by the War On Drugs, such as people of color and low-income individuals, to help them enter the industry and build successful businesses.

Diverse Hiring Practices: Cannabis businesses can promote diversity and inclusivity by implementing hiring practices that seek employees from underrepresented communities. This can create a more diverse and inclusive workplace and encourage opportunities for people from all backgrounds to succeed in the industry.

Community Engagement: Cannabis businesses can promote inclusivity by engaging with and supporting local communities. It can involve initiatives such as sponsoring local events, supporting local charities, and working with local organizations to promote education and awareness around cannabis use.

By promoting diversity and inclusivity within the cannabis industry, we can help to break down stereotypes and promote a more positive and inclusive view of cannabis consumption. It can create a more just and equitable society that recognizes the importance of diversity and inclusion in all aspects of life.

Another strategy for breaking down cannabis stereotypes is to focus on harm reduction and responsible use. It involves promoting accountable and safe use practices while addressing the potential risks associated with heavy consumption. Some harm reduction strategies for cannabis use include:

Education: Education is a critical component of harm reduction, as it can help to promote informed decision-making and responsible use practices. It can involve providing information about dosage and uptake methods of consumption and potential risks associated with heavy use.

Regulation: Appropriate regulation of cannabis consumption can help promote public health and safety while providing a framework for responsible use. It can involve establishing age limits for consumption, implementing quality control standards requiring specific packaging, and restricting advertising and marketing to minors.

Access to Treatment: For individuals who struggle with problematic cannabis consumption, access to treatment and support services can be an essential part of harm reduction. It can involve providing access to counseling, support groups, and other resources to help individuals manage their use and reduce potential harm.

Summary

The history of cannabis is deeply intertwined with cultural, social, and political forces that have shaped its societal perception. From the racially motivated anti-marijuana campaigns of the early 20th century to its association with counterculture movements and eventual mainstream acceptance, cannabis has been subject to a complex and evolving narrative. The perpetuation of stereotypes, such as the "stoner" image, has hindered progress toward a more accurate understanding of this versatile plant and its effects, contributing to unjust policies and discrimination.

Reflecting on the following questions might assist in synthesizing the genesis of cannabis stereotypes and understanding how to change the general public's perception of cannabis consumers:

- How have historical stereotypes around cannabis evolved, and how do they influence contemporary perceptions of cannabis consumers and products?
- How do social, economic, and scientific factors contribute to the perpetuation of stereotypes around cannabis consumption?
- In what ways does the growing cannabis industry impact societal attitudes and cultural representations of cannabis?
- How are education, advocacy, and media representation contributing to breaking down stereotypes and promoting a more informed understanding of cannabis consumption?

There is hope for a more informed, inclusive, and responsible approach to cannabis consumption. Advocacy, education, media representation, and scientific research are helping to challenge stereotypes and promote a nuanced view of cannabis. Moreover, initiatives aimed at social equity and diversity within the cannabis industry, harm reduction strategies, and responsible use practices are paving the way for a future where cannabis is appreciated for its diverse applications while respecting individual choices and public safety. As the global landscape around cannabis continues to evolve, it is vital to remain committed to breaking down stereotypes and fostering a more balanced and compassionate perspective on this remarkable plant.

CHAPTER 5

THE SEEDS OF DISCORD

ROOT ORIGINS: HOW DID WE GET HERE?

The semantics of cannabis are complex and controversial and have been the subject of much debate and discussion in recent years. On the one hand, advocates of cannabis legalization argue that the term "marijuana" is rooted in racist and xenophobic attitudes towards Mexican immigrants in the early 20th century and that its continued use perpetuates harmful stereotypes and stigmatizes the plant and its consumers.

> "There are 100,000 total marijuana smokers in the U.S., and most are Negroes, Hispanics, Filipinos, and entertainers. Their satanic music, jazz, and swing result from marijuana usage. This marijuana causes white women to seek sexual relations with Negroes, entertainers, and others."
> — Harry Anslinger, Commissioner, Federal Bureau of Narcotics

On the other hand, opponents of cannabis legalization argue that the term "marijuana" is simply a common and widely recognized name for the plant and that attempts to replace it with other words like "cannabis" or "hemp" are needlessly confusing and potentially misleading.

The history of the terms "cannabis" and "marijuana" is complex and contested. Both terms have been used to describe the same plant for centuries. Still, their relative usage has shifted over time, with "cannabis" being the more common term in scientific and medical contexts and "marijuana" being the more common term in popular and political discourse.

The term "marijuana" is believed to have originated in the early 20th century, when anti-immigrant sentiment and racism towards Mexican immigrants in the United States was on the rise. At the time, cannabis use was relatively unknown among white Americans but was common among Mexican immigrants, who referred to the plant as "marihuana."

Opponents of cannabis use and immigration capitalized on this association and began using the term "marijuana" to stigmatize and demonize the plant and the people who consumed it. The word "marijuana" became increasingly widespread in the 1930s, when the U.S. government launched a campaign to criminalize cannabis use and associated it with "reefer madness" and other forms of moral depravity.

Advocates for cannabis legalization argue that the continued use of the term "marijuana" contributes to a history of negative associations and stereotypes, particularly around race and ethnicity, that have been used to justify the prohibition and criminalization of cannabis use. They argue that the use of the term "cannabis" is a more accurate and neutral way to describe the plant and that it helps to reduce the stigma around cannabis consumption and consumers.

The controversy over the use of the terms "cannabis" and "marijuana" continues to be a topic of discussion in the legal and political spheres, mainly as more and more states in the U.S. and countries worldwide move towards legalizing cannabis for medical and adult use.

> *"By getting the public to associate the hippies with marijuana and blacks with heroin and then criminalizing both heavily, we could disrupt those communities. We could arrest their leaders, raid their homes, break up their meetings, and vilify them night after night on the evening news. Did we know we were lying about the drugs? Of course, we did."*
> — John Ehrlichman, Asst for Domestic Affairs under Nixon

The debate over the semantics of cannabis is just one aspect of the more extensive discussion over the legalization and normalization of cannabis use. As attitudes and laws around cannabis continue to evolve, the language used to describe the plant and its various benefits will continue to be discussed and debated.

MARIJUANA: THE FAILURE OF AMERICAN POLICY REFORM

Looking back on the history of marijuana in the United States, it is clear that attitudes toward cannabis have shifted dramatically. What was once a widely used and accepted plant became demonized and criminalized in the early 20th century, driven by racial and ethnic stereotypes, fears of drug addiction, and a desire to control and regulate individual behavior.

Despite passing numerous laws and policies to suppress cannabis consumption, the plant has persisted as a cultural force, with advocates and enthusiasts fighting for its decriminalization and legalization. In recent years, as public opinion has shifted in favor of cannabis legalization, a growing number of states have legalized the use of cannabis for medical and adult use purposes.

As the legal landscape around cannabis continues to evolve, it is clear that the history of cannabis in the United States is still being written. Advocates for drug policy reform and cannabis legalization will continue to push for greater acceptance and accessibility. In contrast, opponents will likely continue to argue that "using marijuana" threatens public health and safety.

Several factors drive the shift towards greater acceptance and legalization of cannabis in the United States. One of the primary drivers is the growing body of research demonstrating the potential medical benefits of cannabis. Studies have shown that cannabis can effectively treat various conditions, including chronic pain, nausea and vomiting, multiple sclerosis, epilepsy, and post-traumatic stress disorder (PTSD).

Another factor contributing to the shift in public opinion is the recognition of the disproportionate impact that marijuana prohibition has had on communities of color. Despite similar rates of cannabis consumption across racial and ethnic groups, BIPOC individuals are much more likely to be arrested and prosecuted for cannabis offenses. It has led many advocates to call for an end to the War On Drugs and the adoption of policies that address the racial and social justice implications of cannabis prohibition.

The economic potential of legalized cannabis has also played a role in the changing attitudes towards cannabis. As more states have legalized cannabis, the cannabis industry has become a significant source of tax revenue and job creation. The US cannabis market was valued at USD 15 billion in 2022 and is estimated to surpass around USD 50.91 billion by 2032, growing at a healthy CAGR of 13% from 2023 to 2032. The US cannabis market will expand as a result of the increasing legalization of cannabis in the country.[1]

While the history of marijuana in the United States is complex and fraught with tension, the increasing acceptance and legalization of cannabis suggests that attitudes are changing, and the future of cannabis in America may be one of greater acceptance, accessibility, and equity.

Despite the progress that has been made toward cannabis legalization and decriminalization, there are still many challenges and obstacles that remain. One of the biggest challenges is the continued federal prohibition of cannabis, which makes it difficult for states to legalize and regulate the plant entirely. It has led to a patchwork of policies nationwide, with some states legalizing cannabis for medical and adult use while others maintain strict prohibitions.

Another challenge is the lack of research on the long-term effects of cannabis consumption. While studies have demonstrated the potential medical benefits of cannabis, much is still unknown about the long-term health effects of regular cannabis consumption. It has led to concerns about the potential impact of legalization on public health and safety.

There are also concerns about the commercialization and corporate takeover of the cannabis industry. As the legal cannabis market has grown, large corporations have moved in, raising concerns about the potential impact on small businesses and the equitable distribution of wealth and opportunity within the industry.

As more states legalize cannabis and federal laws evolve, it will be essential to address the complex issues surrounding the plant, including public health, social justice, and economic opportunity, to create a sustainable and equitable future for cannabis.

"I want a Goddamn strong statement on marijuana, and I mean one that just tears the ass out of them. You know, it's a funny thing; every one of the bastards that are out for legalizing marijuana is Jewish."

— Richard Nixon, 37th U.S. President

CANNABIS: THE FUTURE OF AMERICAN POLICY REFORM

As more states in the U.S. legalize the use of cannabis for medical or adult use purposes, the commercialization of cannabis has become a topic of great interest. However, the future of the commercialization of cannabis is also a topic of debate and concern, particularly as large corporations move into the industry.

One of the primary concerns is that the commercialization of cannabis may lead to a shift away from the traditional "mom-and-pop" businesses that have historically dominated the industry. As larger corporations enter the market, they have an advantage in terms of access to capital, marketing power, and distribution networks, which could make it difficult for smaller businesses to compete. It could impact the industry's diversity and inclusivity with smaller firms, particularly those owned by people of color or women.

Another concern is the potential for the commercialization of cannabis to lead to the normalization of the plant and the potential for it to become just another consumer product. While many advocates of legalization see the commercialization of cannabis as a positive development, others worry that it could lead to the same kind of negative impacts that have been associated with other legal drugs, such as alcohol and tobacco.[2]

To address these concerns, some states have implemented regulations designed to promote the participation of small businesses in the cannabis industry and prevent large corporations from dominating the market. For example, some states have implemented caps on the number of licenses granted to large companies and have established equity programs to promote the participation of people of color and other marginalized groups in the industry.

The commercialization of cannabis is a complex and rapidly evolving issue with a range of potential impacts on the industry, public health, and society. As the industry continues to grow and develop, it will be essential to address these concerns and to work towards a future that promotes equity, inclusivity, and responsible commercial practices.

In addition to concerns about the impact of commercialization on small businesses and the normalization of cannabis, there are also concerns about the industry's environmental impact. The cultivation of cannabis requires large amounts of energy, water, and other resources and can negatively affect the environment if not managed responsibly.

Some companies in the cannabis industry are taking steps to become more sustainable and environmentally responsible. For example, some growers use renewable energy sources like solar power to power their operations and implement water conservation practices to reduce their water usage. Additionally, some companies are exploring alternative packaging materials and other sustainable practices to reduce their environmental footprint.

Another issue likely to impact the future of cannabis commercialization is the ongoing debate around federal legalization. While many states have legalized cannabis in some form, it remains illegal at the federal level, which creates a range of challenges for businesses operating in the industry. For example, cannabis businesses often cannot utilize banking services, making it difficult to manage their finances and access capital.[3]

As cannabis becomes more mainstream and widely accepted, there is also a growing interest in exploring the potential therapeutic benefits of cannabis and its various compounds, such as CBD, THC, and other cannabinoids. Some researchers are studying the use of cannabis to treat multiple medical conditions, including chronic pain, anxiety, and epilepsy, while others are exploring its potential as a treatment for addiction or as an alternative to traditional pharmaceuticals.

"The amount of money and legal energy being given to prosecute hundreds of thousands of Americans caught with a few ounces of marijuana in their jeans simply makes no sense - the kindest way to put it. A sterner way to put it is that it is an outrage, an imposition on basic civil liberties and the reasonable expenditure of social energy."
— William F. Buckley, Jr., Founder, The National Review

Much is still unknown about the long-term effects of cannabis use, and more research is needed to understand its potential benefits and risks fully. As the industry continues to grow, it will be essential to prioritize research and education around the consumption of cannabis and to develop responsible regulatory frameworks that ensure safe and equitable access to cannabis products.

In recent years, there has been growing support for the federal legalization of cannabis, with some lawmakers advocating for the removal of cannabis from the list of Schedule I drugs under the Controlled Substances Act – a topic discussed in greater depth in Chapter 9 titled "Reschedule, Deschedule or Decontrol?". If federal legalization were to occur, it could significantly impact the cannabis industry, potentially opening up new opportunities for investment and growth while also creating new challenges and regulatory requirements.[4]

Summary

The history of cannabis in the United States is a complex narrative marked by shifting attitudes, policies, and perceptions. From its roots as a widely used and accepted plant to its demonization driven by racial stereotypes and political agendas in the early 20th century, cannabis has experienced a tumultuous journey. The ongoing debate over semantics, with the terms "cannabis" and "marijuana" carrying different connotations and histories, reflects the broader struggle to accept and normalize cannabis in society.

As we look ahead to the future of cannabis, several key themes emerge. The changing landscape of cannabis policy and growing acceptance are driven by factors such as increasing awareness of its medical benefits, the recognition of the racial disparities in enforcement, and the economic potential of the cannabis industry. However, challenges remain, including federal prohibition, questions about long-term health effects, and concerns about the impact of corporate commercialization.

Thinking through the following questions might help to navigate these complexities and promote a sustainable, equitable future for policymakers, industry stakeholders, advocates, and the plant:

- How did the historical context and racial associations shape the adoption of the term "marijuana," and how has its use affected the perception and legislation around cannabis?
- What factors, including racial biases and changing public opinion, led to the demonization and criminalization of cannabis in the early 20th century, and how have these attitudes shifted in recent years?
- What elements, such as medical research, social justice considerations, and economic incentives, have contributed to the changing attitudes and movements toward cannabis legalization?
- How does the influx of large corporations into the cannabis industry impact smaller businesses, diversity, and the potential normalization of cannabis as a commercial product?

In this unfolding journey, cannabis continues to challenge and reshape American perceptions, policies, and practices. It is a testament to the power of public opinion, evidence-based research, and the dedication of individuals and communities to drive change. As we move forward, it is crucial to learn from the past and adapt to the present while remaining open to the possibilities and responsibilities that the future of cannabis presents.

CHAPTER 6

USE vs. CONSUME

THE USE VS. CONSUME CONTROVERSY

In our journey through the intricacies of cannabis language, we arrive at a crossroads that not only delineates two different words but signifies a significant shift in perception, understanding, and culture. The terms "use" and "consume" may appear interchangeable. Still, when it comes to cannabis, these words carry profound nuances that reflect the evolving nature of our relationship with the plant.

> *"Choosing to 'consume' cannabis over 'using' it signifies a shift towards a more responsible and informed approach. Historically, 'use' has been tinged with stigmatization, linking cannabis to negative stereotypes. Embracing 'consume' reflects our commitment to breaking free from these harmful associations and treating cannabis like any other product with mindful consideration."*
> — Dale Sky Jones, Executive Chancellor, Oaksterdam University

DEFINING THE TERMS

Let's begin by dissecting the meanings of these words:

Use: The term "use" is a broad and neutral word that implies employing or applying something for a specific purpose. Historically, the word "use" in the context of drug policy and addiction has often been associated with negative connotations, particularly during the era of the War on Drugs. "Users" were often depicted as individuals trapped in a cycle of abuse and dependency, perpetuating the stigmatization of cannabis consumers.

Consume: The term "consume" carries a different weight. It refers to ingesting or utilizing something for nourishment, enjoyment, or benefit. It implies intentionality and mindfulness, a purposeful engagement with a substance. In recent years, "consumer" has emerged as a more accurate and respectful way to describe those who interact with cannabis. It implies a conscious choice and separates recreational and medicinal users from the notion of dependency.

HISTORICAL LEXICON

The history of the term "user" in relation to cannabis is fraught with prejudice and bias. During the propaganda-driven War on Drugs, individuals who consumed cannabis were branded as "users" to vilify and criminalize them. This framing perpetuated stereotypes of lazy, unproductive, and morally corrupt individuals, creating a rift between those who consumed cannabis and those who did not.

This stigmatization of "users" has had lasting effects on public perception and policy, contributing to the demonization of cannabis consumers and hindering efforts to end prohibition. One prominent historical example of this demonization is the 1936 film "Reefer Madness," which depicted cannabis "users" as unhinged, criminal, and even violent. Such portrayals fueled public fear and laid the groundwork for harsh drug policies that disproportionately affected communities of color.

The Marihuana Tax Act of 1937 marked a turning point. Cannabis, a common ingredient in various medicines and treatments, suddenly became a feared and vilified substance. The language of prohibition painted "users" as social pariahs, implying moral decay and criminality. This rhetoric justified harsh legal penalties and launched the era of cannabis prohibition.

The term "abuser" came to the forefront during the War on Drugs, declared by President Richard Nixon in the early 1970s. This declaration further demonized cannabis consumers and associated them with criminal behavior. The term "drug abuser" framed cannabis use as a societal scourge, criminalizing countless individuals, particularly from marginalized communities.[1]

THE EMERGENCE OF "CONSUMER"

The paradigm shift from "use" to "consume" is, in part, a response to the harmful historical baggage carried by the term "user." It represents a growing understanding that cannabis consumption, like the consumption of any other product, can be a conscious and informed choice.

As cannabis gradually moves away from the shadows of prohibition, the term "consumer" has emerged as a beacon of hope for a more enlightened discourse. The shift from "user" to "consumer" represents a broader transformation in how society perceives cannabis and those who engage with it. The reasons behind this shift are multifaceted, reflecting cultural evolution and the growing understanding of cannabis.

This shift aligns with the broader trend in society towards a more mindful and responsible approach to consumption. People increasingly seek transparency in what they consume, whether food, beverages, or cannabis. They want to understand the products they're using, their benefits, and potential risks. Using "consumer," we acknowledge that individuals make informed choices about their relationship with the plant.

> *"The term 'use' simplifies the plant's function to ingesting or inhaling THC. On the other hand, 'consumption' implies a deliberate and anticipatory approach. Successful brands provide a 'consumption experience' that prioritizes the journey over the destination."*
> — Benjamin Kennedy, Co-Founder & CEO, Fable Libations

The choice between "use" and "consume" may seem subtle, but it holds immense significance in the journey toward cannabis normalization. "Consumer" emphasizes autonomy, responsibility, and choice. It removes the shackles of stigmatization and challenges outdated stereotypes associated with cannabis "users."

Using the word "consumer" encourages open dialogue, research, and understanding. It signals a departure from the Prohibition era and ushers in a new period where individuals are free to make educated choices about their cannabis consumption, whether for medicinal, therapeutic, or spiritual purposes.

THE RISE OF MEDICAL CANNABIS

The legalization of medical cannabis played a pivotal role in altering perceptions. Patients and caregivers sought a more respectful term reflecting the plant's therapeutic potential. "Consumer" accurately represents individuals making informed decisions regarding their health and well-being, dispelling the misconception that all cannabis use falls strictly under the "recreational" category – another term often misused.

The diversification of cannabis products has further solidified the term "consumer." It encompasses not only those who smoke or vape but also individuals who use tinctures, topicals, edibles, and other form factors. "Consumer" conveys a sense of intentionality, suggesting that individuals make conscious decisions about how they consume cannabis and for what purposes.

DESTIGMATIZATION AND DECRIMINALIZATION

The shift to "consumer" aligns with broader efforts to destigmatize and decriminalize cannabis. By rejecting the derogatory connotations of "user" and adopting a term that conveys responsibility, society takes a step toward more rational and humane drug policies.

This linguistic shift is vital in destigmatizing cannabis and redefining how society views those who engage with the plant. It's not merely a matter of semantics; it's about recognizing the agency of individuals to make choices about their cannabis consumption.

Furthermore, it reflects the changing legal landscape surrounding cannabis. As cannabis legalization spreads, framing cannabis consumption as a matter of conscious choice rather than addiction or dependency becomes increasingly essential. This linguistic change aligns with policies that treat cannabis more like a regulated consumer product than a dangerous substance.

EMPOWERING RESPONSIBLE CHOICES AND FOSTERING INCLUSION

Adopting "consumer" over "user" isn't merely a linguistic adjustment; it's emblematic of a broader societal shift in how we view cannabis and those who engage with it. As we delve deeper into the implications of this terminology, we uncover how this change shapes cannabis culture and the path forward.

> "The term 'consume' transcends the shadow of historical biases that have plagued cannabis enthusiasts labeled as 'users.' By adopting 'consume,' we dismantle the unjust stigmas that have unjustly portrayed cannabis enthusiasts as societal threats. It's a small linguistic shift with a profound message of empowerment and self-determination."
>
> — John Shute, Co-Founder & CEO, PufCreativ

The word "user" has long carried a heavy stigma, conjuring images of addiction, dependency, and societal harm. In contrast, "consumer" normalizes cannabis use by presenting it as a rational choice informed individuals make. This shift helps break down the unjust stereotypes that have plagued cannabis enthusiasts for decades.

"Cannabis consumer" is an inclusive term encompassing a wide range of people with diverse backgrounds and reasons for using cannabis. It recognizes that the cannabis community is not homogenous but consists of patients, enthusiasts, advocates, entrepreneurs, and those seeking relief, relaxation, or creativity. This inclusivity is essential for building a more diverse and equitable cannabis industry.

One of the most significant shifts brought about by "consumer" is its alignment with the medicinal and wellness aspects of cannabis. It acknowledges that many people consume cannabis as a tool to manage medical conditions, alleviate symptoms, or enhance their well-being. "Consumer" respects their intentionality in choosing cannabis as part of their treatment or self-care regimen.

COMMUNITY AND ADVOCACY

Within the broader cannabis advocacy movement, "consumer" has become a rallying point. It symbolizes a shared commitment to responsible use, advocacy for legalization, and the rejection of harmful stereotypes. As cannabis continues gaining acceptance, the term "consumer" provides a unifying identity for those advocating its normalization.

Summary

In the evolving landscape of cannabis acceptance and reform, words matter. The choice between "use" and "consume" is not merely about semantics but reflects a fundamental shift in how society perceives and interacts with cannabis. "Consumer" better encapsulates the spirit of a responsible, informed, and diverse cannabis community. It recognizes the progress and path toward a more inclusive and enlightened future.

While transitioning from "user" to "consumer" is a significant step forward, it's essential to recognize that it's part of a more extensive journey. The cannabis movement is about more than just language; it's about equity, social justice, and responsible industry practices. The term "consumer" aligns with these values, but concrete actions must accompany it to ensure that the cannabis industry benefits all.

The following questions aim to explore the nuances of the linguistic shift in cannabis terminology, its historical context, and the broader societal implications in shaping perceptions and community dynamics:

- How does the shift from "use" to "consume" represent a more enlightened and responsible approach?
- How has the historical usage of the term "user" contributed to the stigmatization and demonization of cannabis consumers, particularly during the War on Drugs era, and what impact has it had on public perception and policies?
- What societal shifts and cultural changes have led to the emergence of the term "consumer" in relation to cannabis, and how does this term reflect evolving attitudes towards responsible and informed engagement with the plant?
- In what ways does the adoption of "consumer" over "user" in cannabis language challenge stereotypes and promote a more inclusive and responsible approach to cannabis consumption?

It's essential to recognize that this linguistic shift is just one aspect of a more significant movement toward cannabis normalization, equity, and social justice. The cannabis industry must continue prioritizing inclusivity and responsible practices to ensure that all benefit from cannabis legalization. As we progress on this journey, let "consumer" serve as a reminder of the progress made and the path towards a more enlightened and equitable future for cannabis.

CHAPTER 7

LEGALIZE vs. DECRIMINALIZE

WHAT'S THE DIFFERENCE?

Legalization typically involves creating a legal market for cannabis, allowing for the production, sale, and consumption of cannabis products within a regulated framework. In a legalized market, cannabis is treated similarly to other regulated consumer goods, with taxes, age restrictions, and other regulations in place to ensure safety and accountability. Legalization can also involve expunging the criminal records of individuals convicted of non-violent cannabis-related offenses.

> *"Federal legalization is much less desirable than decriminalization. The federal government has dragged its feet so long that most states already have a regulation system. The only things that legalization would bring now are the possibility of more tax, more regulation, and the chance of reduced scheduling on the CSA (Controlled Substance Act), which would be disastrous for small and medium-sized operators. Handing the industry to big pharma, alcohol, and tobacco."*
> — Bill Levers, Co-Founder, Beard Bros. Pharms

Decriminalization, on the other hand, typically involves reducing or eliminating criminal penalties for possession and use of cannabis. Decriminalization can take many forms, but it generally consists of reducing the severity of criminal penalties or replacing them with civil fines or other administrative measures. In a decriminalized system, cannabis possession is no longer subject to criminal prosecution, but the production, sale, and distribution of cannabis is still illegal.

The critical difference between legalization and decriminalization is that legalization creates a legal market for cannabis, while decriminalization reduces or eliminates criminal penalties for possession and use. Some see legalization as a more comprehensive approach that could generate significant economic benefits and increase safety by bringing cannabis into a regulated market. In contrast, decriminalization is often seen as a step towards reducing harm and ending the criminalization of cannabis consumers.[1]

"Decriminalization and legalization are often confused, yet they carry distinct implications. Decriminalization means reduced penalties, but civil consequences can still apply. Legalization, on the other hand, will always include some degree of regulation."
— Luke Scarmazzo, Co-Founder, California Healthcare Collective

It's worth noting that the terms "legalization" and "decriminalization" can be used differently in different contexts, and the specific policies and regulations associated with each approach can vary widely. Ultimately, the choice between legalization and decriminalization will depend on various factors, including social and political attitudes toward cannabis, the economic and public health implications of reform, and the legal and regulatory challenges of implementing each approach.

In the US, several states have chosen to legalize cannabis for adult use, creating a legal market for cannabis products. Other states have opted for decriminalization, reducing or eliminating criminal penalties for possession and consumption while maintaining restrictions on production, sale, and distribution, and still others remain in prohibition.

Legalization has significant economic potential, creating a legal market for cannabis products that can generate tax revenue, create jobs, and stimulate economic growth. Further, legalization can also reduce law enforcement costs associated with cannabis-related arrests and prosecutions, freeing up resources to focus on more serious crimes. In addition, legalization can mitigate the harms associated with illegal drug markets, such as violence, corruption, and the sale of adulterated or contaminated products.

It also poses some risks, including the potential for increased cannabis consumption, especially among vulnerable populations, such as youth and people with a history of substance abuse. There are also concerns about the impact of legalization on public health, including the potential for increased traffic accidents, mental health issues, and addiction. Moreover, the legal and regulatory challenges associated with implementing a legalized market for cannabis can be significant.

Decriminalization, by contrast, focuses primarily on reducing the harm associated with cannabis criminalization, such as the impact on individuals and families affected by cannabis-related arrests and convictions. Decriminalization can also free up law enforcement resources and reduce the burden on the criminal justice system.[2]

While it alone may not address the broader public health and social concerns associated with cannabis use, it does not generate the same economic benefits as legalization. Decriminalization can also leave intact the illicit markets and associated harms associated with illegal drug production, sale, and distribution.

Further, it does not make a behavior legal but reduces or eliminates its penalties. In the case of cannabis, decriminalization typically means that possessing small amounts of cannabis for personal use would no longer result in criminal charges. Still, it would instead be treated as a civil offense. It often involves replacing criminal penalties with fines or other non-criminal penalties.

> *"We need to exercise patience with federal legalization and urgency with federal decriminalization to cease the unjust disruption of lives for a plant that poses less risk than readily available substances. Federal legalization should adopt a gradual approach, considering that no state has yet established a system that sufficiently lowers the barriers for communities affected by cannabis prohibition to thrive and maintain their progress. Widespread fear still influences state legislatures, resulting in excessive regulation that generates an ever-evolving maze of compliance for cannabis businesses. Consequently, we must ask ourselves: if states are still grappling with these issues, what confidence do we have in the federal government's ability to handle them better?"*
>
> — Jessica Gonzalez, Esq., Rudick Law, PLLC

In recent years, there has been a growing movement towards legalizing cannabis in various parts of the world. Other countries, including Canada, Uruguay, Thailand, and several European nations, have also legalized cannabis to varying degrees.

Critics of both approaches argue that legalization and decriminalization could lead to increased use and abuse of cannabis, as well as negative social and health impacts. Others say that the regulation and taxation of cannabis may not be practical or lead to unintended consequences.

The debate around cannabis legalization and decriminalization is complex and multifaceted, with solid arguments on both sides. As laws and attitudes towards cannabis continue to evolve, it will be necessary to consider the potential benefits and drawbacks of different regulation approaches.[3]

> *"Decriminalization is like giving cannabis a hall pass, making it less likely to end up in detention. Legalization, on the other hand, is like letting it graduate, complete with a cap and gown, ready to join the grown-up world of taxes and regulations."*
> — Debra Borchardt, Executive Editor, Green Market Report

TO EXPUNGE OR NOT TO EXPUNGE?

The expungement of criminal records related to cannabis use and possession is highly debated, and opinions on its importance vary.

Expungement refers to the process of erasing or sealing a criminal record. In the context of cannabis, expungement typically refers to the clearing of criminal records for individuals convicted of low-level, non-violent cannabis offenses, such as possession, cultivation, or distribution, that are now legal or decriminalized.

Proponents of expungement argue that it is a critical step towards addressing the harm that criminalization of cannabis has caused to individuals and communities, particularly to BIPOC communities disproportionately impacted by drug enforcement policies. Expungement can help to remove barriers to employment, housing, and other opportunities that individuals with criminal records face and can also help to restore justice and reduce the stigma associated with cannabis consumption.

Opponents of expungement argue that it is unnecessary and that individuals who break the law should not be given special treatment. They also say that expungement could be challenging, expensive, and time-consuming, and the resources could be better spent elsewhere.

Research suggests that the benefits of expungement outweigh the costs. A study by the Drug Policy Alliance[4] found that expungement can lead to increased employment opportunities, higher wages, and reduced recidivism rates. Furthermore, several states and cities that have implemented expungement programs have successfully reduced the harm caused by cannabis criminalization.

> *"Full legalization is important for the cannabis industry to be treated as a real industry and provided banking, credit, and taxation like all other industries. Scientific research is also difficult without federal funding and approval, which won't happen until full legalization. Until the United States overcomes the effects of 'reefer madness,' consumers, patients, and businesses are stuck in an increasingly complex and difficult environment that echoes the American Revolution's 'no taxation without representation' principle."*
> — Marianne Cursetjee, Co-Founder & CEO, Alibi Cannabis

Ultimately, whether or not expungement is seen as an essential aspect of cannabis legalization will depend on the jurisdiction's specific legal and social context. In some cases, expungement is necessary to address the harm caused by criminalization. In contrast, in others, it is an insufficient response to broader racial and social justice issues.

The debate over expungement reflects broader debates over the future of cannabis legalization and the role of criminal justice reform in addressing social and economic disparities. As cannabis legalization continues to spread, debates over expungement will likely continue to play a vital role in shaping the contours of cannabis policy and its broader social impact.

WHY IT MATTERS

Whether to legalize or decriminalize cannabis depends on various factors, including cultural attitudes, political considerations, and public health concerns. Both options have advantages and disadvantages, and policymakers must carefully weigh these factors when deciding on drug policy.

While legalization and decriminalization can have positive impacts, policymakers should carefully consider their goals and priorities and potential unintended consequences when deciding which approach to take. It is also essential to recognize that cannabis policy is a complex issue that involves multiple stakeholders, including law enforcement, public health experts, and community members. Successful policy implementation requires collaboration and ongoing evaluation.

> *"Looking at this through the perspective of cannabis as a consumer branded product, there is an undeniable stigma casting a shadow over the cannabis industry, as evidenced by – and exacerbated by – its longtime (and only recently changing) presence on Schedule I of the Controlled Substances Act. In order to gain legitimacy and make itself more financeable, the entire industry has had to embark on a re-brand. Legalization will make greater strides toward bringing the industry and its brands into a more favorable light than would decriminalization, where the underlying product would remain illegal."*
> — Christiane Schuman Campbell, Esq., Partner, Duane Morris, LLP

It is worth noting that the debate over legalization versus decriminalization is not limited to cannabis. Many other drugs are subject to similar debates and discussions, and policymakers must weigh the various approaches, potential benefits, and risks. Some argue that decriminalization of all drugs could reduce drug-related harm, such as overdose deaths, and free up resources for treatment and harm reduction services. However, others argue that decriminalization could increase drug use and associated harms and that legalization would create a regulated market and reduce the harm associated with the illegal drug trade.

Summary

In conclusion, the choice between cannabis legalization and decriminalization is a complex and multifaceted issue, with each approach offering its advantages and disadvantages. Legalization typically involves creating a regulated cannabis market, which can generate significant economic benefits, increase safety, and reduce the harms of illegal drug markets. However, it also poses risks, such as the potential for increased cannabis consumption and public health concerns.

Decriminalization, however, primarily focuses on reducing the harm associated with cannabis criminalization, particularly for individuals and communities disproportionately impacted by drug enforcement policies. It can free up law enforcement resources and reduce the burden on the criminal justice system. However, it does not create a legal market for cannabis and may not fully address public health and social concerns associated with cannabis use.

The questions below aim to delve into the nuances of cannabis policy, exploring the economic, social, and legal implications of the choices between legalization and decriminalization while also considering the broader social justice implications:

- How do the approaches of legalization and decriminalization differ in terms of their impact on criminal records, social justice, and the broader economic and societal aspects of cannabis regulation?
- What are the challenges posed by the federal government's stance on cannabis, and how have various states in the U.S.

responded in terms of legalization, decriminalization, or remaining in prohibition?

- What are the economic potentials associated with legalization, such as tax revenue and job creation, and what potential risks, like increased consumption and public health concerns, are associated with both approaches?
- What arguments exist for and against the expungement of cannabis-related criminal records, and how does it tie into broader discussions about racial justice, opportunities, and social stigma?

The choice between these approaches depends on various factors, including cultural attitudes, political considerations, and public health priorities. The expungement of cannabis-related criminal records is a related issue that can significantly impact the justice and equity aspects of cannabis policy. As cannabis legalization and reform efforts continue to evolve, policymakers must carefully consider their goals and the specific needs of their communities when making decisions about cannabis policy. Ultimately, it is essential to create a balanced approach that addresses both the economic potential of the cannabis industry and the social and health implications of cannabis consumption.

CHAPTER 8

BLACK, LEGACY, TRADITIONAL & LEGAL MARKETS

DEFINING THE MARKETS

The terms "black market," "traditional," and "legacy market" are all deeply intertwined with the history and evolution of the cannabis industry. The term "black market" is often used to describe the illicit cannabis market before legalization. Illegal sales, underground networks, and criminal activity characterized this market. While legalization has helped to reduce the size and scope of the black market, it continues to exist in some parts of the country where cannabis remains illegal.

"The transition from legacy to regulated markets is often viewed through a legal lens, but it is equally important to view it through the lens of scientific revolutions. Today, we are witnessing the age of cannabis discovery, where the dark ages of cannabis prohibition, knowledge suppression, and social injustice seemingly end. Through this transition, we shall bear witness to scientific breakthroughs that were previously unimaginable, and the healing powers of the cannabis plant will finally unlock and impact people across all ends of the globe. We stand on the shoulders of pioneers and risk-takers who paved the roads we now traverse, and it is up to us to honor their sacrifices while ushering in a cannabis renaissance that will revolutionize the world of plant-based medicine".
— Claudio Miranda, Co-Founder, Guild Extracts

On the other hand, the terms "traditional" and "legacy market" are often used to describe the pre-legalized market for cannabis that was not associated with criminal activity. This market was driven by small-scale growers, processors, and sellers who were often part of close-knit communities and deeply connected to the plant. While legalization has created new economic opportunities for some of these individuals, it has also led to the consolidation of the industry and the emergence of prominent corporate players with the resources to dominate the market.

These terms are not just about economics. They also reflect the social and political dimensions of the cannabis industry. The black market has been associated with the criminalization of cannabis and the disproportionate impact of drug laws on BIPOC communities. On the other hand, the traditional and legacy markets have been associated with the cultural and social significance of cannabis, as well as the deep knowledge and expertise of those who have been involved in the industry for decades.[1]

The use of the terms "black market," "traditional," and "legacy market" in the cannabis industry reflects broader social, political, and economic issues related to drug policy and legalization. From a social perspective, the term "legacy market" acknowledges the role that individuals and communities of color have played in the cannabis industry, often at significant personal risk due to the plant's illegal status.

Politically, the term "legacy market" can also be seen as a way to push for more significant equity in the legal cannabis industry by calling for policies that provide opportunities for those previously excluded. Conversely, the term "black market" can be used to justify continued law enforcement efforts and crackdowns on illegal activity.

Economically, the term "legacy market" can be seen as acknowledging the economic contributions of those involved in the cannabis industry before legalization and the potential benefits of bringing those individuals into the legal market. However, the continued existence of the "black market" can also have negative economic impacts, such as lost tax revenue and increased competition for legal businesses.

It is important to note that the transition from the term "black market" to the "legacy market" is not a straightforward process, and many individuals and communities may continue to rely on illegal markets due to barriers to entry into the legal market. Therefore, policies prioritizing equity and access to the legal market are necessary to address the root causes of the black market and ensure a smooth transition to the traditional and legacy market(s). The terms have complex social, political, economic, and public health implications, and their use should be considered carefully.[2]

The black market and legacy market terminology is not unique to the cannabis industry, as it can be applied to other illegal or unregulated markets. However, legalizing cannabis in many jurisdictions has brought these terms to the forefront of public discourse and policy discussions.

The distinction between the black market and the legacy market also raises questions about the role of law enforcement and regulatory agencies in regulating the cannabis industry. While some argue that cracking down on the black market is necessary to protect public safety and prevent criminal activity, others say that excessive enforcement measures can perpetuate harm and further marginalize those involved in the illegal trade.

The terms are essential for understanding the evolution of the cannabis industry and the challenges facing the transition to a legal and regulated market. While the terms have different connotations and implications, they both highlight the need for policies prioritizing equity, justice, and safety and addressing the historical injustices of drug policy.

In addition to the social, political, economic, and public health implications of the black market, traditional, and legacy market, there are also implications for the legal industry itself. The legacy market challenges licensed businesses as they struggle to compete against lower prices and unregulated cultivation practices. It can create a disincentive for legal businesses to comply with regulations and operate transparently, ultimately undermining public trust and confidence in the legal market.

On the other hand, the legacy market can also present opportunities for legal businesses to collaborate with and learn from those with experience in the industry. Policymakers can support a more diverse and resilient industry by acknowledging the contributions of those in the legacy market and providing opportunities for them to enter the legal market.

It is important to note that the black market, traditional, and legacy markets are not static categories but dynamic and evolving phenomena. As the legal cannabis industry continues to evolve and expand, the boundaries between the black market and traditional and legacy markets will likely shift, and new challenges and opportunities will emerge.

While the terms reflect different aspects of the industry, they highlight the need for policies prioritizing equity, justice, and safety. By acknowledging the historical and current realities of the cannabis industry, policymakers can work toward creating a legal market that is inclusive, equitable, and sustainable.[3]

The term "legal market" refers to the industry involved in producing, distributing, selling, and consuming cannabis products within a legal framework established by regional, national, or international government regulations. It encompasses various segments, including:

Cultivation and Production: Licensed cultivation facilities that grow cannabis plants for medical or recreational purposes. This includes indoor and outdoor cultivation, processing, and manufacturing of cannabis products.

Retail and Distribution: Licensed dispensaries, retail stores, or online platforms authorized to sell and deliver cannabis products to consumers. Distribution networks involve transporting and delivering these products to authorized retailers and consumers where applicable.

Medical and Adult Use: Cannabis is used for both medical and adult use purposes. Medical cannabis is prescribed by healthcare professionals for treating various health conditions, while adult use cannabis is consumed for therapeutic or non-medical purposes.

Ancillary Services: Supporting services such as cannabis-focused technology, consultancy, legal services, packaging, marketing, and compliance, which cater to the needs of the cannabis industry.

Regulatory Compliance: The legal cannabis market operates under specific regulations set by governing bodies to ensure compliance with laws related to licensing, product quality, testing, labeling, taxation, and overall industry standards.

Investment and Finance: Involving investors, financial institutions, and venture capitalists in funding cannabis-related businesses, research, and development within the legal framework established by local, state, and federal regulators.

The legal cannabis market varies significantly across different regions and countries due to diverse regulatory frameworks. Some jurisdictions have fully legalized both medical and adult-use cannabis, while others may allow only medical use or have partial legalization with strict regulations. The market continues to evolve as more regions consider or enact legislation to legalize cannabis, leading to an expansion of legal cannabis-related activities and industries.[4]

"The term' legacy' has lost its significance in this industry. As soon as corporate entities became involved, their focus shifted to commercialization for capital gain rather than recognizing and respecting their original community. 'Traditional' also needs to catch up, as anyone can easily manipulate it. So, the transition from legacy to legality feels insincere. These terms have been twisted, requiring us to self-police to safeguard our true intentions."

— Mary Prior, Founder, Cannaclusive

ACKNOWLEDGING PIONEERING WORK

As cannabis legalization continues, there is a growing recognition of the contributions made by legacy cannabis pioneers in developing the industry. Many of these individuals faced significant risks and legal consequences for their involvement in the illegal cannabis trade but also helped to create the cultural and social infrastructure that has supported the growth of legal cannabis.

Some advocates argue that it is essential to acknowledge these pioneers' contributions and include them in the emerging legal market. It may consist of offering pathways for individuals with cannabis-related criminal records to participate in legal cannabis businesses or ensuring that communities most impacted by drug enforcement can benefit from the economic opportunities created by legalization.

At the same time, there are also concerns that the emerging legal market may displace or exclude many individuals involved in the legacy cannabis trade. Some worry that the high costs of entering the legal market, regulatory barriers, and competition from larger, established firms may make it difficult for these individuals to transition to the legal industry.

The question of how to integrate legacy cannabis pioneers into the legal market is part of a more extensive debate over the social and economic impact of cannabis legalization. As the legal market continues to grow, this debate will likely continue to play a vital role in shaping the future of the cannabis industry.

Some organizations and lawmakers have recognized this issue and are working to address it. They have proposed programs to help legacy cannabis pioneers transition to the legal market, such as offering training and funding, expunging criminal records, and prioritizing licensing for individuals previously involved in the legacy market. These efforts aim to acknowledge and honor these pioneers' contributions and promote equity in the legal cannabis industry.[5]

Some legal cannabis companies actively seek out and partner with these pioneers to help them bring their skills and expertise to the legal market. These partnerships can benefit both parties, as the pioneers can share their knowledge of cannabis cultivation and distribution, and the legal companies can provide resources and support to help the pioneers thrive in the legal market.

Acknowledging the contributions of cannabis pioneers is an essential step in promoting equity and justice in the legal cannabis industry. By offering support and opportunities to these individuals, we can honor their legacy and promote a more inclusive and fair industry for everyone.

Recognizing the contributions and sacrifices of cannabis pioneers can also help to shift public perception of cannabis away from negative stereotypes and towards a more positive understanding of the potential of this plant. By acknowledging the history of cannabis and the individuals who helped to shape its cultural significance, we can create a more equitable and inclusive legal cannabis industry.

> *"Embedded within the historical narrative of cannabis are the enduring stories of Black, Legacy, and Traditional Markets. Often marginalized and underestimated, these markets have been the wellspring of innovation, cultural exchange, and community resilience. Exploring their legacy unveils a rich tapestry of heritage, highlighting their pivotal role in shaping cannabis culture and emphasizing the need for equity and inclusion in the modern cannabis landscape."*
> — Roz McCarthy, Founder & CEO, Black Buddha Cannabis

THE ROAD TO LEGALIZATION

For decades, the illegal cannabis market has thrived in countries where cannabis is illegal. In the United States, the underground cannabis market is estimated to be worth billions of dollars annually, making it one of the largest illicit industries in the country. Despite the threat of criminal prosecution, many people continue to buy and sell cannabis outside the legal system, citing various reasons such as accessibility, affordability, and quality.

According to a New Frontier Data[6] report on U.S. cannabis consumption, illicit sales exceeded $74 billion in 2022, outpacing legal sales of $28 billion by a staggering 164 percent. This stark gap presents a clear opportunity for legal retailers who can appeal to those who purchase from unregulated channels.

One of the primary reasons people continue to buy and sell cannabis illegally is the lack of access to legal cannabis. Even in states where cannabis is legal, many people still have limited access due to the high cost of legal cannabis products. In most cases, the illegal market can provide cannabis products at a lower price, making them more accessible to individuals with lower incomes.

Another factor that contributes to the popularity of the illegal market is the quality of the products. Many illegal cannabis dealers claim to offer higher quality products than legal dispensaries. While there is some truth to this claim, the lack of regulations in this market can also lead to dangerous products, such as those contaminated with harmful chemicals and pesticides.

The illegal market also poses significant challenges for law enforcement officials. Due to the illegal nature of the market, it is difficult to track and regulate, making it more challenging to ensure that products are safe for consumption. Moreover, the illegal market often perpetuates criminal activities, including drug trafficking, organized crime, and money laundering.[7]

Legalization can also provide greater access to cannabis products for those who need it for medical reasons. In many countries, medical cannabis is legal, but patients still face significant barriers to access due to the cost and limited availability of legal products. By legalizing cannabis, governments can ensure that patients can access safe, high-quality cannabis products at an affordable price.

Despite the benefits of legalizing cannabis, there are also significant challenges that must be addressed. One of the primary issues is the competition between the legal and illegal markets. Illegal dealers may continue to offer lower prices, making it difficult for legal markets to compete. Additionally, many illegal dealers have established loyal customer bases, which may be challenging to convert to legal markets.

The road to cannabis legalization is complex and multifaceted, requiring the cooperation of multiple stakeholders, including policymakers, industry players, law enforcement officials, and the general public. One of the critical factors in the success of cannabis legalization is public education and awareness. Many people are still uninformed about the potential benefits and risks of cannabis consumption, which can lead to misunderstandings and misconceptions.

One possible solution to the competition between the legal and illegal markets is to implement policies that promote the affordability and accessibility of legal cannabis products. It can be achieved by reducing taxes and licensing fees for legal cannabis businesses and providing subsidies or grants to low-income consumers. Policymakers can also work with legal cannabis businesses to develop innovative pricing models that are more competitive with the illegal market.

Another potential solution is to increase enforcement efforts against illegal cannabis operators. Law enforcement officials can work with legal cannabis businesses to identify and target illegal operators, disrupting their operations and reducing their ability to compete with legal markets. Moreover, law enforcement officials can prioritize and address the most severe criminal activities associated with the illegal cannabis market, such as drug trafficking and money laundering.

> *"How we refer to cannabis industry pioneers who have defied Prohibition for decades is loaded with context. Many unwittingly refer to it as the 'Black Market,' never considering the racial undertones of that description or the marginalized groups that built this industry from the ground up. I prefer to use the term, 'Legacy Market.'"*
>
> — Justin Johnson, Founder & CEO, BudsFeed

Further, policymakers can work to improve public perception of legal cannabis markets. This can be achieved through public education campaigns that promote the benefits and safety of legal cannabis products. They can also work with the industry to develop marketing and branding strategies that appeal to and educate a broader audience, including the canna-curious and those who may be hesitant to try legal cannabis products.

LEVELING THE LANDSCAPE

Below are some key factors contributing to the friction between the legal cannabis industry and traditional/legacy/black market players, as well as potential solutions for addressing these issues and promoting collaboration[8]:

Contributing Factors

Perceptions Of Legitimacy

Legal market players may view traditional, legacy, and black market players as representing criminal activity and a threat to public safety, while traditional, legacy and black market players may view the legal market as representing corporate greed and the commodification of a plant with spiritual and medicinal significance.

Economic Impact

The legalization of cannabis has the potential to generate significant tax revenue and create jobs. Still, it can also lead to the displacement of traditional, legacy, and black market players who have relied on cannabis as their livelihood.

Quality And Safety

The legal market is subject to rigorous testing and quality control standards. In contrast, the traditional, legacy, and black market often lacks such regulations, leading to concerns about the safety and potency of their products.

Cultural And Social Factors

Historical and cultural factors significantly shape attitudes toward the legal, traditional, legacy, and black market players. Some traditional, legacy and black market players view the legal market as a threat to their way of life, and some legal market players view traditional, legacy, and black market players as representing criminal activity.

Potential Solutions

Prioritize Equity And Inclusion:

Create opportunities for traditional, legacy, and black market players to participate and succeed in the legal market through policies such as social equity programs that provide resources and support to individuals from marginalized communities to enter and succeed in the legal market.

Promote Collaboration And Open Communication
Foster an environment of mutual understanding and respect by creating opportunities for dialogue and engagement between legal, traditional, legacy, and black market players.

Address Economic Impact
Provide support and resources to traditional, legacy, and black market players to transition to the legal market, such as training on business best practices and standard operating procedures.

Ensure Quality And Safety
Provide education and resources to traditional, legacy, and black market players to improve the safety and quality of their products, such as training on best practices for testing and analysis.

Recognize Cultural And Social Factors
Engage in meaningful dialogue and mutual understanding by creating opportunities for traditional, legacy, and black market players to share their perspectives and experiences with the legal market. Conversely, educate legal market players to help them better understand the historical and cultural significance of cannabis.

The angst between the legal cannabis industry and traditional, legacy, and black market players is a complex issue requiring a comprehensive and multifaceted approach. By prioritizing equity and inclusion, promoting collaboration and open communication, addressing the economic impact, ensuring quality and safety, and recognizing cultural and social factors, the cannabis community can create a more sustainable and equitable industry that benefits all stakeholders.[9]

It is essential to recognize that the legal cannabis industry and traditional, legacy, and black market players share a common goal of advancing the legalization and destigmatization of cannabis. By working together towards this shared goal, both groups can create a more cohesive and united cannabis community.

Another way to promote collaboration between the legal cannabis industry and traditional, legacy, and black market players is through community outreach and engagement. By working together to educate the public about the benefits of cannabis and combatting stigma, both groups can promote the normalization of cannabis consumption and expand the overall market.

The tension between these groups is not unique to the cannabis industry. Similar divides have existed in other industries undergoing significant regulatory changes, such as the alcohol industry during Prohibition. By learning from these experiences and taking a collaborative approach, the cannabis community can navigate these challenges and emerge more robust and united.

> *"In recognition of the profound shifts within the industry, I stopped using the term 'traditional.' Most of the former practices and customs we employed have undergone adjustments to accommodate the post-recreational model of cannabis consumption. Now I categorize these prevailing market sides as 'private' and 'retail,' differentiated by the degree of engagement required to access them."*
> — Matt Jackson, Cannabis Journalist and Consultant

Summary
The transition from the black market to regulated cannabis markets is a complex and multifaceted process that goes beyond the realm of legality. It encompasses scientific discovery, social justice, and economic considerations. As we witness the end of the dark ages of cannabis prohibition and knowledge suppression, we are poised for a cannabis renaissance driven by scientific breakthroughs and the healing potential of the plant.

The terminology used to describe the various aspects of this transition, such as "black market," "traditional market," "legacy market," and "legal market," reflects not only economic distinctions but also deep-rooted social and cultural dimensions. Acknowledging the contributions and sacrifices of those who operated in the illegal markets is vital for promoting equity and justice in the emerging legal industry. Finding ways to bridge the gap between legal and traditional players, addressing economic disparities, ensuring product safety, and fostering open communication are critical to creating a more inclusive and sustainable cannabis industry.

The following questions aim to help explore the complex shift from illegal to legal cannabis markets by delving into the multifaceted nature of the transition, taking into consideration the social, economic, and cultural implications while exploring potential avenues for collaboration and equity within the industry:

- What are the challenges faced by individuals and communities transitioning from the black or legacy market to the emerging legal cannabis industry, and how can policies address these challenges?
- What social, economic, and public health implications arise from the distinctions between the black and legacy markets, and how can policymakers navigate these complexities?
- How does the legalization of cannabis impact the dynamics between the legal market and traditional, legacy, or black market players, especially in terms of economic viability and access?
- What measures could bridge the divide between legal and traditional players in the cannabis industry, addressing economic disparities, ensuring product safety, and fostering open communication?

The transition from prohibition to legalization represents a significant societal shift in the grander scheme. It demands careful consideration of the historical injustices associated with cannabis criminalization and a commitment to righting those wrongs. As cannabis policy continues to evolve, collaboration, understanding, and a shared commitment to cannabis's potential as a force for healing and innovation will be essential for realizing the promise of the cannabis renaissance.

CHAPTER 9

RESCHEDULE, DESCHEDULE OR DECONTROL?

AN ONGOING DEBATE

The ongoing debate regarding the status of cannabis under the Controlled Substances Act (CSA) has long been a subject of contention, confusion, and anticipation. At the heart of this debate lies the complex interplay between "rescheduling," "descheduling," and "decontrolling" cannabis — terms that, despite their nuanced differences, carry profound implications for the legal landscape of cannabis consumption, research, and commerce in the United States. The conversation is uncertain as experts grapple with a tangled web of legal definitions, regulatory implications, and shifting public sentiments. As federal agencies, policymakers, and stakeholders speculate on outcomes, one thing remains clear: the potential for change is as promising as it is unpredictable, with each possible decision paving a different path for the future of cannabis policy.

> *"The reschedule vs. deschedule debate revolves around industry control. Rescheduling to Schedule II or III could favor 'Big Pharma' and large corporations, sidelining small and medium businesses. Descheduling would promote equity, reducing entry barriers and facilitating industry growth in sectors like banking and insurance, which currently face restrictions."*
> — Jeff Levers, Co-Founder, Beard Bros. Pharms

DEFINING SCHEDULES AND TERMS

The Controlled Substances Act (CSA) is the statute prescribing federal U.S. drug policy regulating the manufacture, importation, possession, use, and distribution of certain substances. Enacted as part of the Comprehensive Drug Abuse Prevention and Control Act of 1970, the CSA consolidates previous drug laws into a single, more comprehensive statute.

The CSA categorizes drugs into five Schedules (I-V) based on their potential for abuse, status in international treaties, and any medical benefits they may provide. Here's a brief overview of each schedule:[1]

Schedule I

Schedule I drugs, substances or chemicals are defined as drugs with no currently accepted medical use and a high potential for abuse. Some examples of Schedule I drugs are heroin, lysergic acid diethylamide (LSD), marijuana (cannabis), methamphetamine, methaqualone, and peyote.

Schedule II

Schedule II drugs, substances, or chemicals are defined as drugs with a high potential for abuse, with use potentially leading to severe psychological or physical dependence. These drugs are also considered dangerous. Some examples of Schedule II drugs are combination products with less than 15 milligrams of hydrocodone per dosage unit (Vicodin®), cocaine, methamphetamine, methadone, hydromorphone (Dilaudid®), meperidine (Demerol®), oxycodone (OxyContin®), fentanyl, Dexedrine®, Adderall®, and Ritalin®.

Schedule III

Schedule III drugs, substances, or chemicals are defined as drugs with a moderate to low potential for physical and psychological dependence. Schedule III drugs abuse potential is less than Schedule I and Schedule II drugs but more than Schedule IV. Some examples of Schedule III drugs are products containing less than 90 milligrams of codeine per dosage unit (Tylenol® with codeine), ketamine, anabolic steroids, and testosterone.

Schedule IV

Schedule IV drugs, substances, or chemicals are defined as drugs with a low potential for abuse and a low risk of dependence. Some examples of Schedule IV drugs are Xanax®, Soma®, Darvon®, Darvocet®, Valium®, Ativan®, Talwin®, Ambien®, and Tramadol®.

Schedule V

Schedule V drugs, substances, or chemicals are defined as drugs with lower potential for abuse than Schedule IV and consist of preparations containing limited quantities of certain narcotics. Schedule V drugs are generally used for antidiarrheal, antitussive, and analgesic purposes. Some examples of Schedule V drugs are cough preparations with less than 200 milligrams of codeine or per 100 milliliters (Robitussin AC®), Lomotil®, Motofen®, Lyrica®, and Parepectolin®.

The Schedule I classification of cannabis has significantly impacted cannabis legalization efforts. It has limited the ability of researchers to conduct studies on cannabis, hindered medical access for patients, and created legal ambiguities and inconsistencies between state and federal laws. The federal prohibition of cannabis has also led to social and economic disparities, particularly for BIPOC communities disproportionately affected by the War On Drugs.[2]

> *"The distinction between rescheduling and descheduling is crucial in understanding the implications for the legal status and regulation of cannabis. While rescheduling would acknowledge some medical benefits and potentially ease restrictions, descheduling would eliminate most federal control and treat it more like alcohol or tobacco, allowing states to determine their own cannabis policies and would open the door for broader uses of cannabis, including for medical, recreational, and industrial purposes, without federal interference, and therefore easier access to investment capital, especially from institutional investors who have been mostly absent from the sector."*
> — Michael Schwamm, Esq., Partner, Duane Morris, LLP

The DEA and FDA are responsible for determining which substances are added to or removed from the various schedules, though the process may also involve Congress. The CSA also provides a mechanism for substances to be controlled or for their scheduling to be changed or removed. This is where the terms "rescheduling" (moving a drug from one schedule to another), "descheduling" (removing a drug from the scheduling system altogether), and "decontrolling" (a less formal term that generally means the same as descheduling) come into play.

Changes to a drug's scheduling can have significant impacts on how it's regulated, ranging from research opportunities to how it's taxed and prescribed. Rescheduling a drug to a less restrictive schedule can increase access for medical research and change the legal landscape for its prescription and use. Descheduling a drug can remove federal oversight and allow state governments to establish their regulations, potentially leading to a legal environment similar to that of alcohol or tobacco.[3]

Defining Scheduling, Rescheduling, Descheduling, And Decontrolling

In the context of the Controlled Substances Act (CSA), the terms "scheduling," "rescheduling," "descheduling," and "decontrolling" have specific legal meanings:

Scheduling: This refers to the process by which a substance is classified under one of the five categories (Schedules I-V) based on criteria that include its potential for abuse, known medical use, and potential for addiction or dependence. Schedule I substances are considered the most restrictive, often with no legally recognized medical use in the U.S., while Schedule V substances are the least restrictive.

Rescheduling: This is the act of moving a substance from one schedule to another. For example, if a drug is moved from Schedule I to Schedule II, it is recognized as having a potential for abuse that may lead to severe psychological or physical dependence but also has an accepted medical use under severe restrictions.

Descheduling: This refers to removing a substance from the CSA schedules entirely, thus no longer regulating it as a controlled substance at the federal level. Descheduling is what many advocates for cannabis legalization aim for, as it would represent the federal government's acknowledgement that the substance does not meet the criteria for any of the CSA schedules.

Decontrolling: This term is not officially used in the CSA but is sometimes used colloquially to describe the process of removing a substance from federal control, which effectively means the same as descheduling. It's the process of lifting restrictions imposed by the CSA on a substance.

These actions can have significant implications for legal access to and control of substances, particularly in the debate surrounding cannabis. Rescheduling cannabis could potentially open the door to more medical research and change its tax status, while descheduling it could allow states more autonomy in their cannabis regulations and could signal a move towards treating it similarly to alcohol or tobacco at the federal level.

> *"DEA officials emphasize their ability to reschedule cannabis but not to 'deschedule' it. However, they often omit the fact that they can also 'decontrol' cannabis, essentially referring to the same action with different terminology. If our aim is to eliminate cannabis from the CSA schedule, aligning our language with that of the DEA is imperative."*
> — Chris Conrad, Writer, Consultant, Expert Witness

RESCHEDULING AND ITS IMPLICATIONS FOR CANNABIS

Rescheduling cannabis within the framework of the Controlled Substances Act (CSA) refers to changing its classification from one schedule to another less restrictive schedule. This move is significant as it would represent a shift in the federal government's stance on the plant's potential for abuse, medical utility, and safety under medical supervision.[4]

Currently, cannabis is listed as a Schedule I drug, indicating a high potential for abuse and no accepted medical use. If rescheduled to Schedule III, for instance, cannabis would be acknowledged to have some potential for abuse that is less than Schedule I and II substances, an accepted medical use, and moderate to low potential for physical and psychological dependence. The implications of such a change are manifold.

The Impact On Medical Research
And Pharmaceutical Development

For research, it would likely ease some of the regulatory hurdles that currently make studying cannabis's potential benefits and risks challenging, potentially leading to discoveries about its therapeutic properties.

Pharmaceutical companies might also gain a foothold in the market, as they would be able to develop and market cannabis-based medications under FDA guidelines, which could lead to a broader range of approved medical cannabis products available to patients. However, rescheduling would not equate to federal legalization akin to alcohol or tobacco; it would still be illegal under federal law without a prescription.

Changes To Business Operations,
Including Taxation Under IRC §280E

For businesses, rescheduling could alleviate certain tax burdens, as companies would no longer be subjected to the same stringent Internal Revenue Code restrictions, potentially lowering the effective tax rate for cannabis businesses significantly. Currently, cannabis businesses face significant tax burdens due to IRC Section 280E, which prevents them from deducting standard business expenses. With descheduling, these businesses could be taxed like any other business, potentially lowering their tax rates and contributing to economic growth.

How Rescheduling Would Affect Consumer Access

For consumers, it could mean access to cannabis through prescriptions, changing the landscape of medical cannabis use. Yet, such a federal shift wouldn't automatically align with state laws where cannabis might be legal for recreational use, maintaining a complex patchwork of regulations and potentially continuing the legal discrepancies between federal and state policies.

DESCHEDULING AND
ITS IMPLICATIONS FOR CANNABIS

Descheduling cannabis would involve removing it entirely from the list of controlled substances under the Controlled Substances Act (CSA). Descheduling cannabis would also make it easier to conduct research on the plant, allowing horticulture and plant genetics researchers to work with fewer federal restrictions, potentially leading to the development of new cannabis strains for both medical and recreational purposes.

> *"Why would the industry be more in the hands of Big Pharma when it's Schedule II or III than Schedule I? To state the question is to answer it. If the FDA wanted the industry to be in the arms of 'Big Pharma,' it would have the power to do that now. And it's not."* [5]
> — Howard Sklamberg, Former FDA Regulator

It's important to note that descheduling cannabis would not automatically address the criminal records of those previously convicted of cannabis-related offenses, nor would it solve all of the issues related to banking and taxation without additional legislation, such as the SAFE Banking Act.[6]

In contrast, if cannabis were merely rescheduled, for example, to Schedule III, it would still be regulated by the DEA, and its sale would require a prescription for medical use. It would also mean that the current state-legal cannabis programs must be adjusted to comply with federal regulations, which could be complex.

While many advocate for descheduling as a step towards full legalization, others are concerned about the potential for increased federal regulation that could come with it. Big pharmaceutical companies could also become significant players in the industry if cannabis remains a controlled substance under federal law, even if it's rescheduled to a less restrictive category.

These broader implications highlight the complexity of cannabis law reform and the various factors that must be considered when discussing changes to its legal status under the CSA.

Potential For Regulatory Models Akin To Alcohol Or Tobacco

The potential for regulatory models akin to alcohol or tobacco following the descheduling of cannabis has been a point of discussion among advocates and policymakers. Descheduling cannabis would remove it from the list of substances regulated under the Controlled Substances Act (CSA), thus ending federal prohibition and allowing states to regulate it as they see fit. This could lead to a regulatory framework where cannabis is treated much like alcohol and tobacco, with individual states having the authority to oversee its production, distribution, and sales.

> *"Descheduling must be done through Congress. It is unrealistic to think that cannabis would go from a Schedule I substance to being decontrolled. The best we can hope for at present is a rescheduling to save the industry from the tax implications of IRS Code 280E."*
> — Robert Hoban, Esq., Co-Chair, Cannabis Industry Group

Such a move would also likely make cannabis research more accessible, removing many of the current federal barriers to study and development. It could enable a broader exploration of the plant's potential benefits and lead to advancements in both medical and recreational cannabis markets. However, descheduling cannabis would not necessarily mean an immediate shift to this kind of regulatory model, as there would still be a need for federal and state coordination to establish new systems of regulation.

The descheduling of cannabis could have significant implications for banking, taxation, and the overall structure of the cannabis industry. Currently, cannabis businesses are heavily taxed and have limited access to banking services due to federal restrictions. Descheduling could alleviate these issues, leading to more robust economic growth within the industry. However, without additional legislation like the SAFE Banking Act, some skeptics argue that descheduling alone may not open the doors of banks to cannabis operators due to ongoing federal controls.[7]

It's important to note that descheduling cannabis would not automatically make all cannabis products available over the counter or without regulation. There would still be a need for some level of oversight, likely from the FDA, to ensure safety and quality standards are met, similar to how alcohol and tobacco are regulated.

The Pros & Cons Of Rescheduling & Descheduling
Below is a detailed list of the pros and cons of each approach, as well as considerations for achieving cannabis legalization and regulation while reducing the impact on social equity and restorative justice efforts:

Rescheduling
Pros:

Access for Research: Rescheduling cannabis could potentially ease restrictions on research, allowing for more comprehensive studies on its medical benefits and potential risks.

Medical Use Expansion: It may open up avenues for broader medical use of cannabis by making it more accessible to patients and healthcare providers.

Regulatory Flexibility: Rescheduling could allow for more nuanced regulations, potentially providing a middle ground between strict prohibition and complete legalization.

Reduced Stigma: A shift in scheduling might contribute to reducing the stigma associated with cannabis use, leading to more open and honest discussions about its effects and applications.

Cons:

Regulatory Uncertainty: Rescheduling may lead to complex and evolving regulatory frameworks, causing confusion and uncertainty for patients, consumers, and businesses.

Potential Misuse: Easier access resulting from rescheduling might lead to increased recreational use and possible abuse, especially among vulnerable populations.

Industry Challenges: A shift in scheduling could pose challenges for businesses navigating new compliance requirements, potentially leading to increased operational costs.

Public Perception: Rescheduling might not eliminate the negative stigma associated with cannabis, leading to continued social biases and prejudices.

Descheduling
Pros:

Reduced Legal Restrictions: Decontrolling cannabis would remove legal barriers, allowing for free market competition and potentially reducing the criminal justice system's involvement.

Economic Opportunities: Decontrol could stimulate the growth of a new industry, creating job opportunities and fostering economic development in various sectors such as agriculture, retail, and manufacturing.

Tax Revenue: Decontrolling cannabis could generate substantial tax revenue for governments, which could be allocated to public services, education, and healthcare.

Consumer Accessibility: Removing control could make cannabis more accessible to those seeking alternative treatment options, potentially leading to improved health outcomes for specific individuals.

Cons:

Regulatory Void: Decontrol might result in a lack of comprehensive regulations, leading to potential quality control issues, inconsistent product standards, and public health concerns.

Increased Accessibility: Freer access to cannabis might lead to higher usage rates, potentially leading to public health challenges and concerns over substance abuse.

Youth Protection: Decontrol might make it more challenging to restrict access to minors, potentially increasing the risk of youth exposure to cannabis.

Social Implications: Decontrol could perpetuate existing social disparities, leading to unequal access and consumption patterns among socio-economic groups.

While descheduling cannabis at the federal level could pave the way for regulatory models similar to those for alcohol or tobacco, it would also require careful consideration and implementation to address various legal, economic, and social factors. The process would involve significant changes to existing state and federal laws and must ensure a balance between access, safety, and control.

FEDERAL AND STATE LAW CONFLICTS

Descheduling cannabis would lead to significant changes in how it is treated under federal and state laws. Currently, the conflict between state laws, where cannabis is legal in some form, and federal law, which still classifies it as illegal, creates a patchwork of regulations that businesses and consumers must navigate.[8]

If cannabis were descheduled, it would no longer be regulated under the Controlled Substances Act (CSA), potentially making it legal at the federal level. This change would allow states to regulate cannabis, much like alcohol or tobacco, without the risk of federal intervention. For businesses, this could resolve many of the banking and taxation issues that currently complicate operations due to cannabis's Schedule I status.

Descheduling cannabis doesn't automatically harmonize federal and state laws. It would require reevaluating and restructuring existing state regulations to ensure compliance with new federal standards. It would also necessitate the establishment of a new federal framework for regulating cannabis, which could involve agencies such as the Food and Drug Administration (FDA) for cannabis products or the Alcohol and Tobacco Tax and Trade Bureau (TTB) for taxation and trade.

"The complete descheduling of cannabis is paramount for public health and advancement. This action would foster extensive growth prospects for the industry and consumers while expediting global cannabis legalization efforts. Conversely, rescheduling might impose new entry hurdles, restricting small business entrepreneurship in cannabis commerce, traditionally the cornerstone of this industry's growth."
 — Michael Zaytsev, Director, Business of Cannabis, LIM College

The impact on the pharmaceutical industry could be significant as well. With descheduling, pharmaceutical companies might be able to develop and market cannabis-based medications under less stringent regulations. However, this also raises concerns about the potential for these companies to dominate the market, which could threaten the survival of existing cannabis operators.

The conversation about descheduling is complex and intersects with issues of criminal justice, public health, and commerce. While it may seem like a straightforward path to resolving federal and state conflicts over cannabis, it involves careful consideration of a multitude of factors and would mark a significant shift in the nation's approach to cannabis policy.

"Schedule III would be a very historic and very major victory because it would be, basically, the tide turning at the federal level for the first time in U.S. history for cannabis."
 — Shane Pennington, Esq., Porter Wright Morris & Arthur, LLP

LEGAL AND ECONOMIC CONSIDERATIONS FOR CURRENT CANNABIS BUSINESSES

The descheduling of cannabis would have significant ramifications for the legal and economic landscape of cannabis businesses in the United States. If cannabis were removed from the Controlled Substances Act's schedules, it would no longer be regulated as a controlled substance at the federal level, akin to the changes that occurred for hemp and CBD products with the 2018 Farm Bill.

However, descheduling cannabis does not automatically resolve the complexities of banking in the industry. Financial institutions may still be hesitant to engage with cannabis businesses due to other federal laws and regulations that could be perceived as barriers. Passage of legislation like the SAFE Banking Act could provide clearer protections and incentives for banks to service the cannabis industry confidently.

Furthermore, descheduling could lead to increased FDA oversight, which may impose new regulatory challenges and costs for cannabis businesses. If cannabis were to be treated as a prescription drug, all products would need to comply with FDA regulations, which could be particularly burdensome and potentially push out smaller operators in favor of larger pharmaceutical companies.

Descheduling would likely not make existing operations automatically legal under federal law for adult use; that would remain a state-regulated matter. Medical cannabis, on the other hand, would see changes, as state programs would need to align with federal regulations, requiring a reevaluation of how medical cannabis is recommended or prescribed. There are also international treaty considerations to take into account, as the United States' obligations under these treaties could impact how cannabis is reclassified or descheduled.

While descheduling could open up new opportunities and reduce some legal barriers for cannabis businesses, it also introduces a new set of regulatory considerations and potential shifts in the market dynamics, particularly with the possible entry of more prominent pharmaceutical players into the space.

Comparison Of Other Substances That Have Been Decontrolled

In the context of substances decontrolled or rescheduled in the United States, one notable example is hemp, as defined in the Agricultural Improvement Act of 2018 (also known as the Farm Bill). This act removed hemp, which is defined as the Cannabis sativa L. plant and any part of the plant with a delta-9-tetrahydrocannabinol (THC) concentration of not more than 0.3 percent on a dry weight basis, from the Controlled Substances Act's definition of marijuana. Consequently, "tetrahydrocannabinol in hemp" was also excluded from the list of controlled substances.[9]

Over the years, the CSA has been amended to reflect new scientific knowledge and public health considerations. Rescheduling cannabis has been a subject of petitions and debate for decades. Despite findings from various studies and recognition of medical uses in treatment, such as nausea and vomiting resulting from chemotherapy, cannabis remains a Schedule I substance. That said, the process for rescheduling or decontrolling substances is dynamic and subject to change as new research emerges and as societal and political attitudes evolve.[10]

Current Taxation Challenges Under IRC §280E For Cannabis Businesses

Cannabis businesses in the United States face unique taxation challenges under Internal Revenue Code (IRC) §280E. This tax code section restricts businesses dealing in controlled substances from deducting typical expenses. Since cannabis is classified as a Schedule I controlled substance at the federal level, cannabis businesses cannot deduct expenses such as employee salaries, utility costs, health insurance premiums, marketing and advertising costs, repairs and maintenance, facility rental fees, and payments to contractors from their taxable income.[11, 12]

However, cannabis businesses can deduct the Cost of Goods Sold (COGS), which includes direct costs associated with producing or acquiring cannabis products. These deductible expenses can consist of items such as seeds, soil, water, nutrients, and costs related to the cultivation and harvesting of the plant.[13]

Despite the legality of cannabis for medicinal or recreational use in many states, the federal tax burden remains heavy due to the inability to deduct most operating expenses. Cannabis businesses are essentially paying taxes on gross profit rather than net income, which can result in effective tax rates that are significantly higher than those of businesses in other industries – often reducing the interest of investors.

The IRS has made efforts to help cannabis business owners understand and comply with their tax responsibilities. They have issued guidance on income reporting, cash payment options for unbanked taxpayers, estimated federal income tax payments, and the importance of robust recordkeeping. The IRS has also established a dedicated webpage to provide resources and answers to frequently asked questions specifically for the cannabis industry.[14]

The ongoing discussion about potentially rescheduling cannabis from Schedule I to Schedule III could provide significant relief from IRC §280E in the future. If rescheduled, the tax implications for cannabis businesses would change, allowing them to take deductions like other legal businesses. This change could improve the financial viability of these businesses and attract more investment capital into the sector.

THE BUSINESS LANDSCAPE
POST-RESCHEDULING OR DESCHEDULING

The potential rescheduling or descheduling of cannabis could have wide-ranging implications for the business landscape. Here are some of the key changes that might occur:

Research Opportunities: Rescheduling would likely lead to expanded research opportunities. Currently, the stringent restrictions on cannabis research are tied to its Schedule I status. A change in classification would mean fewer regulatory hurdles for scientific studies, potentially leading to more innovation and product development in the industry.

Federal Enforcement and Regulation: Even with rescheduling, the DEA would still enforce the Controlled Substances Act (CSA), and the FDA would maintain oversight over drug safety. This could result in a situation where state-legal cannabis businesses continue to operate in a grey area, much like the current hemp-derived CBD market. There could be increased federal oversight but not necessarily a complete overhaul of the existing regulatory structures.

Impact on State-Legal Markets: Rescheduling or descheduling would not directly legalize the sale of cannabis for recreational use or automatically align state programs with federal law. However, it could lessen the conflict between federal and state laws, allowing states more autonomy to regulate cannabis within their borders.

Business Operations: Descheduling could allow cannabis businesses to operate more like traditional businesses, with better access to banking and capital markets. It could also enable interstate commerce, significantly altering the competitive landscape and potentially benefiting businesses in states with surplus production.

Big Pharma's Role: If cannabis is rescheduled, pharmaceutical companies could play a larger role in the industry, especially if cannabis-based medications require FDA approval. This could have both positive and negative effects: increased research and development of cannabis-based drugs, but also potential market challenges for smaller cannabis businesses not equipped to meet FDA requirements.

Interstate Commerce and Trade: Rescheduling or descheduling could pave the way for interstate commerce, allowing states with excess cannabis to export to other states, creating a national market. This would also necessitate a robust discussion among states with differing views on cannabis legalization and regulation.

Taxation: If cannabis is reclassified as a Schedule III drug, it would likely mean the end of the application of IRS Code Section 280E, which currently prevents cannabis businesses from taking certain tax deductions.

The movement toward rescheduling or descheduling cannabis is a complex issue with significant business implications. It could result in a more open and profitable industry, but it would also introduce new regulatory challenges and possibly reshape the competitive landscape.

CANNABIS RESEARCH AND HOW IT MAY BE AFFECTED

Rescheduling cannabis could significantly reduce the regulatory barriers currently impeding clinical studies and scientific inquiry. As it stands, Schedule I classification requires researchers to navigate complex bureaucratic processes, but rescheduling would likely streamline these processes, making it easier to obtain cannabis for research purposes. This would facilitate a broader range of scientific studies, potentially leading to new medical discoveries and a better understanding of cannabis's effects on health. It could also open the door to more extensive clinical trials, which are essential for developing cannabis-based medications.

The DEA and FDA play crucial roles in cannabis research. The DEA oversees the enforcement of controlled substance laws and regulations, which includes granting licenses for the legal handling of controlled substances, including those for research. The FDA is responsible for protecting public health by ensuring the safety, efficacy, and security of drugs, which encompasses the approval process for any new medications derived from cannabis. If cannabis is rescheduled, both agencies would likely be involved in creating a new regulatory framework for cannabis research, potentially easing restrictions and facilitating more extensive studies into its medical applications.

In a rescheduled cannabis market, big pharmaceutical companies could play a significant role. With their extensive resources and experience in conducting clinical trials and navigating the FDA approval process, they would be well-positioned to develop cannabis-based medications. This could lead to advancements in the medical use of cannabis and the introduction of new, rigorously tested pharmaceutical products. However, there is also a concern that the entry of big pharma could overshadow smaller cannabis operators and reshape the market's competitive landscape.

POTENTIAL IMPACT ON CONSUMERS

The rescheduling or descheduling of cannabis would most likely affect consumers in several ways:

Increased Access to Research and Information: With the potential for increased research opportunities, consumers would likely have access to more reliable information about the effects, benefits, and risks associated with cannabis consumption, leading to better-informed decisions about personal use.

Product Quality and Safety: A change in federal status could lead to more regulated and standardized industry practices, improving the quality and safety of cannabis products. Federal oversight could mean more consistent labeling, testing requirements, and safety standards across states.

Availability of New Products: With pharmaceutical companies potentially entering the market, consumers might see a more comprehensive array of cannabis-based medicinal products. This could be especially beneficial for those seeking alternative treatments for various conditions.

Cost Implications: Removing tax burdens on cannabis businesses could potentially reduce costs, which might be passed on to consumers in the form of lower prices. However, new federal taxes could also be introduced, which might offset these savings.

Legal and Medical Access: If cannabis is rescheduled, it would still be regulated and not necessarily available without a prescription or other authorization for Schedule III substances. This could change the dynamics of medical cannabis programs and potentially impact how consumers access cannabis for medical use.

Consumer Protection: Federal regulation would likely focus on consumer protection measures similar to those for alcohol and tobacco, potentially resulting in safer consumption environments and practices.

Impact of Big Pharma: The involvement of large pharmaceutical companies might lead to the development of more sophisticated and clinically tested cannabis-based medicines, which could benefit consumers needing specific treatments. However, if pharmaceutical companies dominate the space, this could also limit the variety of products available in the market.

Interstate Commerce: Descheduling could allow for interstate commerce, giving consumers access to a broader variety of products from different states, which might increase competition and innovation within the industry.

In essence, consumers might experience positive changes, such as improved product safety and more research-based information, and challenges, like potential cost increases or changes in how cannabis is prescribed and sold. The overall impact on consumers will depend on how the rescheduling or descheduling is implemented and regulated at federal and state levels.

Changes In The Prescription Requirements For Cannabis

The rescheduling of cannabis from Schedule I to a lower schedule, such as Schedule III, would alter the prescription requirements for cannabis. Currently, as a Schedule I substance, cannabis is not recognized by the federal government for medical use and cannot be prescribed. However, if cannabis were rescheduled:

Medical Recognition: Cannabis would gain recognition as having a potential medical use, which could allow physicians to prescribe it legally under federal law, similar to other Schedule III medications.

Regulatory Compliance: Cannabis prescriptions would need to comply with the regulatory requirements for Schedule

III drugs, which include restrictions on the amount prescribed and the number of refills without a new prescription from a healthcare provider.

Impact on State Medical Programs: States with medical cannabis programs need to consider how federal rescheduling aligns with their regulations and may need to adjust their programs accordingly. This could mean additional regulatory hurdles to ensure state programs meet federal standards.

Pharmacy Distribution: With rescheduling, cannabis could potentially be distributed through pharmacies, requiring a prescription from a licensed practitioner, which would be a significant change from the current dispensary-based model in many states.

Research and Development: Expanded research opportunities could lead to the development of new, standardized, and dosage-specific cannabis-based medications that could be prescribed, further integrating cannabis into the traditional healthcare system.

Insurance Coverage: There's also a possibility that if cannabis is recognized for medical use and can be prescribed, insurance plans may begin to cover it. However, given the legal and regulatory considerations involved, this would likely be a complex and gradual process.

DEA Licensing: Doctors would need a DEA license to prescribe cannabis, and they would be subject to federal guidelines and monitoring for prescribing controlled substances.

It's important to note that the transition to a prescription-based system for cannabis would require significant changes to existing state laws and medical cannabis programs. The exact impact would depend on how federal agencies like the FDA and DEA choose to regulate cannabis post-rescheduling.

Consumer Access To Cannabis For Medical Versus Recreational Use

Post rescheduling or descheduling, consumer access to cannabis for medical use might become more aligned with traditional pharmaceuticals, requiring prescriptions and pharmacy dispensing. For recreational use, it could lead to broader legal access similar to alcohol or tobacco, with fewer legal restrictions and the potential for purchases across state lines if interstate commerce is allowed. The exact details would depend on how the DEA and FDA regulate cannabis post-policy change.

> *"The placement of cannabis on Schedule I of the Controlled Substances Act was racially and politically driven. Merely rescheduling it does not adequately rectify the deep-seated harm inflicted on communities of color by decades of misguided policies. Rescheduling, as opposed to decontrolling, maintains significant barriers to entry for aspiring cannabis entrepreneurs. To truly address the damages caused by prohibition, decontrolling the plant would empower those most affected to start cannabis businesses and foster generational wealth."*
> — Benjamin Rattner, Esq., Cermele & Wood, LLP

Legal Protections And Rights For Cannabis Consumers

Post descheduling or rescheduling, cannabis consumers may see changes in their legal protections and rights. They might gain the ability to legally purchase and use cannabis without fear of federal prosecution if it is descheduled. If rescheduled, consumers using cannabis for medical purposes with a prescription may be protected under federal law, but specific protections would depend on the new scheduling and accompanying regulations. However, rights and protections will vary by state, as each state will have its laws and regulations governing the use, possession, and distribution of cannabis.

INTERNATIONAL TREATIES AND GLOBAL CONSIDERATIONS

Rescheduling or descheduling cannabis could impact international drug treaties to which the United States is a party. These treaties often have strict provisions regarding the control and regulation of certain substances. Any significant changes in the scheduling of cannabis within the U.S. could necessitate a reevaluation of treaty obligations and potentially require negotiations with other countries to align international standards with the new domestic policy. It's worth noting that other nations have changed their cannabis policies without facing international sanctions, suggesting there might be some flexibility within these treaties.

> *"Ultimately, rescheduling would be a step in the direction that the industry wants. An important step. ... I don't think the FDA's enforcement will change very much because it's not doing very much now. And the same is true of DEA. I think the federal government's posture will continue to be that companies that are compliant with state programs, both medical and recreational, are not going to be subjected to federal enforcement. That's been true for years. And I think that will continue to be true."* [15]
>
> — Howard Sklamberg, Former FDA Regulator

Summary

The discourse surrounding the potential rescheduling or descheduling of cannabis is pivotal in determining not only the legal status and research access for cannabis but also in shaping the framework that ensures its safe and equitable distribution within the healthcare and wellness sectors. The following questions seek to delve deeper into the nuances and balance of this important debate:

- How does the debate between rescheduling and descheduling cannabis impact industry control, particularly regarding favoring large corporations (i.e., big pharma) over smaller businesses?

- What are the implications of maintaining cannabis as a Schedule I drug under the Controlled Substances Act in terms of research, medical access, and legal inconsistencies?
- What are the potential advantages and challenges of descheduling and rescheduling cannabis regarding federalism, regulatory clarity, and social equity?
- What considerations should policymakers prioritize in comprehensive cannabis reform legislation to ensure social equity, restorative justice, and public health are at the forefront of the cannabis policy landscape?

Ultimately, both descheduling and rescheduling cannabis have their strengths and weaknesses, and the best approach will depend on various factors, including political and social considerations, regulatory and legal implications, and the goals of those advocating for legalization. Regardless of the approach, achieving cannabis legalization and regulation in a way that promotes social equity and restorative justice will be essential for addressing the harms of cannabis prohibition and creating a fair and just society.

CHAPTER 10

MEDICAL, MEDICINAL OR THERAPEUTIC?

DEFINING THE TERMS

The terms "medical," "medicinal," and "therapeutic" are often used interchangeably in the context of cannabis, but they have distinct meanings.

"Distinguishing 'medicinal, medical, or therapeutic cannabis' is vital for precision. 'Medicinal' conveys a holistic approach to well-being, 'medical' aligns with rigorous treatment, and 'therapeutic' emphasizes symptom management. Perception matters as these terms shape patient expectations."
— Nikki Lastreto, Co-Founder, Swami Select

Historically, cannabis was viewed primarily as a "recreational drug," and its potential therapeutic uses were largely ignored. However, in recent years, as more research has been conducted on the effects of cannabis on the human body, its therapeutic properties have become more widely recognized.[1]

The term "medical marijuana" refers specifically to the use of cannabis for medical purposes. It can include using cannabis to alleviate symptoms of a particular medical condition, such as chronic pain, nausea, or seizures. "Medical marijuana" is often recommended by a doctor and obtained through a licensed dispensary.

The term "medicinal cannabis" is sometimes used interchangeably with medical cannabis. Still, it can also refer to cannabis-based medicines approved by regulatory agencies such as the US Food and Drug Administration (FDA). Currently, only one cannabis-derived medication, Epidiolex®, has been approved by the FDA for treating seizures associated with two rare forms of epilepsy.[2]

The term "therapeutic cannabis" is broader than medical marijuana or medicinal cannabis and encompasses the use of cannabis for various therapeutic purposes, including treating specific medical conditions and promoting general wellness and relaxation.

"Medicine heals the body, but therapeutic practices nourish the soul. Together, they create a symphony of holistic wellness that transcends mere treatment, guiding us on a journey of self-care and self-discovery. Embrace the power of medicinal marvels and therapeutic treasures, for they hold the key to unlocking a healthier, happier existence."

— Nikki Lawley, LPN, Founder, Nikki and the Plant

UNDERSTANDING THE DISTINCTIONS

As the cannabis industry continues to evolve and expand, it will be necessary for regulators and consumers alike to understand the distinctions between these terms and their implications for the safety and efficacy of cannabis products.

As the public perception of cannabis has shifted in recent years, the terms "medical," "medicinal," and "therapeutic" have become increasingly common in discussions of the plant's potential benefits. However, there is often confusion about what these terms mean and how they are applied in the context of cannabis.

"Cannabis is a versatile plant that serves various purposes. It can be medical when scientifically prescribed by healthcare professionals to treat specific diseases. It can be medicinal, aiding individuals in alleviating symptoms even without a doctor's prescription. Lastly, it can be therapeutic, as it often provides a desired benefit to the user, whether real or perceived. Ultimately, cannabis is often whatever the consumer wants, needs, or desires."

— Ali Eftekhari, Community Outreach, Cannabis Talk 101

These terms have important implications for how products are marketed and regulated. For example, products sold as "medical" may be subject to more stringent testing and labeling requirements, while products marketed as "therapeutic" may be subject to different marketing regulations.[3]

As the industry continues to evolve, it will be necessary for policymakers and stakeholders to carefully consider how these terms are defined and regulated to ensure that patients and consumers can access safe, effective, and appropriately labeled cannabis products.

MEDICAL MARIJUANA'S CONUNDRUM

The term "medical marijuana" has become a controversial topic in recent years, with many people arguing that it is hypocritical because doctors don't prescribe it, pharmacists don't dispense it, and perhaps most importantly, insurance companies don't cover it. It has led to a lot of confusion and debate surrounding the use of cannabis for medical purposes.

The main reason that doctors don't prescribe cannabis is because it is still considered a Schedule I drug by the federal government. It is classified as having "no accepted medical use and a high potential for abuse." This classification makes it difficult, if not impossible, for doctors to prescribe it, as they risk losing their medical license if they do so.[4]

Furthermore, pharmacists don't (typically) dispense cannabis because it is not legal at the federal level. While some states have legalized cannabis for medical use, it is still illegal under federal law. It creates a legal gray area that makes it difficult for pharmacists to dispense cannabis without risking legal repercussions.

Insurance companies don't (typically) cover "medical marijuana" because it is not FDA-approved. It means that it has not undergone the rigorous testing and clinical trials that other drugs have gone through to prove their safety and effectiveness. As a result, insurance companies don't cover the costs of medical marijuana, even in states where it is legal.

Despite these challenges, many believe cannabis has significant medical benefits, such as pain relief, reducing nausea, and improving appetite. As a result, some states have passed laws allowing the use of medical marijuana, and there is growing public support for its legalization at the federal level. This discrepancy leads to confusion and frustration for patients seeking relief from their medical conditions.

Without the medical establishment's support, patients are left to navigate the world of medical marijuana on their own. They must find a way to obtain it legally and safely and determine the appropriate dosage and delivery method for their individual needs.

Another issue with the term "medical marijuana" is that it suggests that the plant has been specifically bred and cultivated for medical purposes when, in fact, it is often the same cannabis plant that is used for adult use purposes. It further complicates the discussion around its medical use, as it can be challenging to determine the appropriate cultivars and concentrations for specific conditions.

It's also worth noting that the legality of medical marijuana varies widely by state and country, making it difficult for patients to access it in certain areas. Sometimes, patients may have to travel long distances or even move to another state to access medical marijuana legally.

MEDICAL MARIJUANA AND IT'S ROLE IN HEALTHCARE

While the term medical marijuana may be well-intentioned, the reality is that it is a complicated issue with many layers of complexity. Without the medical establishment's support, patients are left to navigate this world independently, which can lead to confusion. Until the medical community fully embraces medical marijuana, it will continue to be controversial and divisive.

The lack of support from doctors, pharmacists, and insurance companies also raises questions about the safety and efficacy of medical marijuana. While many advocates tout its benefits, the fact is that there is still a significant amount of research that needs to be done to fully understand how it can best be used to treat various medical conditions.[5]

Without medical professionals' involvement and insurance companies' coverage, patients may be left to rely on anecdotal evidence and self-experimentation to determine the best treatment for their needs. It can be dangerous, as cannabis can have side effects and may interact with other medications.

Another issue is the stigma associated with cannabis consumption, particularly when it comes to medical marijuana. Despite its legal status in many states, much misinformation and negative stereotypes exist surrounding cannabis use – making it difficult for patients to access medical marijuana as well as discouraging them from discussing it openly with their doctors.

> *"Cannabis can be an effective form of medical treatment when recommended by a prescribing physician who understands how to apply its medicinal value to alleviate symptoms that often accompany various ailments. However, the true beauty of the plant is the unique therapeutic potential that cannabinoids contribute to holistic care and overall patient wellbeing."*
> — Mary Szomjassy Brown, Founder, SMJ Consulting

While many patients may benefit from medical marijuana, it is not necessarily appropriate or effective for everyone. Patients with certain medical conditions or who are taking certain medications may be at greater risk for adverse side effects, and it can be challenging to determine who is a good candidate for medical marijuana and who is not.[6]

The term "medical marijuana" is a convoluted issue that raises essential questions about the role of cannabis in modern medicine. While growing evidence suggests that cannabis can be an effective treatment for various medical conditions, more research and standardization are needed to ensure that patients can access safe, effective, and affordable treatments. Until these issues are addressed, the debate surrounding medical marijuana will likely continue.

Summary

The evolving and complex nature of cannabis emphasizes the distinctions between "medical," "medicinal," and "therapeutic" cannabis. It highlights how these terms have different meanings and implications. Such distinctions have crucial implications for how cannabis products are marketed, regulated, and accessed by patients and consumers. While the public perception of cannabis is shifting, there is a need for more precise definitions and regulations to ensure that cannabis products are safe, effective, and appropriately labeled. Achieving this requires collaboration between policymakers, stakeholders, and the medical community.

The questions below explore the nuances between these terms that are crucial in shaping not just perceptions but also the accessibility and safety of cannabis-related products in our evolving landscape of healthcare and wellness:

- What role do regulatory agencies like the FDA play in approving cannabis-based medicines, and what implications does this have on access and perception?
- Why has the term "medical marijuana" become controversial, and how do federal classifications affect its prescription, dispensing, and insurance coverage?
- What are the critical concerns regarding the safety, efficacy, and standardization of medical marijuana, especially in comparison to traditional pharmaceuticals?
- How might precise definitions and better regulations around "medical," "medicinal," and "therapeutic" cannabis impact product accessibility, safety, and public perception in the evolving cannabis industry?

Ultimately, the cannabis industry is at a crossroads, with ongoing debates and complexities surrounding the use of cannabis for various purposes. The lack of standardized regulation and the evolving nature of cannabis as a therapeutic substance remain areas of concern. As research and understanding of cannabis's effects expand, it will be crucial to address these complexities to provide safe and effective cannabis products for those who seek its potential benefits.

CHAPTER 11

ADULT USE vs.
RECREATIONAL USE

APPLYING TERMS TO CANNABIS

The debate over cannabis terminology is not simply a matter of linguistic preference but of legal precision, political progressiveness, societal perception, and psychological impact. In the ongoing discourse on cannabis legalization, the terminology we adopt carries significant weight in shaping perceptions, laws, and societal norms. The preference for "adult use" over "recreational" when referring to cannabis is more than a trivial choice of words; it is a deliberate step towards fostering a responsible, respectful, and legally precise approach to cannabis consumption.

> *"As our understanding of cannabis consumption grows, we recognize its wide-ranging appeal, encompassing relaxation, creativity, social interaction, and more. Given these diverse benefits, the term "Adult Use" emerges as a more fitting and inclusive descriptor. This phrase resonates with a broader consumer base seeking to distance cannabis from mere recreation and emphasize its availability to responsible adults for various purposes."*
> — Michael Rosenfeld, Senior Client Partner, Weedmaps

13 REASONS WHY "ADULT USE" IS MORE APPROPRIATE THAN "RECREATIONAL"

Below are thirteen compelling reasons why the term "adult use" is a more appropriate descriptor than "recreational," emphasizing the term's impact on legal accuracy, political discourse, regulatory effectiveness, societal attitudes, and individual psychology, to name a few:

Legal Implications

The legal implications of adopting the term "adult use" for cannabis are profound, providing a clear distinction that aligns with established legal frameworks for age-restricted substances. This terminology unequivocally states that cannabis products are intended for and legally accessible only to individuals who have reached the age of majority. This clarity is essential for enforcing age restrictions and ensuring that only those legally recognized as adults can purchase and consume cannabis. It serves as a legal safeguard, ensuring that cannabis retailers and consumers are fully aware of who is permitted to engage in cannabis transactions. On the other hand, the term "recreational" lacks this legal precision, potentially leading to ambiguity in enforcement and compliance. It fails to convey the importance of age restrictions, which could result in misunderstandings among consumers and retailers about who is lawfully allowed to use cannabis.

Furthermore, the precise legal boundaries set by the term "adult use" assist in the responsible regulation of cannabis. They provide a foundation for the development of policies that govern the marketing, sale, and consumption of cannabis, mirroring the legal structures in place for alcohol and tobacco. By clearly defining cannabis as an adult-only substance, legislators and regulators can more effectively craft laws that address the nuances of cannabis sales, including advertising standards, labeling requirements, and penalties for selling to minors. This legal clarity not only aids businesses in maintaining compliance but also helps to prevent underage access to cannabis, a key concern for public health and safety.

Moreover, the term "adult use" has significant legal ramifications for the broader societal understanding of cannabis. It supports the creation of educational campaigns and public health initiatives that target adults, informing them of their rights and responsibilities under cannabis legislation. By framing cannabis as an "adult use" substance, the legal system acknowledges the substance's legitimate place in adult society while also reinforcing the notion that with adult rights come adult responsibilities. This distinction is crucial for informing the public discourse around cannabis and ensuring that the move toward legalization does not inadvertently encourage underage use. The term sets a responsible tone for the ongoing legal and societal integration of cannabis, emphasizing that its use is a serious adult choice, accompanied by legal obligations and societal expectations.

Regulatory Framework

"Adult use" cannabis reinforces the need for a robust regulatory framework similar to that of alcohol and tobacco. This framework would include licensing requirements, quality control measures, and marketing restrictions, all critical for public safety and consumer protection. By adopting "adult use" terminology, regulators signal the importance of these controls and underscore the substance's legitimacy as a product for adult consumption. This facilitates the creation of comprehensive regulations that address the unique aspects of cannabis production and sales, from seed to sale tracking, to prevent diversion to the illicit market and ensure that products meet health and safety standards.

> *"The choice between 'recreational' and 'adult use' terminology goes beyond semantics; it reflects a shift towards a more inclusive mindset to understanding cannabis consumption. While 'recreational' may carry limiting connotations of frivolity or pleasure-seeking, 'adult use' attempts to strip those assumptions and pragmatically offer a less constraining term. As a result, we are embracing a perspective that acknowledges the broad spectrum of benefits - and motivations- this plant offers to individuals."*
>
> — Mina Johnson, Co-Founder, Highopes

In the context of "adult use," regulations can be developed to address public health concerns, such as driving under the influence or consumption in public spaces, with a clear understanding that these activities are restricted to adults. This helps to establish a social contract of sorts, where adult consumers are expected to engage with cannabis within the boundaries of the law and, in turn, are provided with legal protections for their consumption. Moreover, the term "adult use" aids in setting the tone for regulatory discussions, encouraging a mature, evidence-based approach to policy-making that considers the full spectrum of adult consumer behavior.

Furthermore, regulatory bodies can leverage "adult use" terminology to improve consumer education. Regulations can mandate that educational materials and product labeling indicate that cannabis is for adult use only, helping to prevent underage access. This also opens the door for regulators to require that information about safe consumption practices and potential risks be made available to consumers, fostering an informed public that can make responsible choices about their cannabis use.

Political Context

The term "adult use" transcends political divisions, allowing for a unified approach to cannabis policy. It offers a pragmatic perspective that focuses on the practicalities of regulation and public health rather than getting embroiled in ideological debates. By framing cannabis consumption as an adult right akin to alcohol consumption, the term depoliticizes the issue, making it more palatable across the political spectrum. This neutrality can lead to more productive legislative sessions, focusing on creating sound policies rather than debating morality or personal beliefs about cannabis use. It also allows for more objective consideration of the economic benefits of the cannabis industry, including job creation and tax revenue, without being overshadowed by politically charged rhetoric.

Adopting "adult use" as the standard term can also help bridge the gap between political ideologies, fostering dialogue and cooperation. It shifts the conversation from permission or prohibition to regulation and rights, concepts that can resonate across political lines. By framing cannabis use as a matter of adult choice, policymakers can redirect their efforts to ensure that the legal framework reflects responsible use and adequately addresses public welfare concerns, such as preventing impaired driving and underage access.

Moreover, "adult use" can help to mitigate the impact of political turnover on cannabis policies. When the terminology associated with cannabis is less politically charged, it is less susceptible to the whims of changing political tides and more likely to result in stable, long-term regulatory strategies. Such stability is crucial for businesses operating in the cannabis sector, for consumers who rely on consistent policies for access, and for communities that benefit from the economic stability that a well-regulated cannabis industry can provide.

Psychological Impact

The psychological ramifications of the term "adult use" cannabis are significant. It inherently suggests a level of autonomy and decision-making associated with adulthood. This framing can influence users to approach their cannabis consumption with a greater sense of responsibility and mindfulness. It implicitly reminds adults that their consumption choices should be made with consideration for the potential effects on their lives, health, and responsibilities. This can lead to more responsible usage patterns and decreased behaviors that could harm the individual or their community.

Conversely, "recreational" use implies a lack of seriousness that might affect the way individuals approach consumption, potentially leading to riskier behavior or misuse. The term "adult use" counteracts this by emphasizing the gravity of the decision to use cannabis and the expectation that such a decision is made thoughtfully. This subtle psychological cue can have a broad impact on how cannabis is integrated into adult life, encouraging a culture where cannabis is respected as a substance that requires careful, informed consideration.

The term "adult use" also plays a role in shaping the emerging narrative around cannabis. It supports the idea that cannabis use can be a part of a balanced, responsible lifestyle for many adults. As society's understanding of mental health continues to grow, the term "adult use" aligns with the conversation about self-care and wellness, providing a framework for adults to consider how their cannabis use fits into their overall health and well-being goals. This is a positive step toward a future where cannabis is understood in a more holistic and health-conscious context.

Societal Perception

The transition to "adult use" cannabis is a critical step in destigmatizing cannabis within society. It signals a departure from the days of prohibition and the negative stereotypes that have long been associated with cannabis users. By presenting cannabis as a choice for adults, akin to choosing a fine wine or craft beer, the term fosters a more accepting and respectful attitude towards cannabis and those who choose to use it. This is a necessary evolution in a society that is increasingly recognizing the potential benefits of cannabis, from wellness applications to its use as a social lubricant.

The societal impact of adopting "adult use" cannabis extends to various sectors, including the arts, medicine, and business, where the term can encourage a more nuanced understanding of cannabis's role. For instance, in the arts, "adult use" can inspire a more sophisticated portrayal of cannabis, moving away from cliched representations to more thoughtful and realistic depictions. In medicine, it can open the door to discussions about the therapeutic potential of cannabis without the baggage of the term "recreational," which might not be taken as seriously.

Furthermore, "adult use" can lead to a more inclusive society where the choice to use cannabis is normalized and respected. It can help to dismantle the social barriers that have prevented open conversations about cannabis use and its place in the lives of responsible adults. As society continues to evolve, adopting "adult use" as the standard term can aid in fostering an environment where individuals feel comfortable discussing their use of cannabis, whether for relaxation, creative inspiration, or medical relief, without fear of judgment.

Public Health Messaging

Public health messaging is a critical component in shaping public attitudes and behaviors toward cannabis use. The term "adult use" significantly enhances public health campaigns by framing cannabis use within the context of informed decision-making and mature consumption. This terminology promotes a dialogue rooted in education and awareness rather than prohibition and fear. It allows public health officials to develop messaging that respects the intelligence and autonomy of the adult population, providing them with accurate information about safe consumption practices, potential health effects, and legal guidelines. This approach can lead to more effective public health strategies that encourage adults to engage with cannabis in a way that minimizes risk to themselves and others.

The shift to "adult use" in public health discourse also underlines the importance of targeting the right audience with appropriate messages. It aligns with the broader goals of public health to protect communities by emphasizing the significance of responsible use among adults. By doing so, it avoids inadvertently targeting or appealing to underage individuals, which is a risk associated with the less precise term "recreational." Public health messaging that identifies cannabis as an adult-regulated substance can better focus its efforts on educating adults about how to integrate cannabis use into their lives safely and legally, thereby enhancing overall community health and safety.

Furthermore, "adult use" terminology can pave the way for more nuanced public health initiatives that address the varied reasons adults may choose to use cannabis. Instead of one-size-fits-all messaging, public health campaigns can acknowledge and address the spectrum of adult use, from those who consume cannabis for relaxation to those who utilize it for therapeutic benefits. This level of specificity not only increases the relevance and impact of public health messaging but also fosters a more comprehensive understanding of cannabis as a multifaceted substance with a place in the fabric of adult society. As a result, the public can make more informed choices about cannabis, leading to a healthier relationship with its use.

Economic Considerations

The economic implications of adopting "adult use" cannabis terminology are multifaceted. It can shape consumer confidence in the cannabis market, portraying it as a mature industry. This perception can attract serious investors and professionals, contributing to market growth and stability. The term "recreational" may inadvertently evoke a less professional image, potentially deterring investment and hindering the development of sophisticated market infrastructure. Moreover, "adult use" suggests a regulated industry, which can lead to increased government revenue from taxes and fees, benefiting public services and the overall economy.

"Adult use" also positions the cannabis industry as comparable to other adult-oriented markets, such as alcohol or entertainment. This allows businesses within the cannabis industry to adopt marketing and operational strategies that appeal to a broad adult demographic, potentially expanding their customer base and increasing sales. It also provides a clear demographic target for businesses, enabling them to tailor their products and services to meet adult consumers' specific needs and preferences.

Additionally, the economic benefits of "adult use" cannabis extend to job creation. As the industry is taken more seriously and grows, it will naturally require a larger workforce. This creates opportunities for employment across various sectors, including agriculture, retail, compliance, and beyond. The professionalism implied by "adult use" can make these jobs more appealing and respected, attracting a skilled workforce and promoting higher standards within the industry.

> *"As adults embrace its myriad uses, from therapeutic and relaxation to creativity and focus, the term 'adult use' resonates better with the newfound understanding and respect for cannabis."*
> — Adriana Hemans, Marketing Director, Green Meadows

Cultural Sensitivity

Using "adult use" reflects a sensitivity to cultural diversity in cannabis consumption. It acknowledges that cannabis plays different roles in various cultures and respects the traditions and values associated with its use. This cultural sensitivity is crucial in a globalized world, where respect for diverse perspectives on cannabis can facilitate better international relations and cooperation on cannabis policy. "Recreational" use does not convey the same level of cultural respect, potentially alienating groups who view cannabis through a different cultural lens.

"Adult use" also allows for a more inclusive approach to cannabis education and public health campaigns. It encourages the creation of materials that respect cultural differences, which is vital for effectively reaching and educating diverse populations. By understanding and acknowledging the cultural context in which individuals engage with cannabis, educators, and policymakers can develop strategies that resonate with and respect the values and beliefs of different communities.

Moreover, "adult use" can encourage cultural exchange and understanding. It opens up dialogues about how cannabis is integrated into adult life across different cultures, promoting a broader understanding and appreciation of its role in society. This can lead to a more harmonious coexistence and a richer societal tapestry where the cultural nuances of cannabis use are recognized and celebrated.

Consumer Behavior

The term "adult use" can positively influence consumer behavior by emphasizing the responsible use of cannabis. It encourages adults to make informed decisions about their consumption, considering factors such as dosage, setting, and the potential impact on daily life. This responsible approach can lead to safer consumption practices and reduce the likelihood of misuse or abuse. In contrast, "recreational" use may not evoke the same level of conscientious behavior, potentially leading to adverse outcomes for the individual and society.

The terminology also affects how consumers perceive the risk associated with cannabis use. "Adult use" carries a connotation of a substance that requires careful consideration, similar to prescription medications or alcohol. This can lead to a more cautious approach to consumption, with individuals seeking to educate themselves about the effects of cannabis and the best practices for its use.

Lastly, "adult use" can foster a culture of moderation. By framing cannabis as a substance for adults, it becomes part of a spectrum of lifestyle choices that require moderation and self-control. This can encourage consumers to view their cannabis use as one aspect of a balanced life rather than an unrestricted activity devoid of consequences. This perspective can contribute to healthier patterns of use and a more sustainable relationship with cannabis.

Global Consistency

The term "adult use" in the context of cannabis aligns with a growing global movement towards regulating cannabis through a public health lens. As countries around the world grapple with the best ways to handle cannabis legalization, having consistent terminology helps in creating a shared understanding and set of expectations. This consistency aids in comparing research data, sharing best practices, and formulating international agreements on the control and regulation of cannabis.

Additionally, "adult use" sets a precedent for new markets as they emerge, providing a blueprint for how cannabis can be integrated into society responsibly. It helps in framing international discussions about cannabis, moving away from the punitive legacy of prohibition towards a focus on harm reduction and adult choice. This can foster international cooperation on issues such as drug trafficking, research collaboration, and public health initiatives.

Furthermore, "adult use" provides a neutral platform for dialogue with countries where cannabis has been traditionally used for centuries. It allows for an exchange that respects cultural histories and practices rather than imposing a Westernized concept of "recreational" use that may not align with local customs and understandings of cannabis.

Educational Strategies

The shift from "recreational" to "adult use" cannabis underscores the need for comprehensive education strategies that treat cannabis as a complex substance that requires understanding and respect. Education is critical to ensuring that adults are equipped with the knowledge to make informed decisions about cannabis. This includes understanding the legal landscape, recognizing the risks and benefits, and learning about safe consumption practices.

Educational materials that use the term "adult use" can more effectively target their audience, framing information in a way that is relevant and appropriate for adults. This framing respects the audience's ability to make mature decisions and can lead to a deeper engagement with the content. It also sets a tone conducive to learning rather than one that might be dismissed as irrelevant to those who do not identify with "recreational" activities.

Moreover, "adult use" reinforces the importance of education across all points of the cannabis industry, from the point of sale to consumption. Dispensaries can play a crucial role in educating consumers, with "adult use" signaling the seriousness with which the industry approaches this responsibility. This can help to ensure that as the cannabis market continues to grow, it does so with an informed consumer base that is aware of both their rights and their responsibilities.

Marketing and Branding

The way cannabis is marketed and branded has significant implications for public perception. "Adult use" cannabis allows for sophisticated branding strategies that appeal to a mature audience, similar to those used in the wine or craft beer industries. This type of branding can help to elevate the product's image, distancing it from any lingering negative connotations associated with "recreational" use. By focusing on quality, experience, and the adult consumer, businesses can position themselves as premium brands within the marketplace.

The term "adult use" also allows for targeted marketing efforts that respect legal restrictions and avoid appealing to underage individuals. This careful approach is essential to maintain public trust and avoid potential legal pitfalls. It can also foster a more responsible industry that prioritizes safety and education in its marketing practices. In contrast, "recreational" use might imply a more laissez-faire attitude toward marketing, which could attract scrutiny and regulatory backlash.

Lastly, "adult use" cannabis branding can help normalize the substance in mainstream culture. By using mature, responsible imagery and messaging, the industry can help shift public opinion and make cannabis use more socially acceptable. This can lead to broader acceptance and integration of cannabis businesses into local economies, fostering community support and opening up new opportunities for industry growth.

Ethical Considerations

The adoption of "adult use" terminology reflects an ethical approach to cannabis legalization, emphasizing respect for individual autonomy while recognizing societal obligations. It acknowledges that while adults have the right to choose cannabis for personal use, this choice comes with a responsibility to do so in a manner that does not harm others. This ethical stance is vital in shaping policies that balance personal freedom with public health and safety.

"Adult use" also implies an ethical responsibility on the part of the industry to ensure that products are safe, accurately labeled, and sold in a way that promotes informed decision-making. This contrasts "recreational" use, which may not convey the same ethical commitment to consumer welfare. By promoting "adult use," the cannabis industry can demonstrate its commitment to upholding high standards and contributing positively to society.

Furthermore, the term encourages ethical consumption among users. It serves as a reminder that, as with any substance, cannabis should be used thoughtfully and with consideration for its effects on oneself and others. "Adult use" therefore supports a culture of ethical use, where cannabis is viewed not just as a product for personal enjoyment but as one that requires a conscious, responsible approach to consumption.

Summary

In conclusion, it is clear that the term "adult use" cannabis is vastly superior to "recreational" cannabis. It provides legal clarity, political neutrality, definitional accuracy, societal respect, and a psychological framing that promotes responsible use. As we continue to navigate the complexities of cannabis legislation and integration into society, we must adopt terminology that reflects a mature, responsible approach.

The following questions aim to uncover the connotations and implications each term holds, their impact on consumer attitudes, and whether they serve an appropriate purpose within the broader context of cannabis legalization, societal acceptance, and legal clarity:

- How does the term "adult use" cannabis provide more explicit legal guidance and better align with age restriction laws compared to the term "recreational" cannabis?
- In what ways does using "adult use" instead of "recreational" help in reducing the stigma associated with cannabis consumption and promote a more mature market perception?
- Why is the term "adult use" more effective than "recreational" in fostering a politically neutral environment for cannabis legislation and international policy alignment?
- How does the shift from "recreational" to "adult use" cannabis support more responsible consumer behavior and inclusive societal attitudes towards diverse reasons for cannabis consumption?

Ultimately, the shift towards "adult use" terminology in the context of cannabis not only signifies a legal and societal maturation in our approach to this subject but also ensures clarity, respect, and responsibility in the public discourse. By embracing this term, we acknowledge the plant's place within the adult community, underscore the importance of informed, responsible consumption, and foster an environment where the economic, social, and health-related aspects of cannabis can be managed with the sophistication and seriousness they deserve. The "adult use" designation is a pivotal step in the evolution of cannabis policy, one that moves us closer to a framework that respects individual choice while upholding community standards and public health.

CHAPTER 12

STRAIN, CULTIVAR OR VARIETY?

BOTANICAL ACCURACY AND
HISTORICAL PRECEDENCE

The terminology debate surrounding cannabis "strains," "cultivars," and "varieties" holds significant importance within the cannabis industry and community. This debate stems from the need for accurate and consistent language to classify the diverse types of cannabis. In this chapter, I aim to explore the controversy surrounding the terminology and propose solutions to address the inconsistencies and discrepancies in cannabis taxonomy.

> *"Within the realm of science, the term 'strain' finds its application solely with microscopic entities such as bacteria and viruses, for example. Employing this term for cannabis is a linguistic misalignment. Some experts even advocate for the use of 'chemovar' to more accurately describe cultivated cannabis."*
> — Swami Chaitanya, Co-Founder, Swami Select

This debate is significant because it impacts the understanding, communication, and classification of cannabis varieties. The terminology used to describe cannabis is crucial in shaping perceptions, research and education, consumer experiences, and regulatory frameworks. More accurate and consistent language can lead to clarity and advancements in scientific understanding and societal acceptance.

By examining the terminology debate and proposing standardized usage, I seek to contribute to developing a more precise, accurate, and widely accepted language surrounding cannabis classification.

Through this exploration, I strived to enhance my understanding of the importance of consistent and scientifically grounded terminology. By addressing the challenges posed by the existing discrepancies, I hope to foster a more cohesive and informed cannabis community. Ultimately, the goal is to promote effective communication, scientific progress, consumer education, and regulatory clarity by proposing solutions to the cannabis "strains," "cultivars," and "varieties" terminology debate.[1]

To understand the controversy surrounding the term "strain" in cannabis taxonomy, it is essential to explore its traditional usage and how it has been misapplied within the context of cannabis. Historically, "strain" has primarily been used to describe variations of microorganisms and viruses rather than plant varieties.

In microbiology and virology, "strain" refers to genetic variations within a specific microorganism or virus. These genetic variations may result in differences in characteristics such as virulence, antigenicity, or drug resistance. It is a precise term used to differentiate between closely related subtypes of a microorganism or virus.

However, the misapplication of the term "strain" to cannabis has led to confusion and inconsistencies in its classification. Unlike microorganisms and viruses, cannabis is a plant with distinct botanical characteristics. The concept of "strain," as traditionally understood in microbiology, does not align with the genetic diversity of the cannabis plant.

The misapplication of the term "strain" in cannabis can be attributed to the historical association between cannabis and microbiology in specific contexts. In the early days of cannabis research, scientists examining the plant's properties often drew upon microbiological terminology to describe the different varieties they encountered. Adopting the term "strain" from microbiology created a linguistic connection that has persisted over time.

However, it is essential to recognize that cannabis is a plant species with unique genetic variations and characteristics. Applying a term rooted in microbiology to a plant can lead to a lack of precision and confusion in its classification. As the understanding of cannabis has evolved, so should the terminology used to describe its genetic diversity.

By recognizing the historical precedents and the misapplication of the term "strain" in the context of cannabis, we can move towards more accurate and scientifically sound language. It involves exploring alternative terminology, such as "cultivar" or "variety," that aligns with the botanical nature of cannabis and provides a more precise classification of its genetic variations.

"As a cultivator, I lean towards the terms variety and cultivar, aligning with scientific and horticultural terminology. However, the widespread use of the term 'strain' has prevailed in legacy and regulated markets. Cannabis culture, shaped clandestinely under prohibition, lacks standardized nomenclature due to limited discourse among experts and influencers. The positive evolution of cannabis culture won't happen through excluding words, but rather by drawing people further into the culture inclusively through a deeper understanding and appreciation for the plant."
    — Aaron Salles, VP, Sales & Marketing, MOCA Humboldt

The American Seed Trade Association (ASTA) uses specific terminology to define plant varieties eligible for seed certification and other formal agricultural and horticultural uses. According to ASTA, for a plant variety to be recognized in a more formal sense, it must be "Distinct, Uniform, and Stable"[2] (often abbreviated as DUS):

Distinct: The variety must be distinguishable from any other variety whose existence is a matter of common knowledge at the time of the distinction. This can be determined by expressing the characteristics resulting from a given genotype or combination of genotypes.

Uniform: The variety must be sufficiently uniform in the relevant characteristics, subject to the variation that may be expected from the particular features of its propagation.

Stable: The variety must remain unchanged in its essential characteristics after repeated cycles of propagation or, in the case of a particular cycle of propagation, at the end of each such cycle.

When ASTA refers to "strains" as not being "Distinct, Uniform, & Stable," it suggests that the term "strain," as commonly used in the cannabis industry and other informal settings, does not necessarily meet these criteria. In the context of the cannabis industry, "strain" might refer to a variety of plants that are genetically similar but not identical. These plants might not exhibit the uniformity and stability required by ASTA's standards. This could be due to the methods of propagation, selective breeding, and genetic diversity within the group of plants being referred to as a "strain."

For instance, a "strain" in the cannabis industry might be a group of plants that are similar in terms of the cannabinoids and terpenes they produce. Still, genetic variation among the plants can lead to differences in how these chemicals are expressed. Such variation might make the "strain" not uniform enough to meet ASTA's standards. Additionally, if these characteristics are not maintained over successive generations or cycles of propagation, they would not be considered stable either.

For more formal and regulated sectors of agriculture, where seed certification and plant variety protection are crucial, meeting the DUS criteria is essential. These standards are in place to ensure that when farmers or growers purchase seeds or plant material, they can expect a certain level of consistency and reliability in the product they are growing.

In the context of cannabis, the terms "strain," "cultivar," and "variety" are often used interchangeably, but there are subtle differences in their botanical meanings.

A "strain" refers to a group of plants descended from a common ancestor and have undergone asexual reproduction, typically through clonal propagation. This reproduction method ensures that the offspring are nearly identical genetically to the mother plant, except for random mutations. In the cannabis industry, "strain" is a commonly used term, but it's not the most botanically accurate term to describe plant variations.[3]

A "cultivar," which is short for "cultivated variety," is a group of plants produced in cultivation by selective breeding. These plants share specific characteristics that are consistently inherited within the group, and these characteristics define them. This term is botanically accurate and refers to plants selectively bred for particular traits.

"Variety" in botanical terms often describes a naturally occurring subset within a species. Still, in the context of cannabis, it is used synonymously with "cultivar" to describe a group of plants created sexually through seed propagation. The plants within a variety have characteristics selected for breeding and passed down through the seeds.[4] The following table sums up the topic succinctly:

	STRAIN	VARIETY	CULTIVAR
Definition and Usage	Commonly used in the cannabis community, but scientifically incorrect in the context of plants. Refers to a specific genetic variant or subtype within a bacterial species.	A more accurate and appropriate term to describe different Cannabis variants. It is defined as a species' adaptation due to climate shifts, soil changes, diseases, etc.	A more accurate and appropriate term to describe different Cannabis variants. It is defined as a species' adaptation due to climate shifts, soil changes, diseases, etc.
Characteristics	Primarily used in microbiology for bacteria, viruses, etc. Unique genetic characteristics may be present.	Result of adaptation to habitat changes due to accidental factors. Reflects the diversity within the Cannabis species.	Created through deliberate breeding or agricultural techniques. Human intervention involved in improving and uniform traits.

It's worth noting that some sources[5] suggest that none of these terms are technically correct in the strictest botanical sense when applied to cannabis. Instead, they suggest that "chemovar," referring to chemical variety, might be more appropriate since cannabis plants are often categorized by their cannabinoid and terpene profiles rather than strict botanical classifications.

In practical terms, when it comes to cannabis, whether one uses "strain," "cultivar," or "variety," the intent is generally to describe a specific kind of cannabis plant with particular characteristics that consumers can expect. However, for those more scientifically inclined or involved in the breeding and classification of cannabis, "cultivar" might be the preferred term for its botanical accuracy.

CLARITY AND PRECISION

Clear and precise terminology is essential in any scientific field, and cannabis taxonomy is no exception. Consistency in language helps researchers, growers, and consumers effectively communicate and share knowledge about specific cannabis varieties. With a plant as diverse as cannabis, accurate and standardized terminology is crucial for classifying and identifying different plant types.

Cultivar and chemovar are related terms used in botany and horticulture, particularly in the context of plants like cannabis. However, they refer to different aspects of plant variation:

Cultivar (Cultivated Variety):

Definition: A cultivar is a plant variety deliberately selected and cultivated by humans through selective breeding or genetic manipulation. It typically has distinct characteristics that differentiate it from other varieties of the same species.

Use: Cultivars describe plant varieties through their physical attributes, such as color, size, shape, or growth habit. They are often named and propagated to maintain these specific traits. In the context of cannabis, cultivar names indicate particular varieties with unique characteristics. The term "cultivar" is frequently used interchangeably with "phenotype," elaborated upon in the next chapter, "Indica vs. Sativa."

Chemovar (Chemical Variety):

Definition: A chemovar, on the other hand, focuses on the chemical composition of a plant, particularly in terms of its secondary metabolites. It refers to variations in the chemical profile of plants within a species.

Use: In cannabis, for example, different strains or cultivars can have distinct chemovars, producing varying levels of cannabinoids (like THC and CBD) and terpenes. Chemovar distinctions are critical in the cannabis industry as they impact the plant's effects on consumers and its potential medical applications.

While cultivar emphasizes a plant's physical characteristics and attributes, chemovar focuses on the chemical composition, especially regarding compounds relevant to its usage or effects. Both terms are valuable in describing and categorizing plants, particularly in horticulture and botany.

ADOPTING "CULTIVAR" FOR SCIENTIFIC UNDERSTANDING & STANDARDIZATION

Adopting "cultivar" as the standard term for cannabis varieties offers several benefits, contributing to scientific understanding and effective communication. Firstly, it aligns cannabis classification with established botanical nomenclature, bringing clarity to the field. Researchers and scientists can quickly identify and categorize specific cultivars, leading to more accurate data analysis and comparison.

"Cultivar" also supports the scientific process of selective breeding and genetic research. By recognizing the human intervention in cultivating distinct cannabis varieties, researchers can more precisely investigate and study each cultivar's traits and characteristics. It promotes advancements in breeding programs, disease resistance studies, and the development of desired traits.

> *"Breeders and growers use cultivar to designate a cannabis plant variety deliberately bred for certain traits such as terpene profile, color, and shape. While 'strain' has its place in microbiology, extending it to describe the rich diversity of cultivated cannabis is a misappropriation of scientific terminology."*
> — Angela Pih, CMO, Papa & Barkley, CannaCraft, and StateHouse

Embracing "cultivar" fosters transparency and reliability in cannabis research. Researchers can accurately reference specific cultivars, ensuring that findings are reproducible and consistent across studies. This precision level enhances the credibility of scientific research within the cannabis community and facilitates collaboration and knowledge sharing among researchers.

Further, consumers can better understand and differentiate between different cannabis products. They can make more educated choices based on their preferences, knowing that the specific cultivar mentioned accurately represents the product's genetic makeup and potential effects.

The cannabis industry is a complex and rapidly evolving landscape with diverse stakeholders, including growers, producers, distributors, retailers, and consumers. With such a wide range of participants, it becomes imperative to have consistent terminology everyone can understand and utilize.

Different regions or companies may use varying terms to describe the same cannabis variety, resulting in unnecessary misunderstandings and potential errors in product identification. Achieving industry-wide consistency in language ensures everyone is on the same page and can effectively communicate their intentions and needs.

Consistent terminology enables efficient supply chain management and product traceability. From seed to sale, each stage of the cannabis production process requires accurate labeling and documentation. By using standardized terms, growers, processors, and retailers can effectively track and verify the origins and characteristics of each cultivar, ensuring compliance with regulations and quality control measures.

UNIFORMITY IN COMMUNICATION

Standardizing terminology within the cannabis industry promotes uniformity in communication among all stakeholders. This consistency enables growers, researchers, and consumers to exchange information accurately and efficiently.

Uniform terminology allows growers to access reliable data and insights to improve cultivation practices. By using consistent language, growers can readily share their experiences, techniques, and knowledge, contributing to the industry's collective expertise. It also simplifies the identification and classification of cultivars, making it easier for growers to find specific genetics for their breeding programs or sourcing needs.

For consumers, consistent terminology is essential in seeking accurate and reliable information about the cannabis products they purchase. With standardized language, consumers can better understand and compare different cultivars' genetic profiles, effects, and characteristics. It empowers them to make informed decisions based on their preferences and desired experiences, fostering a more discerning and educated consumer base.

FACILITATING A DISCERNING MARKET

Consumer education plays a crucial role in shaping the future of the cannabis industry. One key aspect of consumer education is providing accurate and informative terminology that empowers individuals to make informed decisions about cannabis products. Educating consumers about genetic diversity and using precise and accurate language can foster a more knowledgeable and discerning consumer base.

By using accurate terminology, such as "cultivar," we can highlight the distinct genetic profiles and traits of each cannabis variety. It empowers consumers to understand the differences between cultivars and make choices based on flavor, aroma, potency, and desired effects. For example, terms like "landrace" or "heirloom" indicate that a cultivar has been preserved in its original form, offering consumers a glimpse into the historical and cultural significance of the plant. By educating consumers about these distinctions, we foster an appreciation for the diversity and heritage of cannabis, encouraging responsible consumption and supporting sustainable cultivation practices.

Accurately labeling and describing these traits, cultivators and retailers can communicate the unique selling points of each cultivar to consumers. For example, one cultivar may be known for its uplifting and energetic effects, while another may be prized for its relaxation and pain-relieving properties. These distinctions allow consumers to choose cultivars that align with their desired experiences and therapeutic needs.

INTERNATIONAL HARMONIZATION

One critical advantage of consistent terminology is that it facilitates global cannabis research. By using the same terminology across different countries and regions, researchers can precisely identify and categorize specific cannabis cultivars, making it easier to compare and share findings. Consistency in terminology enables researchers to build upon each other's work and collaborate more effectively, leading to scientific progress and innovation.

Uniform terminology also promotes harmonization in the cannabis trade. By adopting standardized language, international trade agreements and regulations can be developed with greater clarity and coherence. This harmonization streamlines the exchange of cannabis products across borders, reduces trade barriers, and fosters a more efficient and transparent global market.

FACILITATING EFFECTIVE COMMUNICATION AMONG DIVERSE STAKEHOLDERS

Consistent terminology promotes effective communication and understanding among diverse stakeholders involved in the global cannabis industry. Using standardized language facilitates clear and meaningful dialogue, whether it's policymakers, regulators, researchers, or industry professionals.

International forums and conferences, including those held by the United Nations or similar global entities, often bring together professionals from various countries to discuss various topics, including those related to cannabis. Misinterpretations or misunderstandings can occur due to cultural differences, language barriers, and varying legal frameworks regarding cannabis.

For example, the United Nations Commission on Narcotic Drugs (CND) holds regular meetings where cannabis's status and policies are often on the agenda. The International Drug Policy Consortium (IDPC) also provides a platform for such discussions. During these meetings, the classification of cannabis under international treaties, medical cannabis use, and policies for controlling and legalizing its use for recreational purposes can be topics of debate and confusion.

Different interpretations of international drug control treaties, the terminology used to describe cannabis and its derivatives (such as the confusion between "strains," "cultivars," and "varieties" as discussed earlier), and the experiences of countries that have legalized cannabis can lead to a diversity of opinions and potential miscommunication.

The World Health Organization (WHO) and the Food and Agriculture Organization (FAO) might also engage in discussions on cannabis, especially relating to its medical use, safety, trade, and agricultural aspects.[6]

By embracing uniform and standardized terminology, the cannabis industry can foster a global community where stakeholders can effectively communicate, collaborate, and work towards shared goals. International harmonization through standardized language enables the exchange of knowledge, promotes regulatory coherence, and facilitates the growth of a global cannabis industry that operates with transparency and unity.

Summary

Accurate terminology benefits the industry, researchers, policymakers, and consumers, ultimately contributing to the growth, development, and acceptance of cannabis in society. By collectively working towards accurate and standardized cannabis terminology, we can create a foundation for the continued advancement and success of the industry.

The following questions seek to clarify the definitions and appropriate applications of "strain," "cultivar," and "variety." Through these questions, one can explore the implications of these terms on cultivation practices, legal standards, and consumer perceptions and how they affect the broader conversation on cannabis regulation and market structure:

- What is the historical root of the term "strain" in cannabis taxonomy, and how does its traditional usage conflict with the botanical nature of the cannabis plant?
- How does the debate between "strain," "cultivar," and "variety" affect the clarity and accuracy of communication within the cannabis industry, and why is precise terminology essential?
- What are the implications of standardized terminology, explicitly using "cultivar," on various aspects of the cannabis industry, including cultivation, consumer education, and regulatory frameworks?

- How does embracing consistent terminology, such as "cultivar," facilitate collaboration and advancements in cannabis research on a global scale, and what are the benefits of this standardized language in scientific endeavors?

As we navigate the complexities of the cannabis plant and its rich genetic diversity, embracing "cultivar" as the preferred term allows us to cultivate the plant itself and a culture of clarity, precision, and responsible use. By recognizing the unique nature of cannabis within the world of botany, we pave the way for a future where growers, researchers, policymakers, and consumers can engage in informed discussions and decisions, ensuring a vibrant and thriving cannabis community.

CHAPTER 13

INDICA vs. SATIVA

BEYOND INDICA AND SATIVA

In the ever-evolving world of cannabis, it is essential to reevaluate the conventional labels of "Indica" and "Sativa" that have guided consumers and cultivators for decades. While these terms may have once held value in distinguishing cannabis plants, we now find ourselves in a more nuanced landscape, where these classifications are often misleading and fail to capture the true essence of the plant.

> *"To establish an industry-wide cannabis standard, we must bridge the gap between cultural and scientific viewpoints. Since its chemical composition primarily determines cannabis effects, it's evident that chemistry must play a central role in the terminology used to classify cannabis."*
>
> — Mark Lewis, PhD., President, Napro Research

ORIGINS OF CANNABIS INDICA AND CANNABIS SATIVA

To understand why these classifications are no longer relevant, we must journey back to the origins of Cannabis Indica and Cannabis Sativa. These terms were initially coined by 18th-century European botanists who sought to categorize the diversity of the cannabis plant based on physical characteristics. Cannabis Indica was typically described as a shorter, bushier plant from regions near the Hindu Kush mountain range. At the same time, Cannabis Sativa was seen as taller and slender, hailing from the equatorial areas. Moreover, these early classifications often included descriptions of the effects of each plant type. Cannabis Indica was linked to soothing and relaxing properties, while Cannabis Sativa was believed to induce uplifting and energizing effects.[1] Let's delve deeper into the historical context and the characteristics that led to these classifications:

Cannabis Sativa: The Tall and Agile Wanderer

Geographic Origins: "Cannabis Sativa" was initially coined to describe cannabis plants found in equatorial regions, particularly around the equator, such as parts of Southeast Asia, Africa, and Central America. These regions offered a warm climate and extended growing seasons that suited the growth patterns of these plants.

Physical Characteristics: Cannabis Sativa plants are characterized by their tall and slender stature. They can reach heights of up to 20 feet or more when grown in ideal conditions. Their leaves are typically narrow and elongated, with thinner leaflets than Cannabis Indica.

Effects and Uses: In early classifications, Cannabis Sativa was often associated with effects that were considered uplifting, energizing, and cerebral. These strains were believed to stimulate creativity and were frequently used during the daytime. Cannabis Sativa strains were also utilized for their fiber, seeds, and oil, making them valuable for industrial and agricultural purposes.

Cannabis Indica: The Compact and Resilient Settler

Geographic Origins: Cannabis Indica was initially used to describe cannabis plants in regions near the Hindu Kush mountain range, spanning parts of modern-day Afghanistan, Pakistan, and India. The mountainous and cooler climates influenced the growth patterns of these plants.

Physical Characteristics: Cannabis Indica plants are known for their shorter, bushier stature than Cannabis Sativa. They are better adapted to withstand harsher environmental conditions, including cooler temperatures and faster growing seasons. Indica leaves are broader and denser, with shorter leaflets.

Effects and Uses: Early descriptions of Cannabis Indica suggested that it had relaxing, sedative, and physically soothing effects. This led to its association with nighttime and bedtime use. Medicinally, it was believed to alleviate symptoms such as pain and insomnia. Additionally, Cannabis Indica strains were traditionally used for producing hashish due to their resin-rich trichomes.

COMPLEXITIES IN MODERN CLASSIFICATION

It is essential to note that while these historical classifications provided a starting point for understanding cannabis diversity, the simplistic Indica vs. Sativa dichotomy no longer adequately represents the complex reality of modern cannabis. Over centuries, humans have engaged in extensive crossbreeding and hybridizing of these two subspecies, resulting in various hybrid cultivars with diverse characteristics and effects. As a result, the historical classifications are now considered too limited to categorize the wide-ranging cannabis varieties available today accurately.

> *"The outdated terms 'Indica' and 'Sativa' fall short in capturing the nuanced benefits and effects of the cannabis plant. It's high time we embrace a new language that reflects this remarkable plant's complex chemistry and diverse characteristics, allowing us to understand better and communicate its potential."*
> — Daniel Hendricks, Founder & CEO, HendRx

HYBRIDIZATION: BLURRING THE LINES

However, as humans began to cultivate and crossbreed cannabis varieties for various purposes, the lines between these classifications blurred. Generations of crossbreeding and hybridization have given rise to many diverse cultivars, each with its unique combination of physical and chemical characteristics. Here's a closer look at how hybridization has transformed the cannabis industry:

Cultivation for Specific Traits: Early cannabis cultivators recognized that different cultivars exhibited unique characteristics and effects. These traits were often associated with either Cannabis Sativa or Cannabis Indica. As cultivation techniques evolved, growers began selecting and breeding plants with specific attributes to meet consumer preferences. For example, they might choose plants with a high resin content for hashish production or those with uplifting effects for therapeutic use.

Crossbreeding for Customization: Cannabis enthusiasts and breeders furthered the hybridization process by intentionally crossbreeding Cannabis Sativa and Indica varieties. This was done to create new cultivars that combined the desirable traits of both subspecies. By carefully selecting parent plants with complementary characteristics, breeders produced hybrids that offered a more comprehensive range of effects, flavors, and aromas.

Effects-Based Hybrids: Hybridization allowed breeders to develop cannabis cultivars tailored to specific medicinal or therapeutic purposes. For instance, they could create hybrids that provided pain relief without excessive sedation or hybrids that enhanced creativity without inducing anxiety. By blending the attributes of Sativa and Indica, breeders aimed to offer consumers a more precise and consistent cannabis experience.

Cultural Influences: The hybridization of cannabis was also influenced by cultural and regional factors. As the cannabis industry expanded globally, local cultivators and enthusiasts added their unique cultivars. This resulted in regional specialties and hybrids incorporating genetic material from different parts of the world, including India, Africa, South America, and Southeast Asia.

CHEMOTYPE VS. PHENOTYPE: UNDERSTANDING THE DIFFERENCE

In the world of cannabis, particularly within the context of plant classification and effects, two terms frequently arise - chemotype and phenotype. These terms are pivotal in comprehending the complexities of cannabis. Let's delve into what they mean and how they differ:

Chemotype:
Definition: A chemotype, often abbreviated as "chemo," is a classification of a cannabis plant based on its chemical composition. It primarily focuses on the plant's cannabinoid

and terpene profiles. A chemotype categorizes a cannabis plant based on the types and proportions of compounds it produces.

Components: The chemical components that define a chemotype include cannabinoids (such as THC, CBD, CBG, and others) and terpenes (aromatic compounds responsible for a cultivar's scent and potential therapeutic effects).

Use: Chemotypes are used to understand and predict the potential effects of a cannabis cultivar. They help consumers and researchers identify which varieties might suit specific purposes, such as pain relief or relaxation.

Phenotype:
Definition: A phenotype refers to the observable characteristics of a cannabis plant, which result from its genetic makeup interacting with environmental factors. These characteristics include the plant's appearance, growth patterns, coloration, and aroma.

Components: Phenotypes encompass a wide range of visual and sensory traits, from leaf shape and flower color to the smell and flavor of the plant. They are the external expressions of the plant's genetic potential.

Use: Phenotypes are critical for breeders and cultivators. They help in selecting plants with desired traits for further breeding or propagation. Phenotypes also influence the overall consumer experience, dictating how the plant looks, smells, and tastes.

Chemotype and phenotype are essential concepts in understanding cannabis. Chemotype provides insights into a strain's chemical composition and potential effects, while phenotype helps growers and breeders select plants with desirable physical and sensory traits. Together, they contribute to the diverse world of cannabis varieties available to consumers and researchers. This shift in focus from subspecies to chemical composition reflects a more nuanced and scientifically informed approach to understanding and categorizing cannabis, ensuring that consumers can access cultivars that cater to their unique preferences and needs.[2]

> *"In cannabis's long history, we've tried to employ simplified labels to describe this intricate plant's potential benefits and effects. The issue lies in that terms like indica, sativa, and hybrid are seldom, if ever, precise, and they often fail to capture the plant's complex chemistry. It's time to embrace a more comprehensive lexicon that accurately reflects the diverse characteristics of this remarkable botanical."*
> — Dustin Hoxworth, Founder, Fat Nugs Magazine

THE FALLACY OF INDICA VS. SATIVA EFFECTS

One of the most significant misconceptions perpetuated by the Indica vs. Sativa paradigm is the idea that the effects of a cultivar can be predicted solely based on its classification. In reality, the results of a cannabis variety are determined by a complex interplay of cannabinoids, terpenes, and other chemical compounds.

> *"Labeling cannabis solely as indica or sativa is as limiting and reductive as describing wine in broad strokes of red and white, failing to capture the intricate complexity and diversity present in both. An expanded lexicon needs to be propagated."*
> — Marco Hoffman, Founder, Evergreen Herbal

Every person's endocannabinoid system is unique, leading to variations in how individuals respond to cannabis. Genetics, tolerance, and prior experience all influence how a person experiences the effects of a given cultivar. What may be relaxing for one person could be energizing for another.

The traditional Indica vs. Sativa categorization is an oversimplification that doesn't align with the modern understanding of cannabis science. It's more accurate to assess cannabis strains based on their chemical profiles (chemotypes) to predict their effects. This shift in thinking acknowledges the complexity of cannabis and allows consumers to make more informed choices based on their desired outcomes, whether it's relaxation, pain relief, or creative stimulation.

A NEW APPROACH TO CANNABIS CLASSIFICATION

Recognizing the limitations of the Indica vs. Sativa binary, some experts advocate for a more scientifically informed approach to cannabis classification. This involves analyzing the chemical composition of strains, particularly their cannabinoid and terpene profiles, to provide a more accurate representation of their effects.[3]

As the limitations of the traditional Indica vs. Sativa classification become increasingly apparent, the cannabis industry and scientific community are adopting a more nuanced and accurate approach to classifying cannabis varieties. This new approach centers around a deeper understanding of the plant's chemical composition and the effects it produces. Here's an exploration of this evolving paradigm:

Chemotype-Based Classification: Rather than relying on the plant's physical characteristics, such as its height or leaf shape, a chemotype-based classification system emphasizes the chemical makeup of cannabis cultivars. It categorizes strains based on their unique combinations and ratios of cannabinoids (like THC and CBD) and terpenes, the aromatic compounds influencing aroma, flavor, and effects.

Cannabinoid Dominance: In this new framework, varieties are often categorized based on their dominant cannabinoid. For example, cultivars high in THC are classified as THC-dominant, while those with significant CBD content are CBD-dominant. Other cannabinoids like CBG (cannabigerol) and CBN (cannabinol) are also considered. This approach provides a more accurate prediction of a cultivar's psychoactive and therapeutic potential.

Terpene Profiles: Terpenes play a crucial role in defining the aroma and flavor of cannabis varieties and contributing to their overall effects. Cultivars are classified based on their terpene profiles, with common terpenes like myrcene, limonene, and pinene having well-documented effects. For example, cultivars high in myrcene may be associated with relaxing, sedative effects, while limonene-dominant varieties might offer an uplifting, citrusy experience.

Hybrid Categories: Recognizing the extensive crossbreeding in the cannabis industry, this approach embraces hybrid categories. A hybrid cultivar may be categorized based on its chemotype, such as THC-dominant hybrid or CBD-dominant hybrid. This acknowledges the complexity of modern varieties that often defy the Indica-Sativa binary.

Medicinal and Therapeutic Categories: Within this new paradigm, cultivars are also categorized based on their intended use, whether for therapeutic or medicinal purposes. For example, varieties high in CBD and lower in THC may be classified as "Medicinal CBD," while those with high THC content might be labeled "Adult Use THC."

Scientific Validation: The chemotype-based classification aligns with scientific research, allowing for more precise studies on the effects of specific cannabinoids and terpenes. This scientific validation enhances our understanding of the plant's therapeutic potential and expands its applications in medicine and wellness.

The shift towards a chemotype-based classification system represents a more sophisticated and accurate approach to categorizing cannabis varieties. It moves away from simplistic labels like Indica or Sativa and focuses on the chemical components that define each cultivar's unique effects. This evolution in cannabis classification enables more personalized and effective cannabis consumption, whether for medical, therapeutic, or adult use purposes and encourages further scientific exploration of this versatile plant.

"In today's dynamic legal cannabis market, the terms 'Indica' and 'Sativa' no longer suffice to capture the nuanced benefits and effects of different cultivars. It's not about where the plant originates but rather how it can best serve consumers' diverse needs and preferences, demanding a more precise language that speaks to the plant's complex chemistry and its potential to enhance our well-being."

— Eric Mercado, Founder & CEO, Terpli

REDEFINING THE LANGUAGE OF CANNABIS

In a modern context, perpetuating these outdated classifications can mislead medical and adult-use consumers. The need to redefine the language of cannabis is paramount as we move toward a more informed and responsible cannabis culture. Here are recommendations and solutions to facilitate this essential transformation:

Adopt a Unified Terminology: The cannabis industry, scientific community, and regulators should work together to establish a unified and standardized terminology. This glossary should encompass cannabinoids, terpenes, chemotypes, and their associated effects. This would provide a common language that can be used across the board, from research papers to consumer labels.

Consumer Education: Educating consumers about the new classification system is crucial. Dispensaries and online platforms can provide detailed information on each cultivar's chemotype and terpene profiles, helping consumers make informed choices based on their preferences and needs.

Label Transparency: Cannabis products should be labeled with comprehensive information, including the dominant chemotype, terpene composition, and intended use (medicinal or adult use). This empowers consumers to make choices aligned with their desired effects.

Rebranding Efforts: The industry should initiate rebranding efforts that move away from the terms "Indica" and "Sativa." Instead, brands can focus on promoting chemotypes and terpene profiles. Marketing campaigns can emphasize the nuanced effects and aromas associated with each cultivar.

Scientific Validation: Encourage and fund scientific research on cannabis to validate the new classification system. This includes studying the effects of specific cannabinoids and terpenes on various conditions, from anxiety to chronic pain. Scientific backing legitimizes the new language.

Regulatory Support: Regulatory bodies should recognize and endorse the new classification system. They can mandate accurate labeling and encourage dispensaries and producers to adopt the standardized terminology.

Training and Certification: Dispensary staff, budtenders, and healthcare professionals should undergo training and certification in the new language of cannabis. This ensures they can provide expert guidance to consumers.

Collaboration with Cultural Influencers: Cultural influencers in the cannabis community can significantly popularize the new language. Collaborations with celebrity cultivators, musicians, artists, and celebrities can help spread awareness and understanding.

Consumer Feedback Loops: Establish feedback mechanisms where consumers can report their experiences with specific varieties. This data can contribute to the refinement of cultivar classifications and recommendations.

Global Adoption: Encourage global adoption of the new language. International cooperation can lead to a consistent and universally accepted classification system, benefiting medical and adult-use consumers worldwide.

Legal and Regulatory Advocacy: Advocate for changes in cannabis-related laws and regulations that reflect the new classification system. This includes lobbying for laws that prioritize accurate labeling and information for consumers.

Research and Development: Invest in research and development to create new cultivars that align with the chemotype-based system. Breeders can develop varieties tailored to specific therapeutic needs or desired adult use effects.

Public Awareness Campaigns: Launch public awareness campaigns to educate society about the outdated nature of the Indica vs. Sativa terminology and the benefits of the new classification system.

Continual Evolution: Recognize that language, like the cannabis plant itself, is dynamic and evolving. Periodic reviews and updates to the classification system should accommodate discoveries and insights.

By implementing these recommendations and solutions, we can redefine the language of cannabis, fostering a culture of responsibility, informed consumption, and scientific progress. This transformation not only benefits the cannabis industry but also empowers consumers and contributes to the broader acceptance of cannabis in society.[4]

> *"We would all prefer simple nostrums to explain complex systems, but this is futile and potentially dangerous in the context of a psychoactive drug such as cannabis."*
>
> — Dr. Ethan Russo, MD

The traditional classifications of "Indica" and "Sativa" in cannabis have served their purpose historically. Still, they are now recognized as oversimplified and inadequate for our modern understanding of this remarkable plant. These terms, once rooted in the physical characteristics and perceived effects of cannabis plants, no longer capture the complexity and diversity that exists within the cannabis ecosystem.

The evolution of cannabis cultivation, driven by human intervention and the desire to create cultivars with specific traits, has blurred the lines between these two subspecies. Crossbreeding and hybridization have resulted in a vast array of cannabis varieties with unique chemical profiles, making the traditional Indica vs. Sativa classification insufficient for describing the full spectrum of effects and potential applications of cannabis.

Furthermore, recommendations have been made to facilitate the transformation of the cannabis language. These include the adoption of a unified terminology, comprehensive labeling, consumer education, and regulatory support for the new classification system. Collaboration with cultural influencers, scientific validation, and global adoption are essential steps in this process.

Summary
Ultimately, this evolution in the language of cannabis reflects a maturing industry and a growing body of scientific knowledge. It empowers consumers, fosters responsible cannabis use, and encourages further research into this versatile plant's potential therapeutic and recreational benefits. As we move forward, let us embrace this new lexicon, one that accurately represents the complexities of cannabis, and continue to explore the boundless potential of this remarkable botanical.

The following questions are intended to scrutinize the historical origins, genetic validity, and current relevance of "indica" and "sativa" classifications in shaping user experience and product marketing:

- What were the traditional effects associated with Cannabis Indica and Cannabis Sativa, and why are these classifications considered outdated and oversimplified?
- How have hybridization and crossbreeding affected the distinctions between Indica and Sativa, leading to a more complex array of cannabis varieties?

- What is the significance of the shift from a physical classification (Indica vs. Sativa) to a chemotype-based classification system in understanding cannabis effects?
- What are the critical components of chemotype and phenotype when categorizing cannabis, and how do they contribute to a better understanding of the plant's characteristics and effects?

Understanding the evolution from the traditional classifications of Indica and Sativa to the more nuanced chemotype-based system is crucial in navigating the complexities of cannabis. Embracing this shift towards a more scientific and comprehensive understanding of cannabis not only enhances consumer knowledge but also propels the industry towards a future of informed choices and responsible consumption.

CHAPTER 14

THE ENTOURAGE, ENSEMBLE OR SYMPHONIC EFFECT?

THE GENESIS OF THE "ENTOURAGE EFFECT"

In the continually evolving realm of scientific research, the precision of technical language plays a pivotal role in shaping our comprehension of intricate systems and complex phenomena. As scientific knowledge grows, so does the need for precise terminology to describe and categorize emerging discoveries. Throughout history, the evolution of technical language has been an organic process intricately linked to the advancement of scientific inquiry and the pursuit of knowledge.

> *"Given the intricate nature of cannabis, with nearly a thousand potential compounds, the term 'symphony' appears most fitting. This includes approximately 150 identified cannabinoids and about 200 terpenes present in cannabis, a fraction of the estimated 40,000 terpenes found in the natural world."*
> — Swami Chaitanya, Co-Founder, Swami Select

The realm of cannabis and cannabinoids has been a captivating arena for exploration, where researchers and enthusiasts continuously strive to grasp the intricate interplay between various compounds within the plant. One phenomenon that has captivated the scientific community is the "Entourage Effect." Initially coined to describe the synergistic interactions between cannabinoids, terpenes, and other compounds in cannabis, the term has been foundational in shaping our understanding of the plant's therapeutic potential. However, as research advances and knowledge deepens, the term "Entourage Effect" has evolved into a more comprehensive concept known as the "Ensemble Effect." In this chapter, we delve into the history of the "Entourage Effect," explore the reasons behind its evolution, and discover the significance of embracing the "Ensemble Effect" in our quest to unlock the full therapeutic potential of cannabis.

Scientific research is a dynamic endeavor that constantly challenges and redefines our perceptions of the natural world. As researchers explore new frontiers and pioneer innovative methodologies, they often reveal complexities and nuances demanding accurate expression. Technical terms emerge as indispensable tools to articulate these discoveries, providing a shared language for scientists to communicate their observations, theories, and conclusions precisely and clearly.

However, as the boundaries of human knowledge expand, so do the limitations of existing language. The continuous accumulation of knowledge necessitates the evolution of technical terms to encompass novel concepts and accommodate breakthroughs that transcend conventional paradigms.

With time, the evolution of technical language becomes a testament to the collective growth and maturation of scientific disciplines. As researchers build upon the work of their predecessors and challenge existing theories, the terminology they employ reflects the ever-changing landscape of scientific inquiry. Interdisciplinary collaboration further enriches this process as insights from different fields converge and contribute to expanding our understanding. Ultimately, the evolution of technical terms reflects the remarkable capacity of human intellect and the collective effort of the scientific community to unravel the mysteries of the universe and pave the way for future discoveries.[1]

> *"Cannabis is the single most versatile herbal remedy and the most useful plant on Earth. No other single plant contains as wide a range of medically active herbal constituents."*
> — Dr. Ethan Russo, MD

The "Entourage Effect" concept can be traced back to the July 1998 European Journal of Pharmacology issue. This text, titled *"An Entourage Effect: Inactive Endogenous Fatty Acid Glycerol Esters Enhance 2-Arachidonoyl-Glycerol Cannabinoid Activity,"* was authored by researchers and scientists, including Professor Raphael Mechoulam and Shimon Ben-Shabat, among others. It demonstrated the increase in activity of a given cannabinoid due to the presence of another compound, specifically the esters of a fatty acid.[2]

Their groundbreaking research identified the endocannabinoid system and revealed that cannabis contains various compounds, including cannabinoids and terpenes, which interact with the body's endocannabinoid receptors. Dr. Mechoulam's research led to the discovery of the first known endocannabinoid, anandamide, and identifying the primary phytocannabinoid, THC. As their investigations continued, it became evident that the therapeutic effects of cannabis were not solely attributed to THC but rather a more intricate interplay between its compounds.

In 2010, Dr. Ethan Russo, MD, further explored these findings. His research expanded on Dr. Mechoulam's discoveries and emphasized the importance of cannabinoids, terpenes, and other compounds working synergistically to enhance cannabis's therapeutic potential.

Russo's paper, titled *"Taming THC: Potential Cannabis Synergy and Phytocannabinoid-Terpenoid Entourage Effect,"* focused on examining the interactions between cannabinoids and terpenes specifically. When discussing the relationship between cannabinoids, Russo stated, "CBD regulates the psychoactivity of THC and reduces its adverse event profile." In the latter part of the paper, he explained how terpenes can enhance or minimize the effects of cannabinoids. For example, pinene can counteract short-term memory deficits associated with THC. The "Entourage Effect" implies that the combined action of multiple components in cannabis results in a more profound and balanced therapeutic response than individual compounds in isolation. This concept challenged the traditional belief of focusing solely on THC and CBD and encouraged researchers to consider the potential of the entire plant profile.[3]

While the "Entourage Effect" provided a more holistic understanding of cannabis's therapeutic properties, it had limitations. The term often implied that certain compounds were more significant contributors to the effect than others, potentially overshadowing the importance of lesser-known compounds. Furthermore, the "Entourage Effect" didn't fully encompass the complexity of interactions between cannabis compounds and their impact on the endocannabinoid system and other physiological processes.

THE EMERGENCE OF THE "ENSEMBLE EFFECT"

As cannabis research advanced, scientists recognized the need for a more inclusive and comprehensive term to describe the intricate interactions within the plant. This led to the evolution of the "Entourage Effect" into the "Ensemble Effect." "Ensemble" implies a harmonious collaboration of all components, each contributing uniquely to the whole without favoring any particular compound. This shift in terminology reflects a more refined understanding of cannabis's therapeutic potential and encourages researchers to consider the collective contributions of cannabinoids, terpenes, flavonoids, and other constituents.

As cannabis research continued to flourish, a paradigm shift occurred. Scientists and researchers recognized the need for a more inclusive and neutral term to encapsulate the synergistic interactions within the plant. Thus, the "Entourage Effect" evolved into the "Ensemble Effect." "Ensemble" implies a harmonious collaboration among all cannabis components, with each compound contributing uniquely to the whole, without bias towards any specific constituent.

> *"I think the ensemble is a better idea than entourage because the word 'entourage' implies one item moving in this direction – and it has company."*
> — Dr. Lester Grinspoon, MD, Harvard Medical School

The recognition and acceptance of the "Ensemble Effect" are paramount for developing holistic cannabis therapies. Instead of focusing solely on isolates or individual compounds, researchers and medical practitioners are now exploring whole-plant medicine, where the interplay of all components contributes to the desired therapeutic outcomes. Embracing the "Ensemble Effect" encourages a personalized approach to cannabis-based treatments, where the unique profile of each cultivar can be tailored to meet individual needs.

ELEMENTS THAT INFLUENCE THE EFFECT

Cannabinoids

Cannabinoids are the "naturally occurring, biologically active, chemical constituents of hemp and cannabis." They are also called phytocannabinoids as they mimic the cannabinoids produced by the body, known as endocannabinoids. Cannabinoids are produced by the hemp or cannabis plant's trichomes, which begin to develop when flowers form. The most common cannabinoids produced by the cannabis plant are CBD and THC. However, there are other cannabinoids, sometimes called minor cannabinoids, like CBC, CBG, CBN, and THCv, that are gaining prominence due to their purported health benefits.

Terpenes

Terpenes are fragrant oils secreted from the same glands that produce cannabinoids, the trichomes. They can repel predators and attract pollinators, giving the plant its odor and flavor while enhancing the efficacy of cannabinoids. Terpenes also have antioxidant effects. With over 200 terpenes in the cannabis plant, each cultivar possesses its unique blend. Terpenes are the basis of aromatherapy, a healing treatment using a plant's essential oils for physical and emotional well-being. Terpenes also have therapeutic qualities and can play a role in a plant's medicinal effects by interacting with cannabinoids, potentially increasing their effectiveness in treating conditions like pain, inflammation, anxiety, depression, epilepsy, and infection when working synergistically.

RESEARCH STUDIES ON THE EFFECT

In 2020, The journal Current Neuropharmacology published a paper by a group of scientists entitled *"The Entourage Effect: Terpenes Coupled with Cannabinoids for the Treatment of Mood Disorders and Anxiety Disorders."* The report reviewed various papers covering the Entourage Effect to answer the question, "When paired with terpenes, are cannabinoids more effective in treating some psychiatric symptoms?" They concluded that terpenes' "contribution to the therapeutic effect of cannabinoids may be significant." They called for further research on the relationship between terpenes and CBD in treating patients suffering from anxiety, depression, or bipolar disorder.

Numerous studies[4,5,6] have highlighted the effectiveness of particular combinations of cannabinoids and terpenes in treating specific medical conditions:

- Myrcene + Linalool + Caryophyllene: Effective for sleep disorders.
- Pinene + Limonene + Linalool: Effective in treating acne.
- Limonene + Linalool: Enhances the effects of CBD.

Considering the wide variety of cannabinoids, terpenes, and other compounds present in cannabis, including ketones, esters, lactones, alcohols, fatty acids, and steroids, it becomes evident that there exists an immense range of potential combinations. Each of these combinations can yield specific and well-defined effects, making the possibilities within the realm of cannabis therapy exceptionally diverse and promising.[7]

IMPLICATIONS FOR FUTURE RESEARCH

As the cannabis industry and scientific community continue to evolve, the "Ensemble Effect" opens the door to exciting avenues of research. Understanding how specific combinations of cannabinoids and terpenes interact with the endocannabinoid system and other receptors in the body may unlock new therapeutic applications. Additionally, exploring the impact of different growing conditions and cultivation practices on the plant's profile can further optimize cannabis-based therapies.

Summary

The evolution of technical language in cannabis research, specifically the transition from the "Entourage Effect" to the "Ensemble Effect," reflects the dynamic nature of scientific exploration. The "Entourage Effect" concept was groundbreaking, shedding light on the synergistic interactions between cannabinoids and terpenes within the cannabis plant. However, as our understanding of cannabis deepened, it became evident that this terminology had limitations. The term "Ensemble Effect" emerged to encompass a more inclusive and neutral perspective, emphasizing the harmonious collaboration of all cannabis constituents without favoring any specific compound.[9]

Understanding the evolution from the "Entourage Effect" to the more comprehensive "Ensemble Effect" offers a glimpse into the dynamic world of cannabis research, emphasizing the importance of nuanced language in shaping our comprehension of this complex plant's therapeutic potential. This linguistic evolution is not merely a matter of semantics but carries profound implications for the future of cannabis research and therapy. Embracing the "Ensemble Effect" encourages a holistic approach to cannabis-based treatments, where the unique profile of each cultivar can be tailored to meet individual needs. It recognizes that the therapeutic potential of cannabis extends far beyond individual cannabinoids like THC and CBD, encompassing a rich tapestry of compounds that work in concert to produce nuanced and personalized effects.

The following questions aim to explore how science and language advancements are shaping the way we view and think about cannabis and cannabinoids:

- How can the "Ensemble Effect" inspire researchers to explore the effects of novel combinations of cannabinoids and terpenes?
- What were the limitations of the term "Entourage Effect," leading to the evolution towards the more inclusive "Ensemble Effect"?
- How do cannabinoids and terpenes differ in the cannabis plant, and what is their role in producing therapeutic effects?
- How has the concept of the "Ensemble Effect" influenced approaches to cannabis-based therapies, and what are its implications for personalized treatments?

The "Ensemble Effect" inspires researchers to explore novel combinations of cannabinoids, terpenes, and other cannabis constituents, paving the way for innovative therapies and a deeper understanding of the plant's potential. As we unravel the mysteries of cannabis, the evolution of technical language remains a testament to our unwavering commitment to scientific progress and the pursuit of knowledge in the ever-evolving world of cannabis research.

CHAPTER 15

LANGUAGE AND LEGISLATION

THE ROLE OF LANGUAGE IN CRAFTING LEGISLATION

Language is the cornerstone of lawmaking. Every word, phrase, and clause in legislation carries the weight of meaning and intention. Effective legislation requires precision, clarity, and foresight in language choice. Ambiguity can lead to unintended consequences, while transparency ensures that laws are understood and applied as intended. When we examine the intricate process of crafting legislation, it becomes evident that language is the bedrock upon which the legal framework is constructed. These carefully chosen words translate a society's aspirations, values, and directives into actionable laws.

> *"Without a comprehensive understanding of the racial animosity and the desire to suppress political speech that motivated the classification of cannabis as a Schedule I substance, involvement in the cannabis industry is disingenuous. The most effective way to educate oneself about the industry and its foundations is by learning from the endeavors of patient and restorative justice advocates who have persistently fought against outdated and ineffective drug policies."*
> — Lauren Rudick, Esq., Rudick Law Group, PLLC

In lawmaking, there is no room for ambiguity or loose interpretation. Each word is selected with the utmost precision to convey specific meanings and outcomes. Consider, for example, the distinction between "shall" and "may." When the law states that a public official "shall" take a specific action, it is an unequivocal directive, leaving no room for discretion. Conversely, when "may" is used, it implies permissibility, allowing for discretion and choice.

Moreover, legislators must consider the potential consequences of their word choices. They must anticipate how these words will interact with existing laws and regulations. This foresight is crucial in preventing unintended consequences that could arise from vague or contradictory language.

Effective legislation hinges on the clarity of its language. Laws must be readily understandable by those subject to them, including citizens, businesses, and law enforcement agencies. Ambiguity in legal language can lead to confusion, disputes, and legal challenges that undermine the very purpose of the law. Clarity in legislation is akin to a well-lit path through a dense forest; it guides and informs, making it easier for individuals and entities to navigate the legal landscape. When the language of a law is clear and concise, it provides a solid foundation for its practical application. People can make informed decisions, businesses can comply with regulations, and courts can adjudicate cases more efficiently.

One of the foremost considerations in legislative drafting is the prevention of unintended consequences. The law is a powerful tool, and when wielded without precision, it can produce results that lawmakers never intended. This is where the choice of language becomes paramount. If the language in such legislation is imprecise, it may inadvertently create loopholes. Conversely, if the language is too stringent, it could burden businesses with excessive regulations, potentially leading to economic hardships.[1]

The recent Farm Bill, specifically the Agriculture Improvement Act of 2018, removed hemp defined as cannabis (Cannabis sativa L.) and derivatives of cannabis with deficient concentrations of the psychoactive compound delta-9-tetrahydrocannabinol (THC) — no more than 0.3 percent THC on a dry weight basis — from the definition of marijuana in the Controlled Substances Act (CSA).

This led to the legalization of hemp production in the United States. However, the language of the bill primarily addresses delta-9 THC, the most commonly known form of THC in cannabis. It did not specifically address the many other analogs of THC, such as delta-8 THC, which can be derived from the newly legal hemp.

The consequence of this oversight is that delta-8 THC, which is psychoactive though reportedly less potent than delta-9 THC, falls into a legal gray area. It can be synthesized from legal CBD (cannabidiol) derived from hemp, leading to the proliferation of delta-8 THC products that may not be fully regulated under the current interpretation of the law.

This example demonstrates how specific legislative language is crucial and how its lack of precision can create unintended legal and regulatory gaps.

> *"As global cannabis markets transition from unregulated to regulated, the clarity of legal and regulatory language is the driving factor for flowering successful local and global cannabis industries. By engaging with legacy stakeholders, taking lessons from the past, and minimizing barriers, we lay the groundwork for compliant markets that honor their roots, avoid unnecessary legal complications, and ensure prosperous growth for all."*
> — David Feder, Esq., Founding Member, Weed Law, LLC

In many ways, legislation represents a societal compact, a set of rules and guidelines that govern how individuals and institutions interact within a community. Therefore, the language in crafting legislation must accurately reflect society's values, aspirations, and priorities. It is the medium through which a society expresses its expectations and standards.

The role of language in crafting legislation extends far beyond the surface of words on paper. It is a fundamental element shaping the essence of law and governance. It is the key to precision, clarity, and foresight. In essence, language in legislation bridges a society's ideals to the practical realities of governance.

CHALLENGES IN DEFINING CANNABIS IN LEGAL DOCUMENTS

Defining cannabis in legal documents is no simple task. The challenge lies in capturing the breadth of cannabis diversity, from different cultivars to derivatives like concentrates and edibles. Legislation must balance scientific accuracy with practicality. For instance, should it differentiate between Cannabis Sativa and Cannabis Indica? How does it address hybrid cultivars? These challenges necessitate nuanced language that accommodates future developments.

Defining cannabis in legal documents is a multifaceted endeavor that presents legislators with unique and intricate challenges. At the heart of this complexity is the need to encapsulate the astonishing diversity of the cannabis plant. Crafting legislation that successfully navigates these intricacies is an exercise in balancing scientific accuracy with practicality and foresight.

One of the primary challenges in defining cannabis lies in acknowledging the vast spectrum of diversity within the plant itself. Cannabis is not a monolithic entity; it is an ecosystem of genetic variations, each with its distinct characteristics. Traditionally, cannabis has been classified into two species: Cannabis Sativa and Cannabis Indica. Yet, the modern understanding of cannabis genetics reveals that these distinctions are far from exhaustive.

Scientific Accuracy vs. Practicality

Balancing scientific accuracy with practicality is at the core of defining cannabis in legal documents. While precision is essential, legislation must also be pragmatic and adaptable to the evolving landscape of cannabis cultivation, processing, and consumption. Definitions must be comprehensive enough to encompass the spectrum of cannabis products and uses, from medicinal cultivars to adult-use edibles.

The dynamic nature of the cannabis industry necessitates a forward-thinking approach to legislative language. Lawmakers must anticipate future developments, innovations, and scientific discoveries related to cannabis. The definition crafted today should be robust enough to accommodate the introduction of new cultivars, products, and consumption methods tomorrow. This forward-looking perspective is critical to ensuring that legislation remains effective and relevant in the future.

Defining cannabis is not limited to the plant itself. It extends to derivatives such as concentrates, edibles, beverages, topicals, and tinctures – to name a few. Each of these products presents its own set of complexities. For example, how should a legal framework address the varying potencies of concentrates or the different formulations of edibles? These considerations demand nuanced language that reflects the nuances of cannabis.

LEGAL LANGUAGE:
LESSONS FROM INTERNATIONAL MODELS

International models of cannabis legislation offer valuable insights into effective legal language. Countries like the U.S., Canada, Thailand, and Uruguay have established legal frameworks that balance regulation with consumer access. Examining their approaches to defining cannabis, licensing, and regulation can provide valuable guidance for jurisdictions navigating the path to legalization.

International models of cannabis legislation present a treasure trove of wisdom for jurisdictions seeking to craft their own effective legal frameworks. Countries previously mentioned have pioneered innovative approaches that successfully balance the complexities of regulation with ensuring reasonable consumer access.

One key lesson from international models is precisely defining cannabis and its various forms. These models typically embrace a comprehensive approach, leaving no room for ambiguity. For instance, they often outline distinctions between medical and adult-use cannabis, various consumption methods, and potency levels. The result is a legal framework that is both coherent and adaptable, serving as a robust foundation for effective regulation.

Another critical aspect illuminated by international models is the establishment of licensing and permitting mechanisms. These models often prioritize the creation of well-defined pathways for businesses to operate legally within the cannabis industry and include detailed regulations for cultivation, distribution, and retail alongside stringent quality control measures. The nuanced and comprehensive nature of these legal instruments ensures a controlled and regulated marketplace.

Several international models strongly emphasize social equity and justice within cannabis legislation. They incorporate language that addresses historical disparities, offering opportunities for marginalized communities to participate in the legal cannabis industry. This is achieved by expunging prior cannabis-related convictions and establishing programs facilitating equitable business ownership and employment.

International models also provide valuable insights into effectively regulating cannabis marketing and advertising. These regulations are crafted to prevent cannabis from being glamorized or targeted at vulnerable populations. By examining these models, jurisdictions can identify strategies to balance allowing businesses to thrive and protecting public health.

> *"I've been wondering if this so-called civil war between hemp and cannabis is just a devious ploy on the part of the government to divide and conquer. If so, it's working!"*
> — Ruth Shamai, Chief Vision Officer, BioVida Inc.

One of the most noteworthy takeaways from international models is their capacity for flexibility and adaptability. They often contain provisions that allow for ongoing refinement and amendment of the legislation as the cannabis industry evolves. This forward-looking approach ensures that legal language remains relevant in the face of changing circumstances, such as the emergence of new products or scientific discoveries.

International models of cannabis legislation offer a wealth of valuable lessons, particularly in legal language. By examining those countries that have defined cannabis, licensing, equity, marketing, and adaptability, new jurisdictions can significantly benefit from the wisdom of those who have navigated the path to legalization successfully. These lessons can pave the way for well-crafted, compelling, and adaptable cannabis legislation that serves the best interests of both the industry and the public internationally.

THE EVOLUTION OF
CANNABIS TERMINOLOGY IN LEGISLATION

The evolution of terminology in cannabis legislation is a compelling journey that mirrors the changing attitudes, perceptions, and policies surrounding this plant. It's not merely a matter of semantics; it reflects how society views and interacts with cannabis. This evolution highlights the need for precision and nuance in legislative language.

In the early 20th century, cannabis legislation was steeped in sensationalism and racism. Terms like "marijuana" and "reefer" were intentionally used to stigmatize the plant, associating it with criminality and addiction. The language was emotionally charged, designed to instill fear and justify prohibition.[2]

As societal understanding of cannabis evolved and scientific research expanded, the terminology within legislation began to shift. While many still use the term "marijuana," other jurisdictions started using the more scientifically accurate term "cannabis." This shift signals a move towards a more objective and evidence-based approach to regulation.

The evolution of cannabis terminology isn't uniform worldwide. Cultural and regional factors play a significant role in shaping the language of legislation. In some places, traditional or indigenous names for cannabis are integrated into legal language to acknowledge cultural significance and heritage. This demonstrates the importance of respecting diverse perspectives and histories.

The evolving terminology in cannabis legislation underscores the power of words in shaping public perception. The shift towards neutral and scientifically precise language reflects a growing recognition of the need for rational, evidence-based cannabis policies. It also highlights the responsibility of lawmakers to choose their words carefully, as language can influence policy and public attitudes.

The journey of cannabis terminology is intrinsically linked to shifts in policy. As legislation began to shed sensationalism in favor of accurate, neutral language, it paved the way for more reasoned and informed policy decisions. This evolution has played a vital role in the global trend towards cannabis legalization and regulation.

In some cases, legislation must strike a balance between tradition and progress. Acknowledging indigenous or traditional terms for cannabis in legal language respects cultural heritage while recognizing the need for modern regulation. This nuanced approach demonstrates an evolving understanding of cannabis and its societal role.

> *"Imprecise language can cause confusion and even impede the rule of law. The problem stems largely from legislating and regulating cannabis, cannabinoids, and intoxication without fully understanding the plant, its derivatives, and its consumption. An example of this is defining "hemp" and "marijuana" based on the arbitrary limit of 0.3% delta-9 THC by dry weight. Confusion over the language has led to a nearly unregulated market of hemp-derived cannabinoid products outside of, and competing with the state-regulated medical and adult-use cannabis markets."*
> — Eric Berlin, Esq., Partner & Leader, Cannabis Group, Dentons

THE IMPACT OF LANGUAGE CLARITY ON POLICY IMPLEMENTATION

Clarity in language is not a mere technicality; it directly influences policy implementation. Ambiguities can hinder regulatory agencies and confuse stakeholders. Clear, well-defined language streamlines the regulatory process, fosters compliance, and promotes public safety.

The impact of language clarity on policy implementation within the cannabis industry cannot be overstated. Unambiguous language serves as the cornerstone upon which effective regulations are built. It's not just about choosing the right words; it's about ensuring that every policy aspect is understandable to all stakeholders.

Ambiguities in legislative language are fertile ground for legal disputes. In the world of cannabis regulation, where the line between legal and illegal activities can be razor-thin, clear language safeguards against protracted legal battles. It provides a solid foundation for enforcing the law and ensuring that businesses, consumers, and regulators agree.

Clarity in language empowers regulatory agencies to carry out their duties effectively. When regulators can easily interpret and apply the rules, they can enforce compliance, monitor safety standards, and protect public health. Regulatory bodies can struggle to provide consistent oversight without this clarity, potentially putting consumers at risk.[3]

> *"Laws are expressed with words, the choice of which affects the public perception of the regulated activity. To support a safe, healthy, and profitable cannabis economy, the language used when drafting rules and regulations is critical for communicating that the lawful use of cannabis products is an accepted part of our modern economy."*
>
> — Seth Gardenswartz, Esq., Partner, Blackgarden Law, PC

Summary

Clarity in language plays a significant role in ensuring public safety. Regulations governing the cannabis industry encompass everything from product labeling to security protocols. When these rules are clear, businesses are more likely to implement safety measures effectively. This, in turn, reduces the risk of harm to consumers and the community. Explicit language in policies and regulations promotes transparency by making it easier for stakeholders, including consumers, to understand the rules governing the industry. When everyone knows the rules, trust in the regulatory system grows, and the likelihood of illicit activities diminishes.

The following questions delve into the nuanced aspects of language's role in legislation and the challenges and impacts it poses within the context of cannabis regulation:

- What are the challenges legislators face in defining cannabis within legal documents, and how do these challenges reflect the plant's diverse nature?
- What lessons can jurisdictions seeking to legalize cannabis learn from international models regarding legal language, licensing, equity, and adaptability?
- How has the terminology in cannabis legislation evolved, and what does this evolution signify in terms of societal attitudes and policy changes?
- How does language clarity influence policy implementation within the cannabis industry, and how does it influence stakeholders such as regulatory bodies and businesses?

Language is the linchpin of effective cannabis legislation. It enables lawmakers to navigate complexity, draw inspiration from international experiences, acknowledge evolving terminology, and shape the impact of policies. Clear and precise language is not just a legal requirement; it's a fundamental factor in crafting legislation that aligns with contemporary values, promotes responsible cannabis use, and contributes to the well-being of society as a whole.

CHAPTER 16

CANNABIS AND EDUCATION

THE ROLE OF EDUCATION IN
CHANGING PERCEPTIONS

Education has the remarkable power to change perceptions. As cannabis legalization gains momentum, equipping individuals with accurate information is essential. The history of cannabis Prohibition is riddled with decades of misinformation campaigns. Terms like "reefer madness" and "gateway drug" were propagated to evoke fear and stigma. Education emerges as the powerful counterweight to this barrage of untruths. By presenting evidence-based information, educators effectively debunk these myths and provide individuals with the tools to differentiate fact from fiction.

"Cannabis education is essential for eliminating the stigma around cannabis and those who consume it. The plant has a rich global history of industrial, therapeutic, and spiritual use. It's one of the most versatile, abundant, and powerful natural resources known to man. Sadly, most people have never learned the truth about this amazing gift from Mother Nature and the many ways it can empower and uplift humanity."
– Michael Zaytsev, Director, Business of Cannabis, LIM College

Education lays the groundwork for informed and open-minded discussions about cannabis. It equips individuals with knowledge about the plant's history, various cultivars, chemical composition, and potential uses. Armed with this information, people can engage in conversations beyond stereotypes, enabling them to critically evaluate the merits and drawbacks of cannabis more objectively.

Changing perceptions often involves challenging deep-seated stereotypes. For many years, cannabis was associated with counterculture, deviance, and criminality. Education unravels these preconceived notions by presenting a more comprehensive picture of cannabis. It explores its cultural significance, historical context, and the diverse communities that have interacted with the plant throughout history.

Education fosters empathy and understanding by humanizing the cannabis experience. Personal stories, testimonials from patients who have benefited from medical and therapeutic cannabis, and insights into the cultural significance of the plant all contribute to a more compassionate view of cannabis consumers and their needs. This shift in perspective is vital for reducing the stigma that has long hindered medical and adult-use cannabis consumers.

> *"The language we use and don't reveal a great deal about attitudes towards this often misunderstood plant. Education is the key to how perceptions of it change in the future."*
> — Alex Halperin, Editor and Publisher, WeedWeek

Education also plays a pivotal role in influencing cannabis policies. Informed citizens are more likely to advocate for evidence-based, rational cannabis regulations. They understand the potential benefits and risks associated with cannabis, allowing them to make more nuanced policy decisions. This can lead to implementing laws and regulations that better serve the interests of communities and individuals.

The role of education in changing perceptions of cannabis cannot be overstated. It acts as a beacon of light in dispelling the shadows of misinformation, ignorance, and stigma that have clouded the cannabis landscape for far too long. By presenting facts, promoting open discussions, and challenging stereotypes, education paves the way for a more informed, compassionate, and evidence-based approach to cannabis, ultimately shaping a brighter future for all.

CANNABIS CURRICULUM AND PROGRAMS

The recognition of the need for comprehensive cannabis education has spurred the creation of cannabis curricula and educational programs. These initiatives can now be found at numerous colleges and universities. These programs offer a wide-ranging cannabis exploration, covering aspects like the plant's biology, chemistry, historical significance, and cultural context. While they serve to prepare future professionals for careers in the cannabis industry, they also contribute significantly to the broader goal of enhancing cannabis literacy among the general populace.[1]

In response to the changing landscape of cannabis, educational institutions have embarked on a crucial mission: to offer cannabis curricula and programs that extend beyond the traditional bounds of academia. These initiatives aim to equip students and enthusiasts with an in-depth understanding of cannabis, its diverse facets, and its role in contemporary society.

With the industry expanding rapidly, there is a growing demand for skilled professionals who can navigate the complexities of cannabis cultivation, quality control, retail, and research. Graduates of these programs are positioned to contribute to this burgeoning field, whether as botanists, chemists, entrepreneurs, or policymakers.

> *"Cannabis education is essential to eliminate the stigma surrounding it. Providing truthful and well-researched information about its benefits, risks, and uses can help dispel myths and promote informed discussions. It's essential to emphasize responsible medical and adult use and the legal framework surrounding it to promote and appreciate this amazing gift from nature."*
> – Lou Giannotti RPh., Program Director, Cannabis Studies, PIT

Cannabis curricula and programs are not static; they evolve with changes in legislation, scientific discoveries, and societal attitudes. For example, as new cannabis products and derivatives enter the market, these programs adapt to incorporate the latest information, ensuring that students remain at the forefront of cannabis knowledge.

Developing and maintaining cannabis programs is not without its challenges. Institutions must navigate complex legal frameworks, varying by state and country, which can impose restrictions on cannabis-related education. Furthermore, there's a need to balance teaching scientific facts with responsible use and ethical considerations, particularly in regions where cannabis remains illegal.

Cannabis curricula and programs represent a vital step towards empowering individuals with the knowledge and skills needed to engage with cannabis responsibly. Whether by preparing the workforce for the cannabis industry or contributing to broader cannabis literacy, these initiatives are instrumental in shaping a more enlightened and discerning society in which cannabis is understood, appreciated, and demystified.

ADDRESSING STIGMA THROUGH KNOWLEDGE

Stigma remains a significant barrier to sensible cannabis policy and consumption. Education plays a pivotal role in dismantling this stigma. By humanizing cannabis through personal stories, scientific evidence, and historical context, educators can help individuals see beyond the stereotypes and better understand the plant's complex role in society.

> *"The role of educators is not only to teach our students what is true but also to equip them with critical thinking and research skills to be able to evaluate information. With so many sources out there, it is vital for them to know the difference between a scientifically supported statement and a sales pitch."*
> — Ekaterina Sedia, PhD, Cannabis Studies, Stockton University

The stigma surrounding cannabis persists as a formidable obstacle in the journey toward sensible cannabis policies and responsible usage. While attitudes shift, deeply ingrained stereotypes and misconceptions still color many perceptions. However, education is a powerful beacon to illuminate the path towards dismantling this stigma, ultimately fostering a more informed and open-minded society.

One of the most effective ways to address cannabis stigma is by humanizing the plant through personal narratives. These stories can come from various sources, such as patients who have found relief through medical cannabis, individuals who have experienced personal transformation, or those who have been adversely affected by the War On Drugs. Personal accounts put a face on cannabis consumption, showing that it is not confined to stereotypes but is a diverse and multifaceted experience.

Education is not solely about personal stories; it must also incorporate scientific evidence. Educators can counteract misinformation and provide credible, factual information by presenting rigorous research and clinical study results. This evidence can encompass the therapeutic potential of cannabis for various medical conditions, the safety of responsible consumption, and the potential benefits it offers to society.

Understanding the historical and cultural context of cannabis is another essential aspect of addressing stigma. By exploring the plant's rich history in different cultures and its role as an ancient herbal remedy, educators can help individuals appreciate that cannabis has been a part of human life for centuries. This historical perspective can challenge contemporary biases and stereotypes.

Education also involves the direct debunking of myths and misconceptions about cannabis. Common stereotypes, such as the "lazy stoner" or exaggerated claims about its harmfulness, can be systematically addressed with factual information. This process allows individuals to replace fear with knowledge and skepticism with understanding.

> *"If we treat cannabis and its consumers like any other market, we have lost a great opportunity. As educators, we challenge students to consider the emotional impact of a decades-long war on the cannabis community. We help our students to reflect the spirit of the plant itself, to be trauma-informed and ready to receive people with empathy and grace."*
> — Trey Reckling, Director, Academy of Cannabis Science

Through education, individuals can develop empathy and compassion for those who consume cannabis medically or for adult use. Understanding the reasons behind cannabis consumption, the challenges medical patients face, and the plant's cultural significance can lead to more inclusive and supportive attitudes.

Addressing cannabis stigma through knowledge is not a simple task but a necessary one. By humanizing the plant, presenting scientific evidence, providing historical context, debunking myths, and fostering empathy, education becomes a potent antidote to deeply rooted prejudices. As attitudes continue to evolve, the role of education in dismantling stigma remains indispensable in shaping a society that approaches cannabis with enlightened understanding rather than unfounded fear.

CANNABIS LITERACY AS A TOOL FOR RESPONSIBLE CONSUMPTION

Cannabis literacy extends beyond merely comprehending the plant; it's about empowering individuals to use it responsibly. This entails understanding dosage, potential risks, harm reduction strategies, and the prevailing legal framework. Cannabis education provides individuals with the knowledge necessary to make informed choices.

> *"Context is crucial for cannabis education. Our country was besieged by nearly a century of anti-cannabis stigmatization and propaganda, which modern educators and advocates now need to reverse. As a media professional, I get the reward of seeing people's opinions about cannabis shift in real-time and in ways they might not even recognize until they're inspired to action. All change for good begins with education."*
> — Ronit Pinto, Publisher, Honeysuckle Magazine

In a landscape where cannabis is becoming increasingly accessible, ensuring individuals have the knowledge they need to navigate its complexities is paramount. Cannabis-literate individuals are aware of the possible side effects, including short-term impairments in memory and coordination. They understand the importance of moderation – particularly concerning THC-rich products – to mitigate the risk of adverse reactions.[2]

Informed individuals are equipped with tools to reduce risks associated with cannabis consumption. They understand the significance of responsible consumption practices, such as not driving under the influence, avoiding overconsumption, and being mindful of the setting in which they consume it. Harm reduction knowledge can help prevent accidents and negative experiences.

A critical aspect of cannabis literacy is understanding the legal framework surrounding cannabis consumption in their jurisdiction. This includes knowledge of possession limits, legal purchasing age, and specific regulations for medical cannabis patients. Being aware of and adhering to the law ensures that individuals can consume cannabis without facing legal consequences.

Cannabis literacy is not a solitary endeavor but a communal one. Educated individuals often become advocates for responsible consumption within their communities. They share knowledge, promote safety, and openly discuss it. This grassroots advocacy contributes to a culture of responsible cannabis consumption, benefiting society.

As the cannabis landscape evolves, staying informed and up-to-date becomes increasingly essential. Cannabis literacy is a tool that adapts alongside the industry, providing individuals with the knowledge they need to make choices that align with their well-being and values. By fostering cannabis literacy, we can contribute to a more responsible, informed, and safe cannabis culture.

THE EDUCATOR'S DILEMMA: BALANCING SCIENCE AND ADVOCACY

Educators occupy a unique position when it comes to teaching about cannabis. While scientific evidence is often unequivocal on many aspects of the plant, advocacy frequently becomes intertwined with education, particularly in medical cannabis. Educators are tasked with delicately navigating this fine line. They must ensure that they provide information firmly grounded in evidence while acknowledging the real-world impact of cannabis policy on patients and communities. Striking this balance is essential for presenting a well-rounded and objective educational experience.

Science provides the foundation for any discussion on cannabis. Educators must emphasize evidence-based information, drawing from research on the plant's chemistry, pharmacology, and physiological effects. This scientific grounding ensures that students receive accurate and reliable data, enabling them to make informed decisions.

"In many ways, marketing addresses the ongoing need for cannabis education among consumers, patients, professionals, and the general public. Prioritizing well-researched educational content and precise language empowers individuals to make informed choices, share accurate information, and collectively combat the lingering stigma around cannabis, a crucial step toward advancing the regulated industry."

— Beth Waterfall, Executive Director, Elevate Northeast

However, cannabis is not just a scientific subject—it's also a profoundly contentious and politicized one. Educators encounter gray areas where science alone may not suffice. For instance, in the context of medical cannabis, advocacy frequently enters the equation. Patients' lived experiences, anecdotal evidence, and the compassionate consumption of cannabis challenge educators to balance scientific rigor and empathy. They must be equipped to discuss how cannabis policies affect patients, caregivers, and communities, recognizing that these factors often blur the line between objective science and the human experience.

One approach to addressing the educator's dilemma is to foster critical thinking among students. Educators can encourage students to examine scientific evidence critically, questioning sources, methodologies, and potential biases. They can also explore case studies that illustrate the interplay between science and advocacy, encouraging students to form well-rounded perspectives.

"More patients in the US are grappling with chronic illnesses and consuming cannabis to manage their health. Educating healthcare providers fosters a more open attitude toward non-pharmacological treatments, representing progress in altering the perception of cannabis from a substance of abuse to a valuable medical resource."

— Maureen Smyth, RN, Host, Cannabis Public School

Educators should create a classroom environment that encourages open dialogue. This means welcoming diverse perspectives and acknowledging that opinions on cannabis vary widely. Educators must navigate questions of impartiality and transparency. They should disclose any personal biases or affiliations that may influence their teaching. Transparency ensures that students are aware of potential sources of bias and can evaluate information accordingly.

Summary

By fostering critical thinking, promoting open dialogue, and adhering to ethical principles, educators can equip students with the tools they need to navigate the complexities of cannabis knowledge with wisdom and empathy. In doing so, they contribute to a more informed and compassionate society where science and advocacy coexist harmoniously.

The following questions aim to delve into the various aspects of cannabis education, perceptions, responsible consumption, the educator's role, and the transformative power of knowledge in shaping societal attitudes toward cannabis:

- How does education challenge the long-standing stereotypes and misinformation about cannabis, and what role does it play in altering perceptions?
- In what ways does education address the stigma surrounding cannabis, and what strategies are employed to humanize the cannabis experience?
- What are the essential components of cannabis literacy, and how does this knowledge empower individuals to engage in responsible cannabis consumption?
- How do educators navigate the delicate balance between scientific evidence and advocacy when teaching about cannabis, particularly in the context of medical use?

Education is not just a critical component of cannabis policy; it's a transformative force that can shape the future of cannabis. By fostering understanding, erasing stigma, and promoting responsible use, education paves the way for more informed decisions, better policies, and a society where cannabis is approached with knowledge, respect, and compassion.

CHAPTER 17

GLOBAL PERSPECTIVES
AND TERMINOLOGY

CANNABIS LANGUAGE ACROSS BORDERS

The terminology used to describe cannabis varies significantly around the world. Language is a powerful vehicle for communication, and its nuances can differ drastically across borders and cultures. In the context of cannabis, understanding these global perspectives on terminology is paramount, as it can have far-reaching implications for policy, trade, diplomacy, and public perception.

"Whether defining quality standards, labeling requirements, or packaging regulations, a shared language streamlines the exchange of cannabis products across borders, ensuring that consumers receive safe and consistent products and that businesses can operate smoothly in the international market."
— Pawin Charoen-Rajapark, Taratera, Thailand

Language is both a bridge and a barrier in the global cannabis discourse. While it enables communication and collaboration among diverse stakeholders, it can also be a barrier when different terms are misunderstood or have varying connotations. For example, "marijuana" is widely used in North America but is less common in Europe, where "cannabis" is the preferred term. Recognizing these linguistic nuances fosters more transparent communication.

Cultural factors exert a profound influence on how cannabis is described and understood. In regions with a long history of cannabis use, such as parts of Asia and the Middle East, terminology often reflects traditional and medicinal aspects. On the other hand, countries with solid prohibitionist histories may employ pejorative slang terms that carry a negative stigma. This cultural lens underscores the need for a culturally sensitive approach to terminology.

Standardizing cannabis terminology across borders is a complex undertaking. Efforts to create a universally accepted lexicon face challenges due to cultural, historical, and legal differences. For example, while some countries may have embraced terms like "cannabis" for their neutral and scientific connotations, others may resist this shift due to entrenched slang or regulatory frameworks. Striking a balance between standardization and cultural respect is crucial.

Cannabis terminology plays a significant role in international diplomacy, particularly in drug policy and trade discussions. Diplomatic cannabis negotiations often center on the wording of international agreements and treaties. The choice of terminology can influence a country's stance on cannabis-related issues and impact its international relationships. Consequently, diplomats must be acutely aware of the linguistic nuances in these negotiations.

> *"Language forms the foundation of all communication. The choice of phrasing, slang, or words employed can significantly alter the intended connotation and tone of a message. In the context of the Thai language, there exists no single term that encapsulates cannabis as a comprehensive species. Instead, distinct terms are used for marijuana (ganja) and hemp (ganjong). The term 'ganja' inherently carries its own societal stigma, thereby presenting an immediate challenge when combating the stigmatization of cannabis. I prefer to use the English term 'cannabis' in my statements, rather than 'ganja,' when conveying the nature of our operations."*
> — Gaurav Seghal, Co-Founder, Siam Green, Thailand

Fostering international understanding is imperative to navigate this intricate landscape of global cannabis terminology. This involves recognizing linguistic differences and appreciating the historical, cultural, and legal contexts underpinning them. By acknowledging and respecting these diverse perspectives, the global cannabis community can engage in more productive and respectful dialogue, ultimately advancing the responsible and informed use of cannabis worldwide.

The study of global cannabis terminology examines the world's cultural, historical, and political intricacies as they intersect with this ancient and complex plant. Understanding this intersection is essential for anyone involved in the global cannabis conversation, from policymakers and diplomats to educators and advocates. It reminds us that words are not just communication tools but windows into the diverse and nuanced worldviews that shape our understanding of cannabis.

THE INFLUENCE OF CULTURE ON CANNABIS TERMINOLOGY

Cannabis is a plant that knows no borders, yet its terminology often differs dramatically from one region to another. Understanding this linguistic diversity is essential for fostering effective communication and collaboration within the global cannabis community.

The words used to describe cannabis carry cultural significance, reflecting each region's unique historical and social contexts. In addition to formal terminology, the cannabis lexicon is rich with slang and street names. These often vary widely from one region to another and even between different communities within the same country. These colloquialisms highlight the complex relationship between cannabis and the societies that consume or prohibit it. Understanding these linguistic preferences is vital when discussing policy reform and harmonization across borders.[1]

As the legal cannabis industry expands globally, the choice of terminology also influences trade and commerce. Companies seeking to export or import cannabis-related products must navigate the linguistic preferences of different markets. Understanding terminology's cultural and legal nuances can be a strategic advantage for businesses operating in the global cannabis marketplace.

Effective cross-cultural collaboration within the cannabis industry and advocacy movements relies on a shared understanding of terminology. The diversity of words used to describe cannabis should be celebrated and respected as a reflection of the plant's universal appeal and the uniqueness of each culture's relationship. Recognizing and honoring these linguistic differences can promote cooperation and mutual respect among stakeholders worldwide.

Cannabis language across borders is a dynamic and multifaceted aspect of the global cannabis landscape. It is a testament to the plant's ability to transcend geographical boundaries while highlighting the intricate tapestry of human culture and history. As the world grapples with cannabis regulation and policy, acknowledging and appreciating this linguistic diversity is essential for fostering effective communication, breaking down stereotypes, and advancing responsible cannabis consumption globally.

> *"Confusion often arises due to variance in language — be it the language of regulation, legislation, cultivation, production, or the specific terms and definitions employed. With disconnected pockets of the industry functioning independently across the globe, a metaphorical Tower of Babel has emerged, hindering the effective transfer of knowledge, experiences, and best practices between different areas of the industry. Addressing this issue necessitates the establishment of global industry groups that can facilitate the development of a unified language for cannabis, enabling us all to benefit from the rapidly expanding global knowledge base currently being established."*
>
> — Ron Lipsky, Co-Founder, Cannaccess, Thailand

CULTURAL COLLABORATION IN TERMINOLOGY STANDARDIZATION

Culture is pivotal in shaping how people perceive and talk about cannabis. Often called the "cultural chameleon," cannabis adapts to the societies that cultivate and consume it. The influence of culture on cannabis terminology is profound, as it reflects the plant's integration into diverse cultural contexts.

In regions where cannabis has deep historical roots, such as India or Morocco, cultural terminology often reflects its longstanding use. Words like "ganja" or "kif" carry historical and spiritual connotations that extend back centuries. These terms highlight cannabis's role in religious rituals, traditional medicine, and communal gatherings.

The perception of cannabis as either a medicinal, therapeutic, or recreational substance is heavily influenced by cultural norms. In some societies, cannabis has been used as a medicinal herb for centuries, leading to terminology emphasizing its therapeutic properties. Contrastingly, cultures with a history of casual consumption may have a more diverse lexicon featuring words that evoke leisure and social enjoyment.[2]

Culture's impact on cannabis terminology also extends to legal and policy considerations. In regions where cannabis has a strong cultural presence, policymakers may be more inclined to adopt language that recognizes its historical significance. Conversely, areas with less cultural familiarity may prefer more neutral or scientific terminology.

Cannabis terminology is intertwined with cultural identity. For some communities, using traditional terms like "dagga" or "charas" is a way of preserving their cultural heritage. Language choices can be a form of cultural resistance against external influences.

"The cannabis plant has been a part of various traditions and cultures for millennia. Over time, Western cannabis consumers have often misused many of the terms and processes that are held sacred. Charas and hashish are perfect examples. Hashish is derived from the Arabic word for dried herb. In contrast, charas comes from Sanskrit/Hindi origins and translates to freshly hand-rubbed cannabis resin. Despite their distinct meanings, these terms are often interchanged in today's cannabis culture. As the global cannabis industry expands, it is essential to recognize and respect these cultural nuances to prevent further misappropriation and foster an environment of genuine appreciation."

— Maha Haq, Founder, Cannaclub

Navigating the diverse terminology rooted in cultural contexts can be challenging, especially in the context of international collaborations or standardization efforts. It requires a nuanced understanding of the cultural underpinnings of these words to ensure that cross-cultural dialogue is respectful and productive.

Ultimately, the influence of culture on cannabis terminology is a testament to the plant's adaptability and the rich tapestry of human cultural expression. By acknowledging and appreciating these cultural nuances, we can engage in more meaningful and inclusive conversations about cannabis, respecting its multifaceted role in societies worldwide.

In an increasingly interconnected world, the need for standardized cannabis terminology has become evident. International collaboration in terminology standardization is critical to establishing a common language for cannabis, transcending borders and linguistic diversity.

The United Nations, through its various agencies, such as the World Health Organization (WHO) and the Commission on Narcotic Drugs (CND), has been at the forefront of international efforts to standardize cannabis terminology. These organizations recognize that clear and consistent language is essential for global discussions surrounding cannabis policy, trade, and health.

> *"From an international perspective, consistency is key when referring to cannabis. While terms used may differ locally in colloquial – or official – terms, we have to consider cannabis as a global phenomenon and find accurate words (from a scientific perspective), accessible (from a human perspective), and appropriate (from a cultural perspective). While perceptions of these terms may differ between nations, regions, and languages, consensus speaks volumes."*
> – Dave Barton, Co-Founder, Thermidor, United Kingdom

Standardized terminology is crucial for regulatory harmonization, particularly as more countries move toward cannabis legalization and regulation. When countries share standard definitions and language, it becomes easier to harmonize regulations, which is essential for international trade and the prevention of illicit trafficking. This harmonization helps create a level playing field for cannabis businesses and ensures consistent quality and safety standards.[3]

Cannabis research often requires international collaboration due to the complexity and global significance of the plant. Standardized terminology facilitates such collaborations by eliminating language barriers and ensuring researchers from different countries are on the same page when discussing their findings and methodologies. This cooperation accelerates our understanding of cannabis's potential benefits and risks. As nations navigate the complexities of cannabis policy and regulation, standardized terminology will play a central role in shaping the plant's future globally.

"In the global cannabis conversation, language can unite cultures, industries, and communities and go beyond words to encompass diverse perspectives. The shared journey of terms like 'ganja' from India to Thailand and the US exemplifies how common passion brings people together, showcasing how cannabis language can unite for a shared cause."

— Cenk Cetin, CEO, Cannabox, Thailand

ADDRESSING GLOBAL CANNABIS CHALLENGES

One of the most pressing global cannabis challenges lies in drug policy reform. Cannabis policies vary dramatically across countries, from strict prohibition to full legalization. Navigating these disparities requires a shared understanding of cannabis-related terminology. Whether discussing harm reduction, decriminalization, or legalization, having a shared language ensures that international conversations about drug policy reform are productive and meaningful.

Public health concerns related to cannabis are another global challenge. Cannabis consumption for medical and adult-use purposes necessitates a nuanced approach to regulation and education. Using consistent terminology helps in the development of evidence-based public health strategies. For instance, when discussing the health impacts of cannabis, clear language enables international health organizations to communicate effectively, disseminate guidelines, and coordinate research efforts. As the legal cannabis industry expands globally, the need for harmonized regulations becomes increasingly evident. Standardized terminology is essential for international trade and commerce.

Diplomacy plays a critical role in addressing global cannabis challenges. Negotiations often involve drafting international agreements and treaties related to drug control and public health. These agreements rely on precise and universally accepted terminology. Shared language simplifies the process, enabling countries to work together to find common ground and develop mutually beneficial solutions.[4]

Cannabis research is a global endeavor. Researchers worldwide collaborate to advance our understanding of cannabis's effects, potential therapeutic applications, and safety profiles. A common language ensures that research findings are universally understandable, facilitating cross-border collaboration. This collaborative research, in turn, informs evidence-based policy decisions and public health initiatives worldwide.

THE ROLE OF LANGUAGE IN CANNABIS DIPLOMACY

Effective diplomacy is contingent upon a nuanced understanding of how different terms are perceived and employed across borders. Cannabis diplomacy highlights the pivotal role of language and terminology in the international discourse surrounding cannabis-related issues.

One of the central aspects of cannabis diplomacy revolves around drug scheduling on the international stage. Cannabis, classified as a Schedule I substance under the United Nations Single Convention on Narcotic Drugs of 1961, carries significant implications for international drug control policies.

Cannabis diplomacy, therefore, encompasses discussions on how different countries perceive and categorize cannabis products, from medical cannabis to hemp-derived CBD. Consistent terminology aids in negotiating trade agreements and ensures that products meet international compliance standards.

Cannabis diplomacy showcases the intricate interplay between language and international relations in the context of cannabis-related issues. Diplomatic negotiations surrounding drug scheduling, international trade, and cultural perceptions hinge on effectively using clear, universally accepted terminology. By recognizing the power of language and understanding its cultural nuances, diplomats can foster constructive dialogues and work toward mutually beneficial outcomes in global cannabis diplomacy.[5]

Bridging the linguistic divide in cannabis terminology is essential. Understanding how culture, policy, and diplomacy intersect with language helps facilitate more productive global conversations about cannabis. By appreciating and navigating these international perspectives on terminology, individuals and organizations can work together to address the complex and evolving challenges posed by cannabis on the world stage.

Summary

Understanding the nuances of cannabis terminology across borders is a critical step toward fostering inclusive and informed conversations in the global cannabis community. By embracing linguistic diversity and recognizing its impact on culture, policy, and diplomacy, we pave the way for a more interconnected and harmonious approach to navigating the complex landscape of cannabis worldwide.

The following questions provide food for thought to better understanding the factors influencing the evolution of the language surrounding cannabis, global perspectives, and terminology:

- How does cultural influence shape the terminology used for cannabis across different regions, and why is understanding this linguistic diversity crucial for effective communication?
- What role does language play in international diplomacy concerning cannabis, especially in negotiations surrounding drug policy, trade agreements, and international relations?

- Why is standardizing cannabis terminology important, and what challenges exist in achieving a universally accepted lexicon, given the cultural, historical, and legal differences across countries?
- How does the choice of terminology impact legislative considerations and policy reforms in different regions, and what are the implications for the legal cannabis industry as it expands globally?

In an increasingly interconnected world where cannabis has the potential to impact economies, health, and societies, understanding how culture, policy, and diplomacy intersect with language is paramount. By appreciating and navigating these global perspectives on terminology, individuals and organizations can work together to address the complex and evolving challenges posed by cannabis on the world stage. As we strive for a future where cannabis is better understood, regulated, and integrated into society, let language be the bridge that unites us in this endeavor.

CHAPTER 18

LOST IN TRANSLATION

MULTILINGUAL CHALLENGES IN
THE CANNABIS INDUSTRY

In a globalized world where cannabis is gaining recognition and acceptance, the importance of breaking down language barriers cannot be overstated. Multilingual approaches are emerging as crucial tools in normalizing cannabis, enabling diverse communities to engage with this versatile plant.

The cannabis industry operates in an increasingly multilingual landscape. From product labels to medical guidelines, effective communication is essential. This chapter examines the unique challenges posed by language diversity in the cannabis space, highlighting the need for precision and cultural sensitivity in terminology.

> *"Language stands as a prominent hurdle in the Thai cannabis industry today. Since our main clientele is tourists, our budtenders often grapple with foreign slang and euphemisms. In response, we actively leverage social media to enhance our grasp of standard terms and vocabulary. Incorporating scientific and universally accepted terminology greatly facilitates the translation and standardization of communication."*
> — Kajkanit "Gem" Sakdisubha, CEO, Taratera, Thailand

The global cannabis industry has witnessed an unprecedented expansion in recent years, with products and knowledge transcending borders. However, this rapid growth has introduced a complex web of multilingual challenges that demand attention and innovative solutions.

One of the primary challenges is ensuring product labeling complies with the diverse linguistic regulations in different regions. Cannabis companies must navigate intricate linguistic requirements, such as ingredient lists, dosage instructions, and health warnings, which may vary significantly from country to country. Failing to do so can result in regulatory fines, product recalls, and damage to brand reputation. Striking the right balance between concise labeling and multilingual clarity is an ongoing challenge.

The cannabis lexicon is dynamic and constantly evolving, making translation and adaptation complex. Slang terms, cultivar names, and cannabis-related jargon often lack direct equivalents in other languages. Translators must bridge these linguistic gaps and consider cultural sensitivities and connotations. An innocuous term in one language could have negative implications in another.

Beyond linguistic translation, understanding the cultural nuances surrounding cannabis terminology is crucial. Certain words or phrases that seem neutral in one culture can be highly offensive in another. This sensitivity is paramount, especially in cannabis, where historical stigma has shaped perceptions. Recognizing these subtleties is vital for successful cross-cultural communication and avoiding unintended offense.

As cannabis companies look to expand into international markets, language considerations are fundamental to market research and strategy. This includes understanding local dialects, dialectical variations, and regional preferences. It also extends to grasping the cultural significance of cannabis in each region, which can significantly impact branding and marketing.

Patients and consumers worldwide seek access to reliable medical and educational cannabis resources. However, these resources often originate in regions with distinct terminology and cultural contexts. Bridging the language barrier is essential to ensure accurate, accessible information.[1]

The cannabis industry's multilingual challenges are diverse and ever-evolving. Addressing these challenges necessitates a nuanced understanding of language, culture, and regulatory frameworks. By embracing linguistic diversity and investing in effective communication strategies, the global cannabis industry can ensure that it reaches and serves a worldwide audience while adhering to the highest standards of precision, clarity, and cultural sensitivity.

"Uruguay has adopted an unadorned approach to its cannabis industry by labeling a limited offering of three cultivars using the Greek alphabet (Alpha, Beta, and Gamma) to avoid flashy branding. Registered buyers at any of the 38 pharmacies dispensing cannabis can only choose between A, B, or G flower, informed only of the THC content (3-15%) and the state-approved growers."

— Susan Stoneman, CEO, Susation, Uruguay

CULTURAL ADAPTATION

Translating cannabis terminology goes beyond mere linguistic conversion; it involves cultural adaptation. In an increasingly globalized cannabis industry, effective translation and adaptation of cannabis terminology are pivotal for building bridges of understanding among diverse communities and ensuring accurate communication.

Translating cannabis terminology requires more than finding equivalent words in another language. It involves navigating the intricate linguistic nuances that exist in the world of cannabis. For instance, cultivar names often have no direct translation. Translators must consider the meaning of the term and its cultural and historical context in both languages. This ensures that the translated terminology conveys the intended message without losing its essence.

Cannabis culture and traditions vary significantly worldwide. Effective translation involves finding linguistically suitable terms and culturally adapting them. This means understanding how different cultures perceive and relate to cannabis and adjusting the terminology accordingly. For example, "recreational cannabis" may not accurately represent the cultural and legal context of cannabis use in all regions. In some cultures, it might be more appropriate to use a term like "adult-use" cannabis to emphasize responsible consumption or "medical cannabis" to be explicitly consumed by patients.

In the realm of medical cannabis, precision in translation is paramount. Scientific terms related to cannabinoids, terpenes, and medical conditions must be accurately conveyed to ensure proper patient education and healthcare. This demands linguistic expertise and a deep understanding of the scientific concepts involved.

Translating cannabis terminology isn't a one-way process. It involves engaging with diverse communities to understand their preferences and sensitivities. This community-centered approach ensures that the translated language resonates with individual segments and fosters a sense of inclusivity.

Examining real-world examples of successful translation and adaptation efforts can illuminate effective strategies. For instance, bilingual packaging and educational materials are a legal requirement in Canada, where both English and French are official languages. This highlights the importance of linguistic and cultural adaptation for compliance and effective communication.

Translation and adaptation of cannabis terminology are intricate processes that encompass linguistic, cultural, and legal considerations. Effective translation conveys meaning, fosters cross-cultural understanding, respects diverse communities, and ensures compliance with regulations. It is crucial in breaking down language barriers and promoting responsible and informed cannabis consumption globally.

BRIDGING THE COMMUNICATION GAP IN DIVERSE COMMUNITIES

Multilingual communication acknowledges cultural nuances, allowing messages tailored to each community's values and beliefs. In regions with historically negative perceptions of cannabis, language can be used to dispel myths and misinformation. Multilingual educational campaigns can address common misconceptions, such as exaggerated health risks or criminal associations. These campaigns present scientific evidence and testimonials in culturally relevant ways, challenging deeply ingrained biases.[2]

Multilingual communication is a dynamic process that involves community engagement. It goes beyond translation to actively involve community members in shaping messages and strategies. Engaging with diverse communities, organizations, and governments can build trust, gain insights, and effectively tailor their approaches.

Such approaches are pivotal for bridging communication gaps in communities with varying degrees of cannabis acceptance. These approaches respect cultural sensitivities, dispel myths, promote responsible use, ensure legal compliance, and foster community engagement. By harnessing the power of language, diverse communities can navigate the evolving landscape of cannabis with knowledge, respect, and unity.

THE POWER OF MULTILINGUALISM IN CANNABIS EDUCATION

Multilingual educational materials break down language barriers, making critical information accessible to a broader audience. In regions with diverse linguistic communities, individuals who may not be fluent in the dominant language can still access vital information about cannabis. This inclusivity ensures that everyone, regardless of their language proficiency, can learn about cannabis in a way that resonates with them.[3]

> "In our advocacy for cannabis policy reform across various EU countries, we consistently use the term 'modernization.' This term is versatile, fitting nearly any policy proposal, regardless of the jurisdiction's progress in policy reform."
> — Alex Rogers, CEO, International Cannabis Business Conference

The ability to communicate in multiple languages enables messaging that is considerate of the linguistic and cultural contexts of different audiences. Educators can ensure their communications are culturally appropriate and pertinent by conveying information in various languages. Such a customized strategy is essential in conversations about responsible cannabis use, where cultural standards and convictions can shape views.

Cultural norms and values frequently influence attitudes toward cannabis. Educational materials in various languages can include examples, narratives, and references pertinent to particular communities, enhancing relatability. Adopting this strategy strengthens the bond and interaction with the information provided.

Providing education in multiple languages aligns with the values of inclusivity and diversity in cannabis education. It acknowledges the variety of languages spoken within a community and upholds the principle that information about cannabis should be available to everyone, irrespective of their first language. This dedication to inclusive practices supports a fairer and more just method of cannabis education.

Summary

The power of multilingualism in cannabis education cannot be understated. It enhances accessibility, tailors communication, improves comprehension, overcomes stigmatization, incorporates cultural sensitivity, and promotes inclusivity and diversity. Multilingual educational materials empower individuals to make informed decisions about cannabis use, fostering a more informed and engaged society.

The following questions encapsulate the core themes of the chapter, providing food for thought to understand better the factors influencing the evolution of the language surrounding cannabis:

- How do multilingual approaches in the cannabis industry address the intricate challenges of diverse linguistic regulations, especially concerning product labeling and compliance?
- What complexities arise in translating and adapting cannabis terminology beyond linguistic conversions, emphasizing the importance of cultural sensitivity and precision?
- What pivotal role does multilingual communication play in dispelling myths, addressing misconceptions, and promoting responsible cannabis use across cultures with varying degrees of acceptance?

- In what ways does multilingual education in the cannabis space enhance accessibility, improve comprehension, and contribute to overcoming stigmatization, particularly in regions where cannabis has been historically prohibited or stigmatized?

As the cannabis industry continues to expand globally, embracing linguistic diversity is not just an option; it's an imperative. By recognizing the challenges and opportunities of multilingualism, we can ensure that cannabis becomes a plant that transcends borders, cultures, and languages, uniting communities worldwide to pursue responsible and informed consumption.

CHAPTER 19

THE FUTURE OF
THE LANGUAGE OF CANNABIS

REDEFINING THE RHETORIC OF CANNABIS

Language is a powerful tool that shapes our perceptions, attitudes, and world understanding. Nowhere is this more evident than in cannabis, where the language used to describe and discuss the plant has evolved significantly over time. As cannabis legalization gains traction and public opinion shifts, it becomes increasingly important to examine the future of the language of cannabis. This chapter will delve into the nuances and complexities of cannabis language, exploring how it will likely evolve in the coming years.

> *"There are two truths about culture as far as we know: first, the future is not fixed, and second, we each have a hand in shaping it. When it comes to the future of language of cannabis, 'they' don't adopt new terminology or eliminate dangerous slang, it's you who normalizes and dictates what comes next."*
> — Matt Klein, Cultural Theorist, Head of Foresight, Reddit

The ever-changing landscape of cannabis language reflects the broader cultural shifts and evolving perceptions towards the plant. In the past, the terms "cannabis" and "marijuana" have been used interchangeably. Still, with the changing attitudes and a push for more accurate terminology, there has been a growing preference for "cannabis" to encompass the entire plant genus. This shift emphasizes a more scientific and neutral approach and aims to distance ourselves from the racially charged history associated with the term "marijuana."

As cannabis continues to gain acceptance for its medicinal properties, we can anticipate an increased emphasis on medical language and terminology. Terms like "medicinal cannabis" and "therapeutic use" will become more prevalent as the medical community acknowledges and embraces the potential benefits of cannabis in managing various conditions. This shift in language reflects a growing understanding of the plant's medicinal value and seeks to reduce the stigma associated with its use.[1]

The ongoing dialogue around responsible consumption and harm reduction will also shape it. As society becomes more educated about the potential risks and benefits of cannabis, language will play a crucial role in promoting responsible use. Terms such as "moderate use" and "conscious consumption" may gain traction as they encourage a mindful approach to cannabis, emphasizing personal responsibility and well-being.

The future of cannabis language is intricately tied to broader societal shifts in perception and understanding. By embracing accurate, inclusive, and responsible language, we can foster a more informed and progressive dialogue around cannabis. As attitudes evolve, our language must adapt to reflect the values of acceptance, compassion, and a commitment to sharing accurate information. In the following pages, we will explore the various aspects and influences that will shape the language of cannabis in the years to come.

CHANGING PERCEPTIONS AND ATTITUDES

The changing perceptions and attitudes towards the plant will influence the destiny of cannabis terminology. As society becomes more informed about the potential medical benefits of cannabis, we can expect a significant shift in language towards a more positive and science-based approach. The emerging research on the therapeutic properties of cannabis is reshaping our understanding of the plant, and this transformation will undoubtedly impact how we talk about it.

"Cannabis's future language is one of inclusivity, where different voices and perspectives unite harmoniously. It's a language that empowers consumers, enlightens researchers, and guides policymakers toward a more informed, compassionate world."
— Aaron Varney, Co-Founder, Dockside Cannabis

The evolving perceptions of cannabis as a plant with diverse uses beyond its psychoactive properties will contribute to a broader lexicon. The language of cannabis will expand to encompass its industrial applications, such as hemp-derived products used in textiles, construction materials, and sustainable alternatives to traditional resources. As these applications gain recognition, we will see the emergence of terms like "industrial cannabis" or "sustainable hemp," reflecting the versatile nature of the plant and its potential in various industries.

CULTURAL INFLUENCES AND EMERGING TRENDS

The language used within cannabis communities and subcultures is dynamic and ever-evolving, constantly reflecting these groups' unique identities, values, and experiences. As we look to the future, it is crucial to acknowledge the profound impact that cultural influences and emerging trends will have on the language of cannabis.

Conversations about cultivar preferences, consumption methods, and the overall experience of using cannabis will become more commonplace. Terms like "vape pens," "edibles," and "budtenders" have already made their way into everyday vocabulary, and we can anticipate that this linguistic integration will continue to expand.[2]

> "The future of cannabis lies in a shared language that transcends stereotypes and welcomes everyone into the conversation. It's a language that unites consumers, researchers, and policymakers, fostering a common ground for progress. It's essential to cultivate a language that inclusively engages all participants."
> — Kieve Huffman, Founder, Engager Global

In addition to the language used within the cannabis community and mainstream culture, emerging trends will also shape the future discourse surrounding cannabis. Concepts such as "cannabis-infused beverages," "microdosing," and "cannabis tourism" have gained traction in recent years, indicating the growing diversity of cannabis-related experiences. These emerging trends not only contribute to the evolving language of cannabis but also reflect the dynamic nature of the industry as it adapts to changing consumer demands and preferences. By recognizing and embracing these cultural influences and emerging trends, we can gain a deeper understanding of the language of cannabis and its impact on our society.

THE IMPACT OF LEGALIZATION AND POLICY

The terminology employed in regulations and laws plays a pivotal role in shaping public perception and understanding of cannabis. The impact of legalization and policy on the language of cannabis cannot be understated, as these laws lay the foundation for how society views and interacts with the plant.

Clarity and consistency in legal language are essential to ensure effective communication and understanding of the rules governing cannabis. As new jurisdictions legalize cannabis, there is a need for precise and standardized terminology to avoid confusion and ambiguity. The development of clear definitions for key terms such as "cannabis," "marijuana," and "hemp" is crucial to establishing a common understanding among lawmakers, industry stakeholders, and the public. We see this now taking root with "adult use" versus "recreational," for example. This clarity in language will facilitate compliance and enforcement efforts and provide a solid framework for responsible and regulated cannabis consumption.

In the past, prohibitionist rhetoric and stigmatizing terminology have contributed to the negative portrayal of cannabis. However, as legalization gains momentum, there is an opportunity to shift the narrative and employ more neutral, informative, and destigmatizing language. By using language that reflects the scientific understanding of cannabis and emphasizes its potential benefits, policymakers can contribute to the normalization and acceptance of cannabis within society.[3]

It is also essential to recognize that the language of cannabis policy extends beyond the terms used in the laws themselves. Public campaigns, educational materials, and public health initiatives all shape the language and discourse surrounding cannabis. These efforts can help dispel myths, provide accurate information, and promote responsible use. By employing inclusive, non-judgmental, and evidence-based language, policymakers can foster a more informed and balanced conversation about cannabis.

"Cannabis terminology is crucial for both consumers and non-consumers alike. With more canna-curious individuals than active consumers, alienating slang could close minds to the potential benefits and normalization of cannabis. Inclusive language is essential in encouraging exploration and acceptance."

— Lara Fordis, Chief Insights Officer, Fordis Consulting

NAVIGATING EUPHEMISMS AND SLANG

While euphemisms and slang can contribute to the evolving language of cannabis, it is essential to approach them cautiously. Euphemisms and slang terms have long played a role in shaping the lexicon of cannabis, creating a unique subculture and fostering a sense of community among enthusiasts. However, as we strive for a more inclusive and respectful language surrounding cannabis, it is crucial to navigate these terms thoughtfully.

Euphemisms and slang terms can be both empowering and limiting. On one hand, they can provide a means of self-expression, allowing individuals to connect and communicate within their cultural and social circles. Slang terms like "ganja," "bud," or "herb" have become familiar and endearing to many cannabis enthusiasts, reflecting a sense of camaraderie and shared experiences. These terms can contribute to a positive and affirming cannabis culture.

On the other hand, euphemisms and slang can perpetuate stereotypes and reinforce negative perceptions of cannabis. Terms like "boof," "dope," or "pot" have been associated with criminality and stigmatization. While some may embrace these terms as a form of reclaiming, it is essential to recognize that they can have harmful implications. Such language may inadvertently reinforce the outdated and harmful notions of cannabis as a dangerous substance. Balancing honoring cultural expressions and avoiding derogatory or misleading language is crucial.

In shaping a more inclusive and respectful language surrounding cannabis, we must challenge ourselves to find alternative, more accurate, nuanced, and inclusive ways of expression. It is essential to consider the impact of our words and the perceptions they may create. By adopting language that reflects the diverse range of experiences and perspectives within the cannabis community, we can foster a sense of belonging and respect for all individuals, irrespective of their relationship with cannabis.

> *"As we reimagine the language of cannabis, we're building bridges between communities, from those seeking wellness to scientists advancing our understanding. It's a linguistic evolution that reflects our collective journey toward normalization."*
> — Kristin L. Jordan, Esq., CEO, Park Jordan

As cannabis moves further into mainstream acceptance, there is an opportunity to reshape the language and discourse surrounding the plant. By embracing terms rooted in scientific understanding and highlighting the potential benefits and therapeutic applications of cannabis, we can contribute to the destigmatization and normalization of its use. Terms such as "medicinal cannabis," "therapeutic use," or "wellness applications" can help shift the narrative, emphasizing the positive aspects of cannabis and promoting a more informed and evidence-based conversation. It is our responsibility to challenge harmful language, honor cultural expressions, and strive for a language that accurately reflects the complexities and potential of the plant.[4]

PROMOTING EDUCATION AND AWARENESS

Education and awareness will play a crucial role in shaping the future language of cannabis. As society continues to evolve its understanding of cannabis, we must provide accurate and reliable information to combat misinformation and challenge existing biases. Doing so can contribute to a more informed and nuanced conversation.

Collaboration among various stakeholders is crucial to promote education and awareness effectively. This includes government agencies, healthcare professionals, educators, and community organizations.

By working together, we can develop comprehensive educational campaigns, conduct research, and provide resources that promote responsible cannabis consumption and language. By providing accurate information about responsible consumption practices, harm reduction strategies, and potential side effects, we can empower individuals to make informed choices regarding cannabis use. This includes promoting messages about responsible use, such as avoiding driving under the influence, using cannabis in moderation, and understanding the potential impact on mental health.

"With the increasing normalization of cannabis, there's a concerted effort to establish clear terms and definitions, aiding new consumers in comprehending cannabis varieties that align best with their needs and preferences."
— Matt Jackson, Cannabis Journalist, Consultant

Summary

The future of the language of cannabis is a dynamic and evolving landscape, reflecting the shifting perceptions, attitudes, and cultural influences surrounding the plant. As cannabis continues its journey toward broader acceptance and legalization, several key factors will shape the language we use to discuss it.

Cultural influences and emerging trends within cannabis subcultures and mainstream culture will also significantly shape the language. The language can adapt and expand as new experiences and consumption methods emerge to reflect these changes.

Legalization and policy will profoundly impact the language of cannabis, as clear and standardized terminology is essential for effective regulation and compliance. Policymakers can employ inclusive, neutral, and science-based language, contributing to the normalization of cannabis within society.

Promoting education and awareness is a critical component of shaping the future language of cannabis. Providing evidence-based information, dispelling myths, and encouraging responsible language use will empower individuals to make informed decisions about cannabis while fostering a more informed and nuanced conversation.

The following questions encapsulate the core themes of the chapter, providing food for thought to understand better the factors influencing the evolution of the language surrounding cannabis:

- What role does medical acceptance play in shaping the future language of cannabis, and how might terms like "medicinal cannabis" and "therapeutic use" contribute to altering societal attitudes toward cannabis?
- How do cultural influences and emerging trends within cannabis subcultures and mainstream culture impact the evolving language surrounding cannabis, and how might this language continue to adapt?
- How do legalization and policy contribute to the language of cannabis, and why is clear and standardized terminology crucial in shaping public perception and understanding?
- What are the challenges and benefits of navigating euphemisms and slang when discussing cannabis, and how can a balanced approach contribute to a more inclusive and respectful language?

As we look ahead, the language of cannabis is poised to evolve further, reflecting our collective journey toward a more informed, accepting, and responsible approach to this remarkable plant. By embracing this evolution and engaging in thoughtful discourse, we can contribute to a language that accurately represents the complexities and potential of cannabis in the modern world.

CHAPTER 20

THE HIGH ROAD

PRESSING ISSUES

Public health stood as the weapon of choice in the early days of the War on Drugs. The nation's first Drug Czar, appointed by President Richard Nixon, championed a system of clinics offering counseling and social services. Most of the drug control budget was allocated to these initiatives, with only a minority directed towards law enforcement. Regrettably, this moment was fleeting as Nixon, seeking to appear tough on crime amidst controversy, shifted the focus to the criminal justice approach. Subsequently, police and prison budgets soared while health, medicine, and social services languished.

> *"Turning over a new leaf for the next generation includes using scientific terminology and performing genetic research. This taxonomy debate is as endless as the studies yet to be conducted. The cannabis vs. marijuana question is among the many topics that need further discussion and understanding as the industry matures."*
> — Jeff Jones, Board Member, Oaksterdam University

In 2021, the Office of National Drug Control Policy (ONDCP) began allocating slightly more funds to treatment and prevention than law enforcement and interdiction, marking a significant shift. The Department of Health and Human Services now grants waivers to states seeking to activate Medicaid for inmates before their release, recognizing the importance of continuity of care. Additionally, the Labor Department is enforcing laws mandating health insurance providers to cover addiction treatment on par with other medical services. These developments signify a positive trajectory but require continued efforts.[1]

Insufficient programs and a lack of trained medical professionals hinder effective treatment for substance use disorders. The criminal justice system often decides who receives care, resulting in suboptimal outcomes. When waitlists for programs become lengthy, individuals with court-ordered treatment jump ahead, leading to a limited understanding of addiction among judges and probation officers, resulting in a punitive rather than therapeutic approach.

Past failures of leading public health agencies to prevent or adequately respond to the opioid epidemic highlight the need for unbiased evaluation and learning from experiences. As funds from opioid settlements and federal resources are deployed and harm reduction programs are initiated, it is imperative that agencies like the Centers for Disease Control and Prevention (CDC) impartially study the effectiveness of different approaches. Evidence-based practices must be at the forefront of responding to this crisis, guiding future policies and interventions.[2]

> "Embracing the future language of cannabis is not just an evolution, but a revolution. By employing precise scientific language, we actively pave the way for a dialogue that transcends outdated and misinformed stereotypes. The discourse on 'cannabis vs. marijuana' is a crucial step in unraveling the plant's potential, fostering collaboration between stakeholders, and ensuring a future where informed choices drive this industry forward."
> — Michael Mejer, Founder, Green Lane Communication

While the nation's leaders are responsible for driving meaningful change, the public must also confront the prejudices perpetuated by the War On Drugs. Recognizing that individuals who use drugs are integral members of our communities and deserving of compassion and care is essential. Simultaneously, understanding the concerns of non-drug users, such as the need for clean streets and safe neighborhoods, is crucial. These goals are not mutually exclusive but somewhat interconnected. To make progress, lawmakers and officials must lead, shaping policies that balance compassion, public health, and community well-being.

ILLUMINATING THE PATH FORWARD

Reversing the failures and hypocrisies of cannabis prohibition and the broader War On Drugs requires a collective effort grounded in compassion, evidence-based approaches, and effective leadership. By restoring public health as the guiding principle of drug policy, revising outdated laws, investing in treatment, addressing root causes, building a comprehensive system, and fostering an environment of understanding, we can create a brighter future. It is a future where individuals with substance-use disorders receive the care they need, communities thrive with support and resources, and drug policy reflects a commitment to public health and social justice. Together, we can move beyond the legacy of the War On Drugs towards a more compassionate and practical approach that genuinely serves the well-being of our society.

The debate surrounding cannabis legalization is not simply about the plant itself but its impact on different groups. While some groups see legalization as an opportunity for economic growth and individual freedom, others fear it will lead to more harm than good. However, there is a need for a balanced approach that considers all stakeholders' concerns.[3]

> *"Opponents and proponents of cannabis have shrouded the plant in weighted language, denying it the ability to speak for itself. Objective terminology—boring and direct—frees cannabis to be explored and exploited for its many benefits. Objective terminology is the tool of educated and constructive cannabis discussion, negating unjust stigmatization through facts and the scientific method."*
> — Mendel Menachem, Co-Founder, High Thailand

The current state of cannabis legalization in the United States is a patchwork of laws and regulations that vary from state to state. While some states have legalized cannabis for medicinal and adult use, others have only legalized it for medicinal use, and some still criminalize it entirely. This inconsistency has created a system that is not only confusing but also unfair, with some individuals and communities benefiting more than others.

To bridge this gap, there needs to be a comprehensive approach to cannabis legalization at the federal level. This approach should address the economic, social, and legal impacts of cannabis legalization and the historical injustices perpetuated through the War On Drugs.

Legalizing cannabis must benefit everyone, not just a select few. This means creating a framework that encourages entrepreneurship and economic growth while ensuring marginalized communities can access the same opportunities. One way to do this is by setting aside a portion of cannabis tax revenue for initiatives that benefit these communities, such as job training, education, and healthcare.

It must be balanced by comprehensive social programs that address the harms caused by the War On Drugs. This includes expunging criminal records for non-violent cannabis offenses and providing resources for those disproportionately impacted by drug enforcement policies. In addition, programs that offer treatment and support for individuals struggling with substance abuse should be expanded and made more accessible.

It should be accompanied by strong regulations that prioritize public health and safety. This includes strict labeling requirements, testing standards, and regulations around advertising and marketing. It also means ensuring that cannabis products are not accessible to minors and that individuals who are under the influence of cannabis are not driving or engaging in other risky behaviors.[4]

It is essential to recognize that cannabis legalization is not a silver bullet that will solve our societal problems. However, it can catalyze change by creating new economic opportunities, providing relief for individuals suffering from chronic conditions, and reducing the burden on our criminal justice system.

"The language that surrounds cannabis now comes from the legacy market. This will fade as cannabis supplants itself as a mainstream ingredient in the health & wellness space."
— Brandon Bobart, Founder, Pisgah Peaks Ventures

It is also important to acknowledge that the legalization of cannabis is just one step in a larger movement toward ending the War On Drugs and promoting social justice. We must continue to address the underlying causes of drug abuse and addiction, including poverty, mental health issues, and trauma. Taking a holistic approach to drug policy can create a more just and equitable society for all.

The goal of cannabis legalization should be to create a fair and equitable system for all Americans. By implementing policies and regulations that prioritize social justice, public health, and economic opportunity, we can build a cannabis industry that benefits everyone and rectifies the wrongs of the past.

ONWARD & UPWARD

In our journey through the complex landscape of cannabis, we have encountered a multitude of competing narratives, misleading information, and historical falsehoods that have clouded our understanding of a remarkable plant. Throughout this book, I have endeavored to shed light on the truth, to separate fact from fiction, and to challenge the stigmas and misconceptions that have plagued cannabis for far too long.

It is essential to acknowledge that change takes time. Over the years, societal perceptions have evolved, scientific research has advanced, and the voices advocating for cannabis reform have grown louder. We have witnessed significant strides towards legalization and regulation as more and more states and countries embrace the potential of cannabis for medicinal and adult use. These developments reflect a shifting paradigm that recognizes the plant's intrinsic value and potential to improve lives.

As we look ahead, we can envision a future where cannabis is fully integrated into our society and treated with the same respect and understanding as any other natural substance. We see a world where individuals can access reliable information about cannabis, empowering them to make informed decisions based on scientific evidence and personal choice. This future is where the stigma surrounding cannabis dissipates, replaced by acceptance and appreciation for its diverse applications.

The path forward involves education and awareness. It is crucial to continue dismantling the webs of misinformation and unfounded fears woven around cannabis. By engaging in open dialogue, promoting accurate research, and sharing personal experiences, we can dispel the myths and foster a more enlightened perspective.

Scientific exploration must remain at the forefront. As we delve deeper into the complexities of cannabis, its various cannabinoids, and their potential therapeutic benefits, we unlock new possibilities for medical breakthroughs and innovative treatments. Rigorous research and clinical trials will pave the way for evidence-based medicine, ensuring that cannabis is utilized safely and effectively to address various health conditions.

> *"As cannabis brands continue to transition into consumer-packaged goods, the vernacular will evolve from plant derivatives (indica/sativa/hybrid) to consumer-centric effects (rise/rest/refresh). This linguistic shift aligns cannabis more closely with mainstream pharmaceutical and wellness products, paving the way for its innovative integration into everyday wellness."*
> — Jason Erkes, Chief Communications Officer, Cresco Labs

The cannabis industry has a vital role to play. The industry can foster trust and credibility by embracing responsible practices, ensuring product quality and consistency, and prioritizing consumer safety. As legalization expands, regulatory frameworks will continue to evolve, striking a balance between safeguarding public health and enabling economic growth. Collaboration between policymakers, scientists, and industry professionals will be vital in shaping a sustainable and equitable cannabis landscape.

Reflecting on our journey through the twists and turns of cannabis history, it becomes clear that the path forward is bright with potential. It is a future where the barriers erected by misinformation and prejudice crumble, replaced by knowledge and acceptance. I envision a society where cannabis is embraced for its versatility, celebrated for its therapeutic properties, and utilized responsibly.

The collective efforts of advocates, researchers, policymakers, and individuals like us will continue to pave the way toward a more enlightened understanding of cannabis. Together, we can navigate the complexities, clarify the uncertainties, and build a future where cannabis takes its rightful place as a valuable asset in our communities.

Ultimately, the cannabis versus marijuana debate is not just about a plant and the words we use to describe it but about the society we want to live and exist in. Is it rooted in fear, misinformation, and punishment or based on science, empathy, and equity?

The choice is ours.

***

GLOSSARY OF TERMS

Adult Use

Definition: The legal use of cannabis products by individuals of legal adult age, typically 21 or older, for recreational purposes without the need for medical justification.

The term "Adult Use," in relation to cannabis, refers to the legal use of cannabis products by individuals who are of legal adult age, typically 21 years or older in many regions, for recreational purposes. Unlike medical cannabis, which is used for therapeutic purposes and often requires a prescription or medical recommendation, adult-use cannabis is available for purchase and consumption by adults without the need for medical justification.

Black Market

Definition: The illegal sale and distribution of cannabis products outside government-regulated systems, operating in violation of legal standards for the production, distribution, and sale of cannabis.

The term "Black Market," when related to cannabis, refers to the illegal sale and distribution of cannabis products outside of government-sanctioned channels. This market operates in violation of laws regulating the production, distribution, and sale of cannabis. It often exists in places where cannabis remains illegal or in regions with legal markets but strict regulatory frameworks, leading to a continued demand for illegal sources.

Note: More recently, the term "black market" is frowned upon, has many implications, and can be offensive to many.

Boof

Definition: Slang for low-quality or poorly grown cannabis, characterized by inferior potency, flavor, aroma, or experience, often due to substandard cultivation or preservation practices.

The term "Boof" in relation to cannabis is slang, often used derogatorily to refer to low-quality or poorly grown cannabis. It implies that the cannabis in question is inferior in terms of potency, flavor, aroma, or overall experience. The term can be used to describe cannabis that is not effective or satisfying for the user, possibly due to poor cultivation practices, improper curing, or being old and stale.

Cannabinoids

Definition: A class of chemical compounds that act on cannabinoid receptors, including those naturally occurring in cannabis, synthetic variants, and endocannabinoids produced within the body, involved in various physiological processes.

The term "Cannabinoids" refers to a class of diverse chemical compounds that act on cannabinoid receptors in cells, altering neurotransmitter release in the brain. While these compounds are most famously associated with the cannabis plant, where they naturally occur, cannabinoids can also refer to a variety of compounds that have similar effects, including synthetic cannabinoids and endocannabinoids produced within the body. These substances interact with the endocannabinoid system, playing a role in various physiological processes, including appetite, pain sensation, mood, and memory.

Cannabis

Definition: A genus of flowering plants in the Cannabaceae family, known for psychoactive and medicinal properties, used for recreational and medicinal purposes in various forms.

The term "Cannabis" refers to a genus of flowering plants in the family Cannabaceae, which includes several species commonly known as marijuana or hemp. These plants are known for their psychoactive and medicinal properties, primarily due to compounds such as Δ9-tetrahydrocannabinol (THC) and cannabidiol (CBD), among others. Cannabis is used for various purposes, including adult and medicinal uses, and comes in several forms, such as dried flowers, concentrates, edibles, and more.

The term "cannabis" refers to any plant in the cannabis genus, including plants grown for their resinous flowers or industrial uses such as paper, fabric, food, lotions, plastics, and building materials. Cannabis taxonomy is not settled. While the genus *Cannabis* L is generally agreed upon in scientific communities, species and subspecies are not as clearly defined.

Legally, it is the overall content of the psychotropic cannabinoid Δ9-tetrahydrocannabinol (THC) that distinguishes "hemp" from "marijuana." Although the distinction is arbitrary and confuses traditional understandings of cannabis varieties, in the United States, plants that contain less than 0.3% THC are legally considered "hemp," and those that contain greater than 0.3% THC are considered "marijuana" or "cannabis." This arbitrary threshold to distinguish "hemp" from "marijuana' and 'cannabis" ranges from 0.3% to 1% worldwide.

Chemotype

Definition: A classification of cannabis plants based on their chemical profile, particularly the ratio of cannabinoids and terpenes, which influences the plant's effects, flavors, and medicinal properties.

The term "Chemotype" in the context of cannabis refers to the distinct chemical profile or the ratio of various cannabinoids (like THC and CBD) and terpenes present in a particular cannabis plant or strain. Different chemotypes in cannabis result in varying effects, flavors, and medicinal properties, making them significant for both adult consumers and medical patients.

Chemovar

Definition: A specific variety or strain of the cannabis plant categorized by its unique chemical composition, particularly the profiles of cannabinoids and terpenes, which determine its effects and potential medical applications.

The term "Chemovar," often used in the context of cannabis, refers to a specific variety or strain of the cannabis plant that is categorized based on its chemical composition. This term is used to describe the different profiles of cannabinoids (like THC and CBD) and terpenes in various cannabis cultivars. Chemovars are important in understanding the diverse effects and potential medical uses of different cannabis cultivars.

Counterculture

Definition: A social movement or subculture that challenges mainstream norms, particularly in the use and perception of cannabis, often associated with the advocacy and widespread use of cannabis in opposition to prevailing attitudes and laws.

The term "counterculture" in relation to cannabis refers to a social movement or subculture that embraces and promotes values and lifestyles that are in opposition to or significantly different from the mainstream culture, especially regarding the use and perception of cannabis. During the 1960s and 1970s, the counterculture movement was strongly associated with the widespread use and advocacy of cannabis, challenging the prevailing attitudes and laws against it. This movement played a significant role in shifting public opinion and policy towards a more tolerant and accepting view of cannabis.

Cultivar

Definition: A plant variety of cannabis that has been selectively bred for specific characteristics like appearance, flavor, effects, and medicinal properties and has been stabilized through cultivation techniques.

The term "Cultivar," in relation to cannabis, refers to a plant variety produced in cultivation by selective breeding. In the context of cannabis, a cultivar is a specific plant variety with distinct characteristics, such as its appearance, flavor, psychoactive effects, and medicinal properties, which have been selected and stabilized over time through breeding and cultivation techniques.

Decontrol

Definition: The process of removing cannabis from strict government controls and regulations, allowing for its production, distribution, sale, and use to be regulated more like common goods, reflecting a change in legal and social attitudes towards the plant.

The term "Decontrol," in relation to cannabis, refers to the process of removing cannabis from government-imposed controls and regulations, particularly those related to its classification as a controlled substance. This involves lifting restrictions on the production, distribution, sale, and use of cannabis, allowing it to be regulated more like common goods rather than a tightly controlled substance. Decontrolling cannabis often implies a significant shift in legal and social attitudes towards the plant, recognizing its safety and utility and removing it from the ambit of strict drug enforcement policies.

Decriminalize

Definition: The process of reducing or eliminating criminal penalties for the possession, use, or non-violent activities related to cannabis, often resulting in civil penalties rather than criminal charges, reflecting a shift towards harm reduction.

The term "Decriminalize," in relation to cannabis, refers to the reduction or elimination of criminal penalties associated with the possession, use, or non-violent activities related to cannabis. Decriminalization does not necessarily mean that cannabis becomes legal but rather that offenses are treated more like minor infractions rather than criminal acts, often resulting in fines or civil penalties instead of criminal charges. This approach represents a shift in how the law treats cannabis users and small-scale possession, focusing more on harm reduction and less on punitive measures.

Deschedule

Definition: The process of removing cannabis from a government's list of controlled substances, changing its classification from a drug with high abuse potential and no accepted medical use, which can lead to changes in legal regulation and use.

The term "Deschedule," when related to cannabis, refers to the act of removing cannabis from the list of controlled substances in a jurisdiction's drug scheduling system. This action signifies that cannabis is no longer classified as a drug with a high potential for abuse and no accepted medical use. Descheduling cannabis effectively changes its legal status, potentially paving the way for legal regulation and use, and reflects a significant shift in the perception of its safety and utility.

Destigmatization

Definition: The process of removing negative perceptions and social stigma surrounding cannabis use, shifting public attitudes from viewing it as harmful to recognizing its potential benefits and accepting its societal use.

The term "Destigmatization" in relation to cannabis refers to the process of removing the negative perceptions and social stigma associated with cannabis use. This involves changing public attitudes and beliefs, often from viewing cannabis as a harmful and illicit substance to understanding its potential therapeutic benefits and accepting its use in society. Destigmatization is a crucial step in the reform of cannabis laws and policies, leading to increased acceptance and normalization of cannabis for both medicinal and recreational purposes.

Ensemble Effect

Definition: A concept similar to the Entourage Effect, emphasizing that the combination of various compounds in cannabis, like cannabinoids and terpenes, produces a synergistic effect different and often more effective than their individual effects, highlighting the benefits of the whole plant.

The term "Ensemble Effect" in relation to cannabis is similar to the more commonly known "Entourage Effect." It refers to the concept that the various compounds in cannabis, such as cannabinoids, terpenes, and flavonoids, work together synergistically to produce a combined effect that is different and often more effective than the sum of their individual effects. This theory suggests that consuming the whole cannabis plant, with its full spectrum of compounds, is more beneficial than consuming isolated compounds alone. The Ensemble Effect emphasizes the importance of the complex interactions between the multiple components in cannabis and how they influence the plant's overall therapeutic and psychoactive properties.

Entourage Effect

Definition: A theory that compounds in cannabis, such as cannabinoids and terpenes, interact synergistically to produce a combined effect greater than their individual effects, suggesting the whole plant's therapeutic impact is more effective than isolated compounds.

The term "Entourage Effect" in relation to cannabis refers to the theory that the various compounds in cannabis (such as cannabinoids and terpenes) work together synergistically to produce a combined effect that is greater than the sum of their individual effects. This concept suggests that the therapeutic impact of the whole cannabis plant is more effective than isolated compounds, like THC or CBD alone. The entourage effect is a critical focus in understanding the complexity of cannabis and its various medical and recreational effects.

Expunge

Definition: The legal process of erasing or removing prior convictions or records associated with cannabis-related offenses, relieving individuals with previous convictions due to changes in cannabis laws.

The term "Expunge" in relation to cannabis refers to the legal process of erasing or removing prior convictions or records related to the possession, use, or sale of cannabis. This process aims to provide relief to individuals who have been previously convicted of cannabis-related offenses, especially in cases where cannabis laws have been reformed or decriminalized. It allows for the clearing of one's criminal record, helping individuals overcome the social and legal consequences of past cannabis convictions.

Genotype

Definition: The genetic makeup of a cannabis plant, encompassing all its genes and DNA sequences that dictate its inherent characteristics, including growth patterns, physical traits, and potential for producing various cannabinoids and terpenes.

The term "Genotype" in relation to cannabis refers to the genetic makeup or the inherited genetic code of a cannabis plant. This includes all the genes and DNA sequences that determine the plant's various potential characteristics, such as its growth pattern, size, resilience to pests and diseases, and potential for cannabinoid and terpene production.

Hemp

Definition: A variety of the Cannabis sativa plant grown primarily for industrial purposes, with low THC and high CBD content, used in producing various products like textiles, paper, and building materials.

The term "Hemp" in relation to cannabis refers to varieties of the Cannabis sativa plant species that are grown specifically for industrial uses of its derived products. Hemp is characterized by having lower concentrations of THC (tetrahydrocannabinol) and higher concentrations of CBD (cannabidiol), making it non-psychoactive. It is used for various products, including textiles, food, paper, body care products, and building materials.

Although "cannabis" and "hemp" are regulated separately, hemp is, in fact, also cannabis. Traditionally, plants referred to as "hemp" or "industrial hemp" were bred to harvest their seeds and stalks, which can be manufactured into a long list of byproducts. Plants bred for their leaves and resinous flowers, specifically the density of therapeutic compounds they contain, have traditionally been referred to as "marijuana." Legally, it is the overall content of the psychotropic cannabinoid (THC) that distinguishes "hemp" from "marijuana." Although the distinction is arbitrary and confuses traditional understandings of cannabis varieties, plants that contain less than 0.3% THC are legally considered "hemp" in the United States, and those that contain greater than 0.3% THC are legally considered "marijuana" or "cannabis."

Indica
Definition: A type of Cannabis sativa plant characterized by broad leaves, short stature, and a faster growth cycle, commonly associated with – whether true or not – relaxing and sedative effects, often used to alleviate anxiety and aid sleep.

The term "Indica," in the context of cannabis, refers to one of the primary types of the Cannabis sativa plant, known for its broad leaves, short stature, and typically faster growth cycle compared to Cannabis sativa (the species name is the same as the genus, but they represent different types).

Legacy Market
Definition: The unregulated, often underground market for cannabis that existed prior to its legalization and regulation, comprising traditional growers, sellers, and advocates who operated outside legal channels.

The term "Legacy Market" in the context of cannabis refers to the original, unregulated cannabis market that existed before the legalization and regulation of cannabis in various jurisdictions. This term often encompasses the traditional, underground market where cannabis was sold and distributed outside legal channels. It recognizes the historical and ongoing contributions of original cannabis growers, sellers, and advocates who operated in a time when cannabis was largely illegal.

Loud
Definition: Slang for high-quality cannabis characterized by a strong, pungent aroma, indicating potency and superior cultivation and curing, used to express its exceptional quality and desirability.

The term "Loud," in relation to cannabis, is slang used to describe high-quality cannabis that has a strong, pungent aroma. It implies that the cannabis is potent and has been well-grown and adequately cured, often indicative of its effectiveness and desirability. The term is used colloquially to express the exceptional quality of cannabis, particularly in terms of its smell and overall sensory experience.

Legal Market

Definition: A cannabis market that operates under the legal frameworks established by governments in regions where cannabis has been legalized, encompassing authorized cultivation, production, distribution, sale, and use, subject to regulation and taxation.

The term "Legal Market" in relation to cannabis refers to the regulated market for cannabis that operates under the laws and regulations established by governments where cannabis has been legalized. This market includes the authorized cultivation, production, distribution, sale, and use of cannabis products in compliance with specific legal frameworks. The legal market is distinct from the black market or legacy market as it functions within the bounds of legal statutes and is typically subject to government oversight and taxation.

Marijuana (also Marihuana)

Definition: The dried leaves, flowers, stems, and seeds of Cannabis sativa or Cannabis indica plants, containing psychoactive compounds like THC, are used for recreational and medicinal purposes.

The term "Marijuana" refers to the dried leaves, flowers, stems, and seeds from the Cannabis sativa or Cannabis indica plant, which contain psychoactive compounds like tetrahydrocannabinol (THC). Marijuana is used for both recreational and medicinal purposes due to its psychoactive and therapeutic effects. The term is often used interchangeably with cannabis, though some prefer to use "cannabis" due to "marijuana" having historical connotations associated with the early 20th-century prohibition campaign in the United States.

Medical

Definition: The use of cannabis and its components, like THC and CBD, for therapeutic purposes to treat symptoms of various medical conditions, often prescribed by healthcare professionals and regulated differently from recreational cannabis.

The term "Medical," when related to cannabis, refers to the use of cannabis and its constituents, such as THC and CBD, for therapeutic purposes. Medical cannabis is used to treat symptoms of various medical conditions, such as chronic pain, nausea, epilepsy, and others. A healthcare professional typically prescribes it and may be subject to different regulations than recreational cannabis.

Medicinal

Definition: The use of cannabis and its active components for health and healing purposes, often prescribed to treat symptoms of various medical conditions, differing from recreational cannabis in legality, concentration, and administration.

The term "Medicinal," in relation to cannabis, refers to the use of the cannabis plant and its active compounds, such as THC and CBD, for health and healing purposes. Medicinal cannabis is utilized to alleviate symptoms of various medical conditions, ranging from chronic pain and epilepsy to glaucoma and nausea caused by chemotherapy. Healthcare professionals often prescribe it, and it may differ from recreational cannabis in terms of legality, concentration, and mode of administration.

The MORE Act

The MORE Act stands for the Marijuana Opportunity Reinvestment and Expungement Act. This piece of legislation aims to decriminalize marijuana at the federal level. Some of the key provisions of the MORE Act include:

- Removing marijuana from the list of controlled substances under the Controlled Substances Act, which would effectively end federal criminalization of cannabis.

- Eliminating criminal penalties for individuals who manufacture, distribute, or possess marijuana.
- Replacing statutory references from "marijuana" to "cannabis" to align with current nomenclature.
- Creating a trust fund to support various programs and services for individuals and businesses in communities impacted by the war on drugs.
- Imposing an excise tax on cannabis products produced in or imported into the U.S. and an occupational tax on cannabis production facilities and export warehouses.
- Making Small Business Administration loans and services available to legitimate cannabis-related businesses or service providers.
- Prohibiting the denial of federal public benefits or immigration benefits due to cannabis-related conduct or convictions.
- Establishing a process to expunge convictions and conduct sentencing review hearings related to federal cannabis offenses.
- Directing the Government Accountability Office and other agencies to study the societal impact of cannabis legalization on aspects such as the workplace, traffic safety, and education.

Note: I can't help but call out the irony in the name of the Act – Marijuana Opportunity Reinvestment and Expungement Act – as one of its objectives is literally to "Replace statutory references from "marijuana" to "cannabis" to align with current nomenclature." Perhaps it should be renamed the CORE Act – Cannabis Opportunity Reinvestment and Expungement Act.

Phenotype

Definition: The observable physical and biochemical characteristics of a cannabis plant, determined by the interaction of its genetic makeup with environmental factors, including traits like plant height, leaf shape, and potency.

The term "Phenotype" in relation to cannabis refers to the observable physical characteristics and traits of a cannabis plant, which result from the interaction between its genetic makeup (genotype) and the environment. This includes traits such as plant height, leaf shape, color, bud structure, aroma, and potency. The phenotype can vary widely even among plants with the same genotype due to differences in environmental conditions like light, temperature, and nutrients.

Pot
Definition: A colloquial term for marijuana, referring to the dried leaves, flowers, stems, and seeds of the Cannabis sativa or Cannabis indica plants, known for their psychoactive effects due to THC and other compounds.

The term "Pot," in relation to cannabis, is a colloquial slang term commonly used to refer to marijuana, which is the dried leaves, flowers, stems, and seeds of the Cannabis sativa or Cannabis indica plants. These parts of the plant contain psychoactive substances like THC (tetrahydrocannabinol), making marijuana popular for its mind-altering effects. "Pot" is one of the many informal terms used in reference to cannabis, especially in recreational contexts.

Prescription/Recommendation
Because cannabis is a Schedule I drug, it cannot be prescribed in the United States and most of the world. The term "prescription" is often incorrectly used in reference to suggested consumption by a doctor. Doctors write letters of recommendation where the medicinal consumption of cannabis is legal. FDA-approved pharmaceutical synthetic cannabinoid medicines like Marinol® and botanically-derived cannabinoid medicines like Epidiolex® are prescribed rather than recommended.

Prohibition
Definition: The legal forbidding of the manufacture, transportation, sale, and possession of cannabis products, often associated with a

historical period and characterized by strict enforcement and penalties for cannabis-related activities.

The term "Prohibition," in the context of cannabis, refers to the legal act of forbidding the manufacture, transportation, sale, and possession of cannabis products. This term is commonly associated with a period in history when cannabis, along with other substances, was made illegal in various countries. Prohibition typically entails strict legal enforcement and penalties for cannabis-related activities, reflecting governmental and societal attitudes towards the substance at the time.

Recreational

Definition: The use of cannabis products for enjoyment, leisure, or non-medical purposes, distinct from medicinal use and often regulated differently in terms of legal status and age restrictions.

The term "Recreational," in relation to cannabis, refers to the use of cannabis products for enjoyment, leisure, or other non-medical purposes. This contrasts with medicinal or therapeutic use, where cannabis is used to treat specific health conditions. Recreational cannabis is often subject to different legal regulations and age restrictions compared to medical cannabis.

Note: Although the term "recreational" is commonly used to refer to the consumption of cannabis by adults 21+ who do not have a doctor's recommendation, the more appropriate term is "adult use." "Adult use" can and should be used in place of "recreational" because the term is most often associated with "play" or "non-professional" activities.

Regs

Definition: Slang for average or lower quality cannabis, characterized by lower potency, less pronounced flavors and aromas, and often less meticulously cultivated or processed, representing a more economical option.

The term "Regs" in relation to cannabis is slang for "regular" or average-quality cannabis. It refers to cannabis that is generally considered to be of lower quality than top-shelf or premium varieties. "Regs" typically implies cannabis with lower potency, less pronounced flavors or aromas, and may be less carefully cultivated or processed. It is often less expensive and used by those seeking a more economical option.

Reschedule

Definition: The process of altering the classification of cannabis within a controlled substance scheduling system, often moving it to a less restrictive category based on its abuse potential, accepted medical use, and safety profile.

The term "Reschedule," in relation to cannabis, refers to the act of changing the classification of cannabis within a government's controlled substance scheduling system. This process involves reassessing and altering the category under which cannabis is listed, typically based on factors such as its potential for abuse, accepted medical use, and safety. Rescheduling can result in cannabis being moved to a less restrictive schedule, acknowledging its medicinal value or lower risk compared to other substances in more restrictive categories.

Ruderalis

Definition: A subspecies of the Cannabis sativa plant characterized by its small size, rugged nature, and auto-flowering trait. It is typically lower in THC content and valued in crossbreeding for its hardiness and auto-flowering characteristic.

The term "Ruderalis" in relation to cannabis refers to Cannabis ruderalis, a subspecies of the Cannabis sativa plant. It is known for its small size, rugged nature, and ability to automatically flower based on age rather than light cycle, a trait known as "auto-flowering." Cannabis ruderalis is less common in the cannabis cultivation world compared to Cannabis indica and Cannabis sativa, and it is typically lower in THC content. However, it is valued for its hardiness and is often crossbred with other cannabis subspecies to introduce the auto-flowering characteristic.

The SAFE Banking Act

The Secure and Fair Enforcement Banking Act of 2023 is legislation intended to protect financial institutions that provide services to cannabis-related businesses in states where such operations are legal. Under current federal law, cannabis remains a Schedule I substance, which poses legal risks to banks that service the cannabis industry. The SAFE Banking Act seeks to remove these risks by prohibiting federal banking regulators from penalizing banks for providing services to state-legal cannabis businesses. Specifically, the SAFE Banking Act would:

- Ensure that financial transactions with a state-licensed cannabis business are not considered as proceeds from illegal activity.
- Protect banks from federal prosecution or penalties solely for providing services to the cannabis industry.
- Require the Financial Institutions Examination Council to develop guidance to help credit unions and banks understand how to provide services to cannabis businesses legally.

Sativa

Definition: A type of Cannabis sativa plant characterized by long, narrow leaves and taller growth, typically having a longer flowering cycle, and associated with – whether true or not – energizing and uplifting effects, often preferred for daytime use or activities requiring mental stimulation.

The term "Sativa," in relation to cannabis, refers to one of the primary types of the Cannabis sativa plant species. Cannabis sativa plants are known for their long, narrow leaves and taller stature. They generally have a longer flowering cycle compared to Cannabis indica plants.

Strain

Definition: A specific variety or breed of the cannabis plant cultivated to possess certain desired traits, such as potency, flavor, and cannabinoid composition, each with unique characteristics and effects.

The term "Strain" in relation to cannabis refers to a specific variety or breed of the cannabis plant, which has been cultivated to enhance certain desired traits, such as potency, flavor profile, or the balance of cannabinoids (like THC and CBD) and terpenes. Each cannabis strain has its unique characteristics and effects, and they are often given distinctive names by their breeders.

Note: The term "Strain" in a general context refers to a genetic variant or subtype of microorganisms, plants, viruses, or any other organism. It denotes a variation within a species that results from a natural genetic mutation or is produced through selective breeding. Strains are identified based on morphology, behavior, or biochemical properties.

Terpene

Definition: Aromatic compounds in cannabis responsible for the plant's diverse scents and flavors are believed to influence its effects and contribute to the therapeutic properties of cannabinoids through the "entourage effect."

In relation to cannabis, the term "Terpene" refers to the aromatic compounds found in the essential oils of the cannabis plant. Terpenes are responsible for the distinctive scents and flavors of different cannabis strains, ranging from citrusy and fruity to earthy and piney. Beyond their aromatic qualities, terpenes in cannabis are believed to influence the plant's effects. They may contribute to the overall therapeutic properties of cannabinoids through a phenomenon known as the "entourage effect."

War On Drugs/Drug War

Definition: A segment of the broader government-led initiative aimed at the prohibition and control of cannabis use, distribution, and production, involving strict legal measures and law enforcement, significantly impacting legal, social, and public health aspects related to cannabis.

The War On Drugs is a global campaign led by the United States federal government of drug prohibition, military aid, and military intervention to reduce the illegal drug trade in the United States. The initiative includes a set of drug policies intended to discourage the production, distribution, and consumption of psychoactive drugs that the participating governments and the United Nations have made illegal. The term was coined by President Richard Nixon and popularized by the media shortly after a press conference given on June 18, 1971 – the day after the publication of a special message from President Nixon to the Congress on Drug Abuse Prevention and Control – during which he declared drug abuse "public enemy number one."

Weed

Definition: A slang term for marijuana, referring to the dried parts of the Cannabis sativa or Cannabis indica plants, known for their psychoactive properties, primarily due to the presence of THC.

The term "Weed," in relation to cannabis, is a colloquial slang term used to refer to marijuana. It encompasses the dried leaves, flowers, stems, and seeds of the Cannabis sativa or Cannabis indica plants, known for containing psychoactive compounds like THC (tetrahydrocannabinol). "Weed" is a commonly used term, especially in recreational contexts, and is one of many informal names for cannabis.

***

ACKNOWLEDGEMENTS

I want to extend my heartfelt gratitude to the remarkable individuals who contributed to the creation of this book. Your support, invaluable insights, and dedication have been instrumental in bringing this project to fruition. You are, in alphabetical order:

Kristina Aducci, Anthony Alegrete, Angela Bacca, Dave Barton, Eric Berlin, Esq., Dawn Black, Michael Blatter, Brandon Bobart, Warren Bobrow, Mary Szomjassy Brown, Solonje Burnett, Sam Burton, Jason Erkes, David Feder, Esq., Christiane Schuman Campbell, Esq., Cenk Cetin, Swami Chaitanya, Chris Conrad, Marianne Cursetjee, Amy Deneson, Ali Eftekhari, Tyme Ferris, Lara Fordis, Seth Gardenswartz, Esq., Christian Gray, Dr. Lester Grinspoon, MD, Jessica Gonzalez, Esq., Alex Halperin, Maha Haq, Adriana Hemans, Daniel Hendricks, Robert Hoban, Esq., Marco Hoffman, Dustin Hoxworth, Kieve Huffman, Jordan Isenstadt, Matt Jackson, Justin Johnson, Mina Johnson, Dale Sky Jones, Jeff Jones, Kristin Jordan, Esq., Benjamin Kennedy, Billi Kid, Matt Klein, Nikki Lastreto, Nikki Lawley, Bill Levers, Jeff Levers, Dr. Mark Lewis, PhD., Ron Lipsky, Carolyn Matthies, Roz McCarthy, Mendel Menachem, Eric Mercado, Mike Mejer, Lylian Miller, Claudio Miranda, Stuart Narduzzo, Benjamin Paleschuck, Shane Pennington, Esq., Angela Pih, Ronit Pinto, Kim Prince, Mary Pryor, Pawin Charoen-Rajapark, Benjamin Rattner, Alex Rogers, Michael Rosenfeld, Lauren Ruddick, Esq., Dr. Ethan Russo, MD, Kajkanit "Gem" Sakdisubha, Aaron Salles, Luke Scarmazzo, Susan Stoneman, Michael Schwamm, Esq., Kathy Sedia, PhD., Gaurav Sehgal, Ruth Shamai, Jocelyn Sheltraw, John Shute, Howard Sklamberg, Rick Snyder, Gary Stein, Patrick Toste, Wensdy Von Buskirk, Beth Waterfall, Juliana Whitney, Rusty Wilenkin, Stephanie Wright, Stu Zakim, and Michael Zaytsev.

I sincerely thank Dale Sky Jones and the dedicated team at Oaksterdam University, who shared their profound knowledge and inspired this book. Special thanks to Ruth Shamai for her editing and attention to detail. To my family and friends for your patience. And to the countless others who offered their expertise and encouragement, thank you for participating in this endeavor. This book would not have been possible without your collective efforts and unwavering belief in its message. For that, I thank you.

REFERENCES

CHAPTER 1: CANNABIS vs. MARIJUANA

1. High On Words: Exploring The Diverse Stoner Slang Of Marijuana Culture
    https://www.stiiizy.com/blogs/learn/diverse-stoner-slang-of-marijuana-culture

CHAPTER 2: CANNABIS, CULTURE & CONTEXT

1. What Is Culture?
    https://www.livescience.com/21478-what-is-culture-definition-of-culture.html

2. Cannabis Culture
    https://en.wikipedia.org/wiki/Cannabis_culture

CHAPTER 3: A BRIEF U.S. CANNABIS HISTORY

1. Branding Bud: The Commercialization Of Cannabis
    https://brandingbud.com/

2. Survey of Marijuana Law in the United States: History of Marijuana Regulation in the United States
    https://libguides.law.uga.edu/c.php?g=522835&p=3575350

3. MORE Act Reintroduced in U.S. House!
    https://blog.mpp.org/prohibition/more-act-reintroduced-in-us-house/

4. A Brief History of Cannabis in the U.S.
    https://thecannabisindustry.org/a-brief-history-of-cannabis-in-the-u-s/

CHAPTER 4: THE CREATION OF CANNABIS STEREOTYPES

1. Branding Bud: The Commercialization Of Cannabis
   https://brandingbud.com/

2. The Mysterious History Of 'Marijuana'
   https://www.npr.org/sections/
   codeswitch/2013/07/14/201981025/the-mysterious-history-
   of-marijuana#:~:text=A%20common%20version%20of%20
   the,homicidal%20mania%20touched%20off%20by

3. Cannabis Stereotypes And Why They're Wrong
   https://hightopscannabis.com/cannabis-stereotypes-and-why-
   theyre-wrong/

CHAPTER 5: THE SEEDS OF DISCORD

1. "Yahoo Finance
   https://finance.yahoo.com/news/us-cannabis-market-
   demand-set-103000033.html#:~:text=The%20US%20
   cannabis%20market%20was,of%20cannabis%20in%20the%20
   country.

2." "A Brief History of Cannabis in the U.S.
   https://thecannabisindustry.org/a-brief-history-of-cannabis-
   in-the-u-s/

3. "The Mysterious History Of 'Marijuana'
   https://www.npr.org/sections/
   codeswitch/2013/07/14/201981025/the-mysterious-history-
   of-marijuana#:~:text=A%20common%20version%20of%20
   the,homicidal%20mania%20touched%20off%20by

4. "The Complicated History of Cannabis in the US
   https://www.history.com/news/marijuana-criminalization-
   reefer-madness-history-flashback

CHAPTER 6: USE vs. CONSUME

1. What You Need To Know If You Choose To Consume Cannabis
   https://www.canada.ca/en/health-canada/services/drugs-medication/cannabis/resources/what-you-need-to-know-if-you-choose-to-consume-cannabis.html

CHAPTER 7: LEGALIZE vs. DECRIMINALIZE

1. The Difference Between The Decriminalization And Legalization Of Substances
   https://www.aclu-wa.org/story/difference-between-decriminalization-and-legalization-substances%C2%A0

2. Legalization Vs. Decriminalization Of Marijuana
   https://www.reddinsinger.com/legalization-vs-decriminalization-of-marijuana.html

3. Decriminalization vs. Legalization of Cannabis: What's the Difference?
   https://leafwell.com/blog/decriminalization-vs-legalization

4. Statement On Marijuana Opportunity Reinvestment And Expungement (MORE)
   https://drugpolicy.org/news/statement-marijuana-opportunity-reinvestment-and-expungement-more-act-being/

CHAPTER 8: BLACK, LEGACY, TRADITIONAL & LEGAL MARKETS

1. From Underground Legacy To Legal Industry: The Global Shift In Cannabis
   https://www.rollingstone.com/culture-council/articles/from-underground-legacy-legal-industry-the-global-shift-in-cannabis-1234820957/

2. Six Years After Legalization, Cannabis Black Market Still Thriving
   https://www.pacbiztimes.com/2022/09/15/six-years-after-legalization-cannabis-black-market-still-thriving/

3. Why Black Market Weed (still) Beats NJ Dispensaries
https://www.insidernj.com/black-market-weed-still-beats-nj-dispensaries/

4. Why New York Legalizing Recreational
https://www.forbes.com/sites/willyakowicz/2021/03/19/why-new-york-legalizing-recreational-cannabis-wont-kill-the-illicit-market/?sh=58b7550c6bb5 Cannabis Won't Kill The Illicit Market

5. Legalize It Right: Federal Cannabis Regulation
https://drugpolicy.org/resource/legalize-it-right-federal-cannabis-regulation/

6. Cannabis Consumers in America 2023 Growing the Legal Market: Expanding the Consumer Base
https://info.newfrontierdata.com/cannabis-consumers-in-america-2023-part-3

7. How New York and California Botched Marijuana Legalization
https://www.wsj.com/articles/marijuana-legalization-dispensary-california-new-york-db1bb11c

8. How 'Equity' Ruined Cannabis Legalization In New York
https://nypost.com/2023/04/08/how-equity-ruined-cannabis-legalization-in-new-york/

9. Marijuana Retail Licenses in NY Are Going First to Those Convicted of Drug Crimes
https://www.wsj.com/articles/marijuana-retail-licenses-in-new-york-are-going-first-to-those-convicted-of-drug-crimes-11663424695

CHAPTER 9: RESCHEDULE, DESCHEDULE OR DECONTROL?

1. Drug Enforcement Agency Drug Schedule
https://www.dea.gov/drug-information/drug-scheduling

2. Rescheduling Marijuana Is Not Enough
https://norml.org/blog/2023/09/05/rescheduling-marijuana-is-not-enough/

3. What Would Descheduling Cannabis Mean? And Other Questions On Federal Cannabis Law, Answered
https://www.greenstate.com/explained/what-would-descheduling-cannabis-mean-and-other-questions-on-federal-cannabis-law-answered/

4. Descheduling Or Rescheduling Cannabis: The Road Ahead
https://www.bhfs.com/insights/alerts-articles/2022/descheduling-or-rescheduling-cannabis-the-road-ahead

5. Former FDA Regulator Predicts Cannabis Rescheduling This Year
https://www.greenmarketreport.com/former-fda-regulator-predicts-cannabis-rescheduling-this-year/

6. Descheduling vs. Rescheduling Marijuana: A Dramatic Difference
https://www.natlawreview.com/article/de-scheduling-vs-re-scheduling-marijuana-dramatic-difference

7. In the Weeds: The States Reform Act of 2021, The Latest Comprehensive Cannabis Reform Bill
https://www.natlawreview.com/article/weeds-states-reform-act-2021-latest-comprehensive-cannabis-reform-bill

8. DEA Diversion Control Division: Controlled Substances Q&A
https://www.deadiversion.usdoj.gov/faq/cs_faq.htm

9. Leafly: A Guide to Federal Drug Rescheduling (And What It Means for Cannabis)
https://www.leafly.com/news/politics/a-guide-to-federal-drug-rescheduling-and-what-it-means-for-cannabis

10. How Section 280E Is Hindering The Cannabis Industry
https://www.bakertilly.com/insights/how-section-280e-is-hindering-the-cannabis-industry

11. Resources to Help Cannabis Business Owners Navigate Unique Tax Responsibilities
https://www.irs.gov/about-irs/providing-resources-to-help-cannabis-business-owners-successfully-navigate-unique-tax-responsibilities

12. How Section 280E Creates Big Tax Challenges For The Cannabis Industry
https://anderscpa.com/how-section-280e-creates-big-tax-challenges-for-the-cannabis-industry/?tag=cannabis

13. IRS (Finally) Issues Guidance For The Cannabis Industry
https://www.bakertilly.com/insights/irs-finally-issues-guidance-for-the-cannabis-industry

14. Federal Rescheduling Of Marijuana Could Lead To State-Level Changes
https://www.marijuanamoment.net/federal-rescheduling-of-marijuana-could-lead-to-cascade-of-state-level-changes/

15. Former FDA Regulator Predicts Cannabis Rescheduling This Year
https://www.greenmarketreport.com/former-fda-regulator-predicts-cannabis-rescheduling-this-year/

CHAPTER 10: MEDICAL, MEDICINAL OR THERAPEUTIC?

1. Legalization, Decriminalization & Medicinal Use of Cannabis: A Scientific and Public Health Perspective
https://www.ncbi.nlm.nih.gov/pmc/articles/PMC6181739/

2. Medical use of cannabis and cannabinoids in adults
https://www.uptodate.com/contents/medical-use-of-cannabis-and-cannabinoids-in-adults

3. Drugs Of Abuse: A DEA Resource Guide
https://www.dea.gov/sites/default/files/2020-04/
Drugs%20of%20Abuse%202020-Web%20Version-508%20
compliant-4-24-20_0.pdf

4. National Conference Of Legislatures
https://www.ncsl.org/health/state-medical-cannabis-laws

5. Medicinal Cannabis: Is Delta-9-Tetrahydrocannabinol
Necessary For All Its Effects?
https://onlinelibrary.wiley.com/doi/epdf

6. The Therapeutic Potential Of Cannabis And Cannabinoids.
https://www.ncbi.nlm.nih.gov/pmc/articles/PMC3442177/

CHAPTER 11: ADULT USE vs. RECREATIONAL USE

1. Oaksterdam Terminology Style Guide
https://oaksterdamuniversity.com/oaksterdam-publishes-
cannabis-style-guide/#:~:text=The%202024%20
Oaksterdam%20University%20Cannabis,writes%20about%20
cannabis%20and%20hemp.

CHAPTER 12: STRAIN, CULTIVAR OR VARIETY?

1. US Department Of Agriculture
https://www.ams.usda.gov/services/plant-variety-protection/
pvpo-frequently-asked-questions

2. ASTA Releases Seed Industry Priorities For 2023 Farm Bill
https://www.betterseed.org/asta-releases-seed-industry-
priorities-for-2023-farm-bill/

3. What's The Difference Between A Variety, Cultivar, and Strain?
https://newwestgenetics.com/faq-items/what-is-the-
difference-between-a-variety-or-cultivar-and-a-strain/

4. Strain? Variety? Cultivar? Which is Which?
https://plantlaw.com/2018/11/18/strain-cultivar/

5. The Cultivar vs. Chemovar Debate
https://moderncanna.com/cannabis-classifications/cultivar-vs-chemovar-debate/

6. Cannabis Strain, Cultivar, or Variety? What Is the Correct Term?
https://thecannabisindustry.org/cannabis-strain-cultivar-or-variety-what-is-the-correct-term/

CHAPTER 13: INDICA vs. SATIVA

1. The Cannabis Sativa Versus Cannabis indica Debate: An Interview with Dr. Ethan Russo, MD
https://www.ncbi.nlm.nih.gov/pmc/articles/PMC5576603/

2. Sativa vs. Indica: What to Expect Across Cannabis Types and Strains
https://www.healthline.com/health/sativa-vs-indica

3. Indica vs. Sativa: The Great Debate
https://www.mamedica.co.uk/indica-vs-sativa-the-great-debate/

4. The Name of Cannabis: A Short Guide for Non-Botanists
https://www.ncbi.nlm.nih.gov/pmc/articles/PMC5531363/

CHAPTER 14: THE ENTOURAGE, ENSEMBLE OR SYMPHONIC EFFECT?

1. An Entourage Effect: Inactive Endogenous Fatty Acid Glycerol Esters Enhance 2-Arachidonoyl-Glycerol Cannabinoid Activity
https://pubmed.ncbi.nlm.nih.gov/9721036/

2. The "Entourage Effect": Terpenes Coupled with Cannabinoids for the Treatment of Mood Disorders and Anxiety Disorders
https://www.ncbi.nlm.nih.gov/pmc/articles/PMC7324885/

3. The Entourage Effect: Synergistic Actions Of Plant Cannabinoids
https://www.researchgate.net/publication/273330402

4. Systematic Combinations Of Major Cannabinoid And Terpene Contents In *Cannabis* Flower And Patient Outcomes: A Proof-Of-Concept Assessment Of The Vigil Index Of Cannabis Chemovars
https://www.ncbi.nlm.nih.gov/pmc/articles/PMC9906924/

5. Taming THC: Potential Cannabis Synergy And Phytocannabinoid-Terpenoid Entourage Effects
https://www.ncbi.nlm.nih.gov/pmc/articles/PMC3165946/

6. A Cannabidiol/Terpene Formulation That Increases Restorative Sleep in Insomniacs: A Double-Blind, Placebo-controlled, Randomized, Crossover Pilot Study
https://www.medrxiv.org/content/10.1101/2023.06.03.23290932v1.full

7. A Tale Of Two Cannabinoids: The Therapeutic Rationale For Combining Tetrahydrocannabinol And Cannabidiol
https://www.ncbi.nlm.nih.gov/pubmed/16209908

8. Cannabis Is More Than Simply D9-Tetrahydrocannabinol
https://www.researchgate.net/publication/10983207_Cannabis_is_more_than_simply_Delta9-tetrahydrocannabinol

9. Taming THC: Potential Cannabis Synergy And Phytocannabinoid-Terpenoid Entourage Effects
https://www.ncbi.nlm.nih.gov/pmc/articles/PMC3165946/

CHAPTER 15: LANGUAGE AND LEGISLATION

1. National Conference Of State Legislatures
https://www.ncsl.org/civil-and-criminal-justice/cannabis-overview

2. Federal Regulations of Cannabis for Public Health in the United States
https://healthpolicy.usc.edu/research/federal-regulations-of-cannabis-for-public-health-in-the-u-s/

3. FDA Regulation of Cannabis and Cannabis-Derived Products, Including Cannabidiol
    https://www.fda.gov/news-events/public-health-focus/
    fda-regulation-cannabis-and-cannabis-derived-products-
    including-cannabidiol-cbd

CHAPTER 16: CANNABIS AND EDUCATION

1. Why Cannabis Education Could Create Better Policy
    https://www.rollingstone.com/culture-council/articles/
    cannabis-education-better-policy-1264011/

2. Cannabis And Education
    https://thecannabisindustry.org/education/

CHAPTER 17: GLOBAL PERSPECTIVES AND TERMINOLOGY

1. International Perspectives on the Implications of Cannabis Legalization: A Systematic Review & Thematic Analysis
    https://www.ncbi.nlm.nih.gov/pmc/articles/PMC6747067/

2. World Health Organization
    https://www.who.int/teams/mental-health-and-substance-
    use/alcohol-drugs-and-addictive-behaviours/drugs-
    psychoactive/cannabis

3. Transcultural Aspects Of Cannabis Use: A Descriptive Overview Of Cannabis Use Across Cultures
    https://link.springer.com/article/10.1007/s40429-023-
    00500-8

4. United Nations Office On Drugs And Crime
    https://www.unodc.org/documents/drug-prevention-and-
    treatment/cannabis_review.pdf

5. Cannabis and the Environment: What Science Tells Us and What We Still Need to Know
    https://pubs.acs.org/doi/10.1021/acs.estlett.0c00844

CHAPTER 18: LOST IN TRANSLATION

1. United Nations Office On Drugs And Crime
   https://www.unodc.org/documents/drug-prevention-and-treatment/cannabis_review.pdf

2. 420 Day: Why There Are So Many Different Names for Weed
   https://time.com/4747501/420-day-weed-marijuana-pot-slang/

3. European Medicines Agency
   https://www.ema.europa.eu/en/documents/other/compilation-terms-and-definitions-cannabis-derived-medicinal-products_en.pdf

CHAPTER 19: THE FUTURE OF THE LANGUAGE OF CANNABIS

1. Word Choice Matters: Divisive Cannabinoid Language Can Impact Consumers and Companies
   https://www.rollingstone.com/culture-council/articles/word-choice-matters-divisive-cannabinoid-language-can-impact-consumers-companies-1234795421/

2. The Future Is Green: How Cannabis Is Infiltrating Mainstream Brand Culture
   https://vault49.com/future-cannabis-brands/

3. It Matters How We Talk About Cannabis
   https://www.ganjier.com/2020/11/11/how-we-talk-about-cannabis-matters-to-be-a-successful-cannabis-sommelier/

4. Marijuana vs. Cannabis: Why Your Language Matters
   https://theemeraldmagazine.com/marijuana-vs-cannabis-why-your-language-matters/

CHAPTER 20: THE HIGH ROAD

1. This Is Your Language On Cannabis
   https://www.bostonglobe.com/ideas/2014/01/26/this-your-language-cannabis/9bguslv7ZkSsHTElfANTTN/story.html

2. A Qualitative Review Of Cannabis Stigmas At The Twilight Of Prohibition
   https://jcannabisresearch.biomedcentral.com/articles/10.1186/s42238-020-00056-8

3. The Future Of Medical Cannabis Development In Europe
   https://www.europeanpharmaceuticalreview.com/article/183928/the-future-of-medical-cannabis-development-in-europe/

4. Americans and the Future of Cigarettes, Marijuana, Alcohol
   https://news.gallup.com/opinion/polling-matters/398138/americans-future-cigarettes-marijuana-alcohol.aspx

DAVID A. PALESCHUCK

With 20+ years of brand-building and consumer marketing experience serving American Express, MasterCard, PepsiCo, and Microsoft, David has participated in developing and marketing many of today's best-known brands. David's career has focused on innovation, brand strategy, brand development, brand management, experiential and integrated marketing. He has developed, activated, and led comprehensive marketing programs designed to connect brands with relevant communities consistently, credibly, and meaningfully. Since entering the cannabis industry in 2012, David has created profitable partnerships while working as the VP, Licensing & Brand Partnerships at DOPE Magazine and crafted award-winning cannabis-infused products as the Chief Brand Officer at Evergreen Herbal. David is perhaps best known for his writings and thought leadership on cannabis branding and marketing. His writings have been featured in Forbes, Kiplingers, The Brookings Institution, The Green Report, Green Entrepreneur, Dope Magazine, High Times, PROHBTD, Cannabis Dispensary Magazine, MG, The Cannabis Industry Journal, A Different Leaf, Skunk Magazine, New Cannabis Ventures, among others. David's book, *"Branding Bud: The Commercialization of Cannabis"* – the first book on cannabis branding was released in April 2021 and became a best-selling book on Amazon in the "Branding & Logo Design" and "Green Business" categories. He writes, speaks, and consults on many projects and products within and outside the cannabis industry. For more information about David and his work, visit www.davidpaleschuck.com.

CONTACT INFORMATION

Author Website:
www.davidpaleschuck.com

Business Website:
www.brandingbud.com

Publisher Website:
www.littlegiantpress.com

Contact:
info@brandingbud.com

ALSO BY DAVID A. PALESCHUCK

If you've enjoyed "Cannabis vs. Marijuana: Language, Landscape And Context," you'll want to read "Branding Bud: The Commercialization of Cannabis" – the first and bestselling book on cannabis branding.

For more information about David's consulting services and online courses or to sign up for his newsletter, scan the code below or visit www.brandingbud.com.

Made in the USA
Columbia, SC
13 May 2024

35241667R10166